THE
HISTORY OF PEACE

A SHORT ACCOUNT OF THE ORGANISED MOVEMENTS FOR INTERNATIONAL PEACE

BY

A. C. F. BEALES, M.A.

SOMETIME INGLIS STUDENT IN THE
UNIVERSITY OF LONDON

" *Comment arriver à créer ce milieu sain dans lequel vivront nos descendants ? Comment accélérer notre arrivée dans cet Éden de justice et d'amour, que fondera l'avenir ? . . . En jetant un regard sur le passé pour ne rien laisser perdre des travaux de nos pères dans l'œuvre de rédemption.*"

E. POTONIÉ-PIERRE

LINCOLN MAC VEAGH

THE DIAL PRESS

NEW YORK   MCMXXXI

COPYRIGHT 1931

Printed in Great Britain by
NEILL & CO., LTD., EDINBURGH

PREFACE

THIS book is not Peace propaganda. It is a study of the historical development of organised efforts towards World Peace since the foundation of the earliest "Peace Societies" in 1815. My interest in the history of the Peace idea was first stimulated by a second-hand copy of a life of Henry Richard which I picked up in 1926. I was surprised to find that every single idea current to-day about peace and war was being preached by organised bodies over a century ago, and that the world-wide ramifications of the present-day Peace Movement can be traced back in unbroken continuity to a handful of forgotten Quakers in England and America at the close of the Napoleonic Wars. Subsequent inquiries revealed that the story had never as yet been related in detail, though historians are working on particular aspects of the history of Peace.

My aim has been to tell that story in outline. I have attempted to show how the first Peace Societies, gradually reinforced by allies who were internationalists but not pacifists, built up a complete theory of Peace with which they succeeded in capturing the attention of the world for a brief period before going into decline; how they were followed, after 1870, by a second Peace Movement organically connected with them which gained the ear of Parliaments and statesmen and organised itself into a world-wide crusade; how far it succeeded, and how far its aspirations were realised after 1918.

Materials for the study are almost inexhaustible. The bibliography at the end of the book contains only the sources I have actually consulted. No final study can be made without access to national archives at present closed, for after 1878 the history of Peace becomes an integral part of the history of international relations; and arbitration and disarmament, once the nostrums of a few cranks, become the commonplaces of diplomacy. Nor has any considerable attempt been made as yet to explore the subject. The history of Peace has at present only four prominent historians at work on it: Dr. Chr. L. Lange at Geneva, Dr. M. E. Curti in the United States, Dr. Jacob Ter Meulen at The Hague, and Professor Paul Koht in Norway. The only "History of the Peace Movement" already in existence, Alfred H. Fried's *Handbuch der Friedensbewegung*, has not been translated, nor re-issued since its second edition in 1911. Apart from this monumental manual there is no work except the present which surveys the whole ground. And so vast, indeed, is the subject that Part Two of the book was originally over half the length of the complete book as now published.

I have to record my grateful thanks to the many organisations which have helped me by giving me access to their libraries and by translating important documents which I could not read in the original. Particular acknowledgments are made in the footnotes; but I wish to thank here the following: Rev. Herbert Dunnico, of the Peace Society, London; Mr. E. G. Smith, of the National Council for Prevention of War; Mr. J. W. Wheeler-Bennett, of the Royal Institute of International Affairs; the Librarians of the Society of Friends, the League of Nations' Union, the German Liga fur Völkerbund, the American Peace Society, the Carnegie Endowment, and the World Peace Foundation; Miss Lucy A. Cox, of the No More War Movement; and, for valuable criticism and advice, Dr. M. E. Curti, Dr. Chr. L. Lange, and Dr. G. P. Gooch. Without this assistance the extent of the subject and the multiplicity of its vernacular sources would have made the task impossible.

A. C. F. B.

CONTENTS

ILLUSTRATIONS

LIST OF ABBREVIATIONS

A. of P. *Advocate of Peace:* Organ of American Peace Society.

H. of P. *Herald of Peace:* Organ of British Peace Society.

N.C.P.W. (Lond.). National Council for Prevention of War, London.

N.C.P.W. (Bost.). National Council for Prevention of War, Boston.

W.P.F. World Peace Foundation, Boston, U.S.A.

U.P. Cong. Universal Peace Congress *Reports*.

I.P. Conf. Inter-Parliamentary Conference *Reports*.

PART ONE

INTRODUCTORY

An enterprise more celestial than human
(HENRY IV OF FRANCE)

A HISTORY OF PEACE

CHAPTER I

THE PHILOSOPHICAL THEORY OF WAR AND PEACE

(a) *Theory of the Nature, Causes, and Justification of War*

WAR has been aptly defined as "the use and predominance of material force in the conflicts between the various human nuclei," "the right to settle disputes between State and State by armed force." [1] It is a human institution, and has been analysed from varying standpoints during the progress of civilisation. To the Roman, war was conditioned by the idea of a *jus gentium*; to the medieval Christian, fighting was judged according to the Just War theory; for the present generation, juridical conceptions of war have reduced its justifications to one. Simultaneously with the change in conception there has developed a tendency both to regulate and to mitigate the use of force in international relations, and to consider war as falling within the science of sociology. It is in this light that Jean Lagorgette carried out his investigation into *Le Rôle de la Guerre*. [2] Lagorgette distinguished four kinds of war, devoting 700 pages to the analysis. They were, first, impulsive war, unprovoked aggression, in both ancient and modern times; secondly, war as a means to a special end, *e.g.* cannibalism, plunder, slave-trading, conquest, commerce, independence, secession; thirdly, war as a means to a juridical end—what he

---

[1] L. Sturzo, *International Community* (1929), p. 89. *The Herald of Peace* (Nov. 1892), pp. 121–2, cites forty-eight different definitions, mostly unscientific.
[2] Paris, 1906.

calls "just wars"; and fourthly, war as a means to a generic end, *e.g.* industrial wars, which he examines in terms of Spencer and Darwin.

The feature common to all four types is that they arise from disputes created by the relationships between States, and are attempts to settle those disputes. It has been pointed out, however, that while the solution of war is a uniform solution, the disputes it is employed to solve may vary exceedingly. This is apparent in Lagorgette. Its truth has been demonstrated more exactly in L. S. Woolf's *International Government*.[1] The causes of war in the modern State are fourfold, according to the species of international relationships from which they emanate. Legal relationships have produced wars concerning the interpretation of treaties and the definition of territorial boundaries; economic relationships, wars of trade and finance; political relationships, wars over minorities and nationality; social relationships, wars concerning "questions of honour." Usually, in the actual life of States, there is present a mixture of all four causes in every war, though one alone may be dominant.

But the vital point, which furnishes at once an explanation and a justification for all the pacifist and internationalist propaganda of the last century, is that war to-day is not fundamentally necessary. "Remote causes provide the substance of the motives of a war, but never cause war. Proximate causes provide the legal and political pretext for a war, but they are not its true causes. Thus there is no necessary and determinant connexion between the motives or excuses of a war and the war itself unless the human will to war intervenes. . . . The wars of to-day are unquestionably *voluntary* in character while presenting themselves to the human mind as products of *necessity*. . . . In the present organisation of the State there can be no necessary war; a nation cannot find itself in a state of necessity obliging it to make war, for there is a juridical system and a permanent system of interstatal relations by which every dispute could be peacably settled."[2] This, of

[1] London, 1916.   [2] Sturzo, pp. 108, 114.

course, was not true in 1815.   It is the purpose of this book to
discover how far the peacemongers of the nineteenth century
were responsible for the change.

(b) *Pacifism and Internationalism*

War has been defended in the past for several distinct reasons.
In the Middle Ages it was held to be just when undertaken in
conditions which made it intrinsically moral.   After the
Renaissance the criterion became that of utility to the State,
and survived into the present century under the titles of
"national efficiency" (*cf.* Hegel) and "national interests,"
claiming for war a supreme value as a test of emergent national
greatness.   After 1800 the conception changed to one of
biological and sociological necessity, emphasising the frailties
of human nature and the complexities of human relationships.
All three theories, in a word, employed the phrase "the common
good" to prove the existence of a right of victory.

They are supported by a curious argument from history
which partakes of more than one form.   Panaceas like arbitration, it is sometimes declared, would not have averted the Wars
of the Roses or the Thirty Years War.   But the objection is
quite irrelevant and futile.   What matters "is not Will our
standards and ideals apply backwards, but Will they not apply
forwards"; not whether the time for an international organisation had arrived by 1455 or 1618, but whether it has arrived
now.[1]   A second form of the argument avers that war has been
in the past a blessing in disguise; that without war Italy and
Germany would never have achieved unification, and American
slavery would never have been abolished.   A sublime utterance
in this strain occurred in the United States Congress in 1912.
"Every step towards what we term civilisation to-day has been
the result of war.   A rule that has been tried out through so
great a period of time is entitled to some respect. . . . We
grow philanthropic, we grow sentimental—I had almost said
maudlin—over the brotherhood of man.   No nation ever

[1] *Cf.* N. M. Butler, *The International Mind* (1912), p. 6.

existed fifteen minutes based on the brotherhood of man." [1] In the third place, history has been made to support the argument from human nature. "I believe with Darwin that violent struggle is a law of nature which rules every being; I believe with Joseph le Maistre that it is a divine law. . . . All the experience of history teaches us that it [war] can never be eradicated while there remain on the earth two men, bread, money, and a woman between them." [2] The argument is important, not for its intrinsic value, but for the opposition to peace propaganda which it inspired during the nineteenth century.

Peace propaganda was of two kinds, pacifist and internationalist; both based on inflexible principles, but the former more dogmatic and uncompromising than the latter.

Pacifism, which is an extremist philosophy and rules out *all* organised war, has several bases. It believes in the fundamental unity of mankind as taught by the Scriptures; homicide is criminal, war nothing but collective homicide. Such was the teaching of the Early Christian Fathers and the seventeenth-century Quakers. Again, pacifism is utilitarian; it emphasises the misery and waste involved in war. But it does not therefore support Red Cross Conventions and efforts to humanise war; such mitigations have usually been held by pacifists, apart from purely humanitarian benefits, to be wrong in principle. Thirdly, pacifism is ethical, denouncing war on the same grounds as the duel—namely, that force is no test of justice. Finally, pacifism is logical; it realises that war is worse than useless as a means of settling quarrels and removing grievances—that in fact it only adds fresh sources of friction; and that peaceful persuasion alone is logically defensible.

Thus pacifists have striven for peace in two organised camps. The first in order of time were those who preached from the first principle, the religious and positive principle, and seldom had recourse to the other three; the second camp comprised

---

[1] Congress, 5th March 1912 : cited by N. M. Butler, p. 108.
[2] Quoted from Vogué, in Rouard de Card, *Destinées de L'Arbitrage International* (1892), p. 6, note.

those who stressed all four principles at once, and religion perhaps least of all. The first group held the field until the necessity for planning some form of world organisation became insistent. Thereafter the lead passed to the second group.

Both crusades were strengthened in action by the co-operation of other reformers working towards the same end (Peace) from very different motives—the internationalists. In this sense pacifism and internationalism are complementary, though in principle they have trenchant differences. Internationalism is definitely a theory of the State, which it conceives as an organic nation-unit existing inside a community of nations— which community is not an aspiration but a sociological *fact*. And this conception does not rule out war altogether. The right of private war, certainly, has no longer any existence in a living community which functions along lines of common interest and obligation; but two forms of war remain—defensive war against unprovoked aggression, and concerted warfare in the name of the entire community of nations to punish any State which flouts its obligations by active aggression. Internationalism, in short, is federative and not unitary.

Within the federation of States the "international mind" thinks in terms of free trade, self-determination, and the rights of minorities; but its thought has faltered at times on the difficult question of intervention and non-intervention. The Concert of Europe had split into two parts in 1822 on the same issue. Canning emphasised the right of States to regulate their own domestic affairs free from outside interference; the Holy Alliance, arguing that the very essence of a Concert lay in collective obligations and collective risks, insisted on a right of collective intervention if and when the domestic concerns of any single State should threaten the general peace. The present century has solved the problem by defining the limits of intervention. Risks of war are now reduced to a minimum, and the terms of the League of Nations system restrict collective intervention to cases of an actual outbreak of war.

Internationalism is, then, "harmony of understanding

established in a world of unassailable diversity." [1] With Aristotle it believes that "the things which make men alike are more important than the things which make them different"; and that the world's heritage of freedom and enlightenment is to be held by each in trust for all. The interests of humanity are rarely *national* to-day; they are rather group interests, which cut across national frontiers and are the concern of world-wide professions, creeds, and classes—for which concerns, indeed, purely national government makes no provision. In providing for these interests a theoretical environment in which they can attain to a maximum realisation, the internationalist thinker has always held that his is the highest form of Patriotism.

(c) *Roads to Peace*

It was not until the religious pacifists of 1815 had been re-inforced by free-trade internationalists that their programme became thoroughly practical. As soon as insistence on the unjustifiability of war began to prompt serious questions as to how the scourge was to be destroyed; as soon as the issue became no longer Should we? but Can we?—concrete methods were sought which might supersede the old haphazard system of foreign alliances and negotiation as bulwarks of peace.

The schemes of the nineteenth century all centred on five fundamentals: arbitration, arbitration treaties and clauses in treaties, an International Authority or Tribunal or Congress, the codification of International Law, and disarmament. These five essentials were regarded as interrelated and inter-dependent; it was held to be extremely doubtful whether, for lack of one of them, any of the others (except arbitration) could be secured. Yet the emphasis in peace propaganda was never on all five equally. Each in turn was made the subject of an intensive campaign lasting several years.

(i) *Arbitration and Arbitration Treaties*

Arbitration, whether domestic or international, has been defined as "the judgment of a litigation by a third party chosen

[1] Alfred Zimmern, in *Foreign Affairs* (N.Y.), June 1923, p. 126.

by the contending parties."[1] The implications contained in such a definition—there have been many to the same general effect—were brought out and legislated upon during the second Hague Conference in 1907: "International arbitration has for its object the regulation of litigations between States by judges of their choice, and on a basis of respect for law. Recourse to arbitration presupposes the engagement to submit to the award in good faith."[2] There must thus be present a desire for peaceful settlement, and the award must be binding on both parties—and impartial.[3]

The merits of such a device were never in dispute. Arbitration gives time for passions to cool, ensuring that problems will be resolved according to reason rather than to prejudice; it costs little and wastes hardly anything compared to the expense of war; it facilitates a search for information, and so ensures that the award shall be built up on sound and adequate knowledge of the facts; and it leaves behind it neither rankling nor devastation, but rather an incentive to sympathy and understanding.[4] Wherefore it is esteemed more highly by democracies than by autocracies, and is most appreciated by all peoples at the end of long and costly wars.[5]

It has never been widely believed that arbitration could settle every dispute. Henry Richard himself, the greatest pacifist in England during the nineteenth century, recognised in 1875 that "cases may be conceived to which it does not apply." The *Edinburgh Review* regarded it (1882) as "an expedient for occasional adoption, not a specific for universal use." Kamarovsky remarked that cases actually arbitrated were none of them of "a true political character," but "principally exhibit a material interest" (1887). Every reputable monograph on arbitration specifies definite limits for the applicability of the principle.

[1] C. Langlade, *La Clause Compromissoire* (1899), p. 16.
[2] Hague (1907), art. 37; (1899), arts. 15 and 18: translated from French texts.
[3] See a valuable paper on the impartiality of awards, by Sir E. Hornby, in *Herald of Peace* (1893), p. 171 *seq.*
[4] *Cf.* B. F. Trueblood, *Federation of the World* (1899), pp. 110–12.
[5] *See* N. Politis, *La Justice Internationale* (1924), p. 17.

Above all, questions touching "national honour" have always been ruled out, by every critic except pacifists, as not arbitrable. Now national honour, like Balance of Power, cannot be measured; nor can it be defined. By 1918 over a hundred alleged definitions had been recorded, but all of them reduced to the single proposition that national honour would "only be defended by arms if, and when, it is believed to coincide with interest. It is, in fact, a word without content, employed to excite or to sustain emotions."[1] Nevertheless the expression provided an insurmountable obstacle to the extension of arbitration after 1873, and was written deep into the two Hague Conventions, wherein also appeared a more honest synonym called "national interests."

Thus it was that juristic analyses of arbitration divided disputes into the two categories, justiciable (which might be arbitrated) and non-justiciable (*e.g.* national interests—which might not). Within the field of justiciable disputes there was a further division into cases judged by canons of international law (legal cases), and political questions which involved no question of legal right and could accordingly be judged only on their merits (equitable cases). This second distinction the friends of Peace frequently ignored. But it was vital; for on it depended the deeper problem of whether arbitration could ever be made compulsory. In point of fact, every arbitration of the nineteenth century concerned a legal and not a political dispute, while every arbitration clause and arbitration treaty (with but a few notable exceptions) excluded political disputes from the sphere of arbitration. Even after 1900, when disputes like that of the Dogger Bank outrage (which was held at first to be a matter involving national honour) were successfully composed by means of arbitration or conciliation, the solution was attempted only by first reducing them to *legal* questions.[2] Pending a certainty that *all* questions of national interests could be so reduced, therefore, the instituting of obligatory arbitration would be dangerous and unwise.

[1] Leo Perla, *What is National Honour?* (1918); G. L. Dickinson, *The International Anarchy*, p. 34.

[2] *Cf.* L. S. Woolf, *International Government* (1916), pp. 43–64.

WILLIAM LADD

(Reproduced by permission of Yale University Press)

These problems were laboriously explored by statesmen as well as by the friends of Peace. During the process the number of cases arbitrated reached, by 1900, one hundred and seventy-seven.[1] At the same time a further difficulty in the theory of arbitration—that of sanctions, or methods of assuring that the award should invariably be accepted—served to separate pacifists from internationalists. Sanctions are discussed below.

(ii) *An International Authority*

As a convenient instrument for use as and when particular crises arose, arbitration needed no framework of international organisation for its maintenance. It was an *ad hoc* expedient. The three other recommendations of the reformers, however, were inseparable. They hinged on the plan, most enduringly propounded by the American, William Ladd, for an International Tribunal or Congress of Nations. The necessity for some form of international consolidation had been an essential point in every international theory evolved in the past, from Pierre Dubois onwards. It seemed that Peace was unattainable without disarmament, and that disarmament was futile without an alternative to war in the shape of a code of law; while no code of International Law could take effect without some sort of juridical tribunal to apply and enforce it. It is in not co-ordinating their efforts towards this supreme end above all else that the later Peace Societies must be denied their claim to omniscience and foresight.

Not that the problem was easy to solve. But the need for a Tribunal was urgent. Treaties of agreement were valuable in so far as they created for the future a legal bond between nations; but treaties embodied a static conception of politics. It would be of infinitely more value to extend the bond of law throughout the entire comity of nations by instituting a Tribunal of Justice acting for one and all. The difficulty lay in the question whether the Tribunal were to be a series of periodical

---

[1] Full list in H. La Fontaine, *Hist. Sommaire des Arbitrages Internationaux*, 1794–1900 (1902).

congresses or a permanent body in constant session; and
further, what limits were to be placed on the right of the
nations collectively to control the behaviour of individual States,
and how that control was to be enforced.   On these three points
a multitude of divergent conclusions were reached during the
century.[1]   The most serious discouragement to further speculation occurred when the outbreak of the American Civil War
seemed to indicate that there were issues which even a supreme
Sovereign Tribunal could not resolve in such a way as to avert
war and dissolution.   One fact only was taken for granted,
namely, that an international court of *criminal* justice was out
of the question.   The number of persons indicted would be
too enormous, and passions would be roused at a time when,
the war being over, there was most need for pacific sentiments
to prevail.

(iii) *The Codification of International Law*

While any form of Judicial Tribunal would necessitate the
formulation of a code of law as a basis of international relations,
the gradual evolution of such a code (which presented obvious
advantages) conversely would necessitate a tribunal to apply
it.   As modern States discovered among themselves an increasing economic interdependence, the need for a steady
development of International Law increased proportionately.
Before 1815 the nearest approach had been diplomatic treaties.
After 1815 the Danube Commission and the Slavery Control
Board bore testimony to a richer conception of international
relations.   But even should permanent international agreements be multiplied for ever, they would have little more
sanctity than treaties unless embodied in a code and dispensed
by an International Tribunal.

Here was a serious difficulty which even the Hague Conferences declined to face squarely.   Until it should be overcome, International Law would remain open to the objection
that it lacked the force of true law; that it amounted to nothing

[1] For an exhaustive discussion see L. S. Woolf, *International
Government* (1916), chap. vii.

stronger than custom and convention. On the other hand, its enforcement by an interstate tribunal raised anew the question of sanctions.

(iv) *Sanctions*

Sanctions constituted the one issue on which there could be no final compromise between internationalist and pacifist. The former definitely conceived of a future world organisation stabilised by combined material force against "outlaws." The latter, whether his pacifism were religious or not, was equally convinced that the only justifiable compulsion was moral and not physical. It will be seen later that one Peace Society barely escaped complete disintegration through internal dissensions regarding sanctions. But in general the distinction between the two groups of friends of Peace was rigid, though it did not interrupt their active co-operation.

Briefly stated, the case for sanctions rests on the belief that, in the present condition of public opinion, no decrees of any International Tribunal can hope to be invariably respected unless they are backed by a material compulsion which exceeds the force at the command of the transgressor. Force has been too long the monopoly of States for any other form of constraint yet to replace it. "There is only one way," said Woodrow Wilson, "to insure the world of peace, that is by making it so dangerous to break the peace that no other nation will have the audacity to attempt it." This is the theory underlying the Covenant of the League of Nations. It is defended, further, by the argument that international material sanctions "lift the war system out of its exclusively nationalistic status and universalise it." [1] Translated into details the system comprises a graded scale of combined constraints, ranging from pacific blockade to open war.[2] Occasional schemes for an

---

[1] *Cf.* C. C. Morrison, *Outlawry of War* (1927), p. 179. The author thereupon refutes the argument.

[2] See analysis by J. Dumas (Paris, 1905), and D. Mitrany (London, 1925).

international army also have been advanced since the days of
the *Great Design*—even as late as 1923.[1]

Evil, however, said Buddha, cannot be overcome by evil, but
only by good. The case against sanctions holds that the
symbol of reform is not a whip; and that coercion, whether
by sanctions or by compulsory arbitration, is bound to perpetuate the old system. Distrust is its very essence. Secondly,
sanctions are not merely pernicious, but useless as well. Without recognising the potency of moral obligations, runs the
argument, even despite the shock of 1914, no lasting world-
federation can be built up. Once moral sanctions *are* recognised
the need for coercion vanishes, and the proverb runs in a new
form—*Si vis pacem, para pacem.* For in the last resort the
application of sanctions, the obligation of the community of
nations to combine one and all against an aggressor, itself rests
on individual good faith.[2]

(v) *Disarmament*

"Simultaneous and proportional disarmament," finally, was
an essential plank in the Peace platform. Its realisation, of
course, was entirely conditional on the prior establishment of
the other organs of international machinery. An assured
substitute for arms was the necessary prelude to disarmament.
The substitute chosen was naturally that of a " Permanent
Court." Even so, it was realised that the will to disarm must
come from within a nation rather than from without. Hence
the intensive educational propaganda of the Peace Societies.
Disarmament would be, not the cause, but the result of Peace;
weapons of war would ultimately disappear not so much
through destruction as through decay for want of use. Their
condemnation rested on three facts—that they were an economic
and financial burden which only increased with time; that they
promoted competition in militaristic preparation, and so produced fear and still greater competition; and that they were
incompatible with any sincere system of international organisation. Given a universal sentiment of national security, created

---

[1] *Friedenswarte* (1923).   [2] Morrison, pp. 175–205.

by the successful functioning of a new World Federation, the reduction and gradual abolition of armaments would be no longer a problem for anybody save technical experts.[1]

(d) *Summary*

The Peace Societies of 1815–16, then, were founded at a moment when Europe, having learnt, as it thought, the lesson of the Napoleonic Wars, had remodelled its political constitution; when there had just emerged into international practice a number of new habits which were capable of being moulded for the good of mankind; and when five centuries of isolated international thought had contributed a mass of literature from which could be extracted the five principles outlined above. All these realities were to serve as raw material for the reformers, who, though they coincided as a rule in choice of means, attacked their common problem—the eradication of war—from a number of incompatible standpoints. Thus we shall find in the story of their labours, besides the inevitable checks administered by their opponents, hesitations and crises due to their own want of cohesion. But we will reserve final judgment until the story has been told.

[1] *See* P. J. N. Baker, *Disarmament* (1926), and S. de Madariaga, *Disarmament* (1929).

CHAPTER II

THE EVOLUTION OF SCHEMES OF WORLD PEACE

ABOUT the middle of the nineteenth century there began to be expounded by western philosophers the theorem that all wars in the future would tend to become world wars. Before the century was out a Russian strategist added a rider to the effect that wars in the future would threaten civilisation itself.[1] Within the next twenty years the world demonstrated both propositions and accepted them as sufficiently proved. In the meantime a counter-proposition had been developed which endeavoured to show that the days were gone in which war as an institution was necessary, and that in the modern world no nation was compelled to go to war. As the theory and practice of settling international disputes otherwise than by resort to arms progressed this belief gained in appeal. The creation of alternative machinery destroyed "the sole juridical and ethical excuse" which was still being advanced by those who believed that war could never be eradicated. Whereupon it was but a single logical step to the Pact of Paris, whereby, though only the most sanguine believed that it would be possible in practice to make armed conflict impossible, war was formally abjured and outlawed. The future of international relations lay thereafter with the machinery of world organisation, which alone could allow the renunciation to be kept, by welding together a living International Community with a personality of its own.

The history of the efforts which produced the present ordering of world politics hardly oversteps a century. Disarmament proposals can be traced as far back as B.C. 546 in China;

[1] Jean de Bloch, *The War of the Future* (1898).

16

universal brotherhood has been the keynote of all organised
religion from the earliest days; the Middle Ages abounded in
schemes for world peace and cosmopolitan unity. But the first
organised and coherent movements towards these ends were
born of the Napoleonic Wars, when world politics had already
long been international in the strict sense of the word, and
when it was at last possible to appreciate the problem of
patriotism *versus* internationalism.

These first movements were not altogether mushroom
growths. Though the founders of organised pacificism
emerged suddenly and were long in earning respect or even
tolerance, and though the economists who became their first
allies were prone to harp on contemporary evils as insistently as
on eternal principles, they had behind them at least fifteen
centuries of thought. They themselves were but disciples:
their Bible and their Prophets extended far back in the past—
from Augustine to Wyclif, and from Pierre Dubois to Kant.
For this reason it is necessary that an account of organised
Peace should be prefaced by a summary sketch of the older
efforts—articulate but inchoate—to fashion a better world.
The prophets furnished not only ideas and catchwords, principles and formulæ, but elaborate and complicated schemes,
and laboured arguments on their practical and everlasting
potency. Much of the argument, and all the plans, survive
largely as academic curiosities. But the nineteenth century
extracted from them a measure of permanent truth and a fund
of maxims for practical guidance.

There emerges from a study of medieval philosophy one
theory of war and peace. In the centuries that followed the
collapse of medieval universality, schemes of world organisation were evolved to accommodate the new system of national
Sovereign States. Arguments were launched for and against
arbitration; a beginning was made at establishing and codifying
International Law; and—supreme achievement—an experiment
among the American Indians was placed on record as an earnest
that ideals may sometimes be realised.

2

(i) *Pacifism*

The earliest thoughts of universal peace were religious and sentimental; they envisaged the unity of mankind and preached humanitarianism as a means thereto. Among the Israelite Fathers, Micah and Isaiah formulated texts which are still the most favourite heirlooms of the Peace Movement, measuring the future in terms of swords and ploughshares, spears and pruning-hooks.[1] Paganism contributed to the same end in the writings of Zeno, Seneca, Epictetus, and Marcus Aurelius; and the birth of Christianity consecrated the whole of ancient pacifist thought in the name of a God who was the Father of all. But Christianity had to condone the principle of military service within the Roman Empire. A decree of A.D. 314 rendered deserters from the imperial armies liable to excommunication, on the argument of Christ's "Render unto Cæsar . . ." The unqualified protests against warfare which had been raised by Justin the Martyr, by Tertullian, and by St. Martin of Tours, ceased on the recognition of Christianity by Constantine, and it became a common practice for priests to accompany the armies.

In time there developed a body of Christian theory which explained and vindicated the change, and which can be regarded as representing the attitude of the Medieval Church towards war. The argument is built up from Augustine, Thomas Aquinas, and Francis de Victoria. It emphasises the horrors of war and all the attendant moral crimes, but stops short of a categorical denunciation of all war. In certain conditions war is "just"; though the conditions prescribed are strict enough to condemn every war that has ever been fought. When there has been an injustice committed on one side only, amounting to moral and not merely material guilt; and when this injustice is known for certain; and when all peaceful methods of settlement have been tried in vain, the aggrieved nation might with justice, says Augustine, resort to arms. But in doing so that nation must intend to further good and relieve evil by war, must

[1] Micah iv. 3 ; Isaiah ii. 4.

be certain of victory beforehand, must conduct the war "rightly" and without excesses of any kind, must make the punishment of the enemy strictly proportionate to the offence, and must scrupulously avoid all unnecessary upheaval among neutrals. Failing any one of these conditions, the war would be unjust.[1]

Such was the medieval theory. Suarez contrived centuries later to conjure with it, balancing degrees of guilt and equating the moral cases put forward by contending princes. He served only to weaken a doctrine that was already diffuse and obscure. Long disputations were held as to who was to make the declaration of war. Augustine's ruling vested the power to do so in "lawful authorised authority exercised in the name of God." In the light of this it was asked further whether the whole of the aggressor nation was to be held morally responsible for the misdeeds of its prince; and further still, whether any aggressive act could be other than immoral.

In this wise, because it empowered the Prince to plunge his people into war, and because it seemed to be using war as a means to its ideal of Peace, the theory of the Just War provoked protests which crystallised into the first true pacifist doctrines. The medieval sects which broke away—Albigenses, Vaudois, Lollards, Paulicians, Manicheans, Waldenses, Mennonites—took their stand firmly on the sanctity of human life, stood out uncompromisingly against all war, and took the whole world for their country. They were pacifist and cosmopolitan. The counterblast to Augustine's *Civitas Dei* is to be found in Wyclif's *Trialogus*. But here again there is a limitation. The sects, having no frontiers, were not interested in the State. Thus they have a survival value for pacifism but not for internationalism.[2]

Translated into action, the medieval theory produced on the one hand the Crusades and the Truce of God, and on the other hand Chivalry. Irrespective of the setting of a Holy War, the conception of Chivalry embodied a lofty Christian ideal. Its

[1] *See* F. Stratmann, *The Church and War*, p. 79 *seq.*
[2] *See* M. E. Hirst, *Quakers in Peace and War*, chap. i; and C. L. Lange, *La Doctrine Pacifique*, chap. i.

four corners were honour, the pledged word, defence of the innocent and weak, and idealised womanhood. It created an ethic and an aristocracy; it helped to humanise warfare and exalt the middle class; and it knew no geographical boundaries. It typifies medieval universality. When that universality had at last collapsed, the fall echoed throughout Europe in the Decree of Eternal Pacification (1495), by which private war among the descendants of the Age of Chivalry was abolished.

(ii) *Organisation*

At a lower level, that of mere political expediency, efforts had been made to regulate intercourse between nations—partly to promote defence, partly to diminish friction. The earliest recorded experiment in interstatal organisation is the Amphictyonic Council of the second century B.C. The twelve tribes of ancient Greece banded themselves together in 1497 B.C., naming their League after Amphictyon, the son of Deucalion. They held an annual assembly at Anthela in the Pass of Thermopylæ, where the rites performed in honour of Ceres gradually changed from a religious to a political character. Affairs common to the twelve tribes were managed by a Council, made up of deputies from each tribe, and by an executive assembly which carried out the Council's decrees. The tribes each took an oath to abstain from internecine plunder or destruction. In the Council each tribe had two votes on all questions discussed, and the Council's decrees were theoretically inviolable—though there was no organised means of enforcing them. Later the League and its machinery developed further. By 191 B.C. there were seventeen members. Under Augustus the regulations were reorganised. The League is last heard of about A.D. 200.[1]

Its importance in history is apt to be overstressed. Undoubtedly the principles of federation and interstatal obligation which it involved were of immense significance for the future. The idea of federation among city States bore fruit in the Confederation of Delos during the age of Pericles, and in the

[1] *See* Eliz. York, *Leagues of Nations*, p. 25 *seq.*

Athenian League. Peaceful settlement of disputes within the League, moreover, due to a community of interests produced by the regular assemblies, gave the Council a reputation as a peace organisation. Arbitrations among the Greeks were numerous, particularly between the Athenians and the Lacedemonians, and between the Lacedemonians and Argos. But the Amphictyonic Council was not so much a National Assembly as it was a religious body, and it had no legal power to settle disputes between the member States. Nor is there anything to show that the principle of arbitration was explicit in the League. There was indeed a form of international law, necessitated by the geographical frontiers of the Peloponnesus, and a system of ambassadors and secret diplomacy based on the balance of power between the various States. But the recorded arbitrations turned sometimes on law and sometimes on the merits of the particular case. And at all times the issue was domestic rather than international.

The truth of this is borne home by the practice of Rome later. The Romans allowed the custom of arbitration to persist where they found it prevalent in Greek colonies; but no Roman dispute was ever submitted to outside judgment. Rome was the arbiter of the world. Similarly, the conditions under which imperial Rome expanded did not allow the development of a code of international law. In no sense were the Greeks or Romans internationalist; for in place of the two fundamentals of internationalism—equality and unity—they postulated slavery and absorption, and a world-empire administered under the *Pax Romana*. The legacy of Rome was thus the struggle in the Middle Ages between Empire and Papacy.

The great work of the medieval Church was to attack the problem of mitigating warfare and organising perpetual peace from another angle. By the Truce of God, proclaimed in 989 at the Council of Charroux (in Poitou) and extended in 1027, fighting among the feudal nobles was prohibited from sunset every Wednesday till dawn on the following Monday, and on certain festivals. Fantastic as it sounds to modern ears, the prohibition was tolerably well respected for close on two centuries, and it serves as an index of the influence exerted by the Papacy. Early in the thirteenth century it waned, owing to the needs of the Popes themselves in the struggle against the Hohenstaufen. But as an attempt to organise war its significance remains.

The Crusades, spread over three centuries, exemplified the same ideal of unity. They girded up the whole of Christendom into an array of warriors, priests, cities, and kings, to conquer and convert Islam. De Quincey saw in them an ecstacy of chivalry and martyrdom, and a triumphant manifestation of Augustine's just war. Modern scholarship emphasises the commercial and æsthetic contact between East and West which they achieved rather than their religious aspirations. Judged by the canons of Augustine and Aquinas, the Crusades do not satisfy the contemporary test of a just war, despite their ostensible motive. They were not the only means available to achieve the end in view; the tide of Islam had been steadily ebbing since before 1095. Nor was there any reasonable certitude that they would be successful. The canonists, however, accepted and glorified them; for their aim transcended everything.

About the time of the Third Crusade the first definite plan was formulated for abolishing war. It was as simple as it was logical. The author, one Gerohus of Regensberg, proposed that the Pope should forbid all war, that differences between princes should be referred to Rome for decision, and that any party who rejected the Pope's award should be excommunicated and deposed. His deposition would be accelerated by the priests in his dominions, who would stir up a popular revolt against him. What is chiefly remarkable in the scheme is the complete assumption of a united Christendom which underlies it. Had it been carried into effect, its insistence on the political power of the Papacy could only have exacerbated an already perennial feud. None the less it was not an isolated piece of extravagance. Contemporary schemes of a similar purport were being aired in both France and Italy.[1]

[1] See R. L. Jones, *International Arbitration*, pp. 85–6.

From the imperial side three treatises on the organisation of the world were written during the fourteenth century. The first, *On the Recovery of the Holy Land*, by Pierre Dubois of Normandy, an adviser of Philip le Bel of France, is significant in so far as it advocated for the first time a federation of Christian Sovereign States.   Dubois held that peace was the *summum bonum* among Christian nations, and that therefore a Council of the Nations should be established, ministering to the needs of the federated member States in their dealings one with another, and deciding quarrels among them by means of arbitration. The appearance of this new principle of federation, however, is discounted by two other features on which Dubois was equally insistent—that France (his own country) was to become dominant in Europe, and that the Council of the Nations should make its first and pre-eminent duty the subjugation of the Turk.   The first of these two features alone would have enabled growing national feeling in the emergent modern kingdoms to wreck his scheme for organisation.

The second imperialist scheme, equally prophetic and far more daring, was similarly restricted by the exigencies of contemporary politics.   The *Defensor Pacis* of Marsiglio of Padua and John of Jandum interpreted peace as stability rather than abstention from war.   Accordingly its provisions for future harmony among the nations made too little allowance for the hardening of national sentiments in the future.   The *status quo* could in practice be modified hardly otherwise than by catastrophic action.   Marsiglio's prime contribution to later thought, apart from his clarification of various theories of Augustine and Aquinas, was his discussion of the representative principle in government, which he vigorously advanced as being morally just, logically inevitable, and practically useful in reconciling "the mass of the citizens" to a government dispensed in their own name by their own elected representatives.

The third scheme is that of Dante's *De Monarchia*, written in 1310–14 but not published until 1559.   Dante wrote at a time when the whole question of the true nature of law had been opened by the imperial struggle against the Papacy, and when Boniface VIII had lately fortified the papal claim to temporal power in the Bull *Uram Sanctam* of 1302. Dante's refutation vindicated the claim of an Empire which, he argued, had existed before the Church and independently of the Church, and which was divinely sanctioned. The Emperor was absolute; the Pope's authority was spiritual only. But by the rule of the Emperor Dante meant the rule of Law. His word monarch connoted government. The actual personal sovereign was an official, removable if he proved unfaithful to the sovereign people (as in Marsiglio). Law was "the rule which directs life." There should be one Law and one Prince, whose principles and conduct should secure that state of "peace and calm" in which alone the human race could live a fullest life. The organisation of the world, in a word, should be a universal Empire based on a universal Law.

Only one other plan of importance was propounded before 1500—by George Podiebrad, King of Hungary. It echoed Dubois in its insistence on a Holy War against the infidel (Constantinople had fallen seven years before the work appeared); and it adopted Dubois' plan for a Parliament or "Consistory" of Nations. What Podiebrad preached was, in essence, the realisation of peace in the Christian world by means of warfare outside its religious frontiers.

Meanwhile the federative principle had been put to the test in two practical interstate compacts. One of them, the Hanseatic League, founded by Lubeck and Hamburg about 1239 among fourteen Baltic cities, on a basis of "peaceful umpirage" sanctioned by force, did not long survive the Reformation. The other, the Swiss Confederation, constituted by the Treaty of Sempach in 1393 on a roughly similar defensive foundation, persisted and flourished—partly because of its geographical homogeneity. One other interesting phenomenon is on record during the same period, of an attempt in 1429 to intercept the advance of the Turks and to compose the rivalry between Slavs and Germans by means of concerted effort on the part of all Europe. An amazing Congress for the purpose was held at Loutsk in Russia. Eight rulers, including the Emperor and the Pope, attended either in person or by delegates. But no common basis of agreement could be found, and the enterprise collapsed.[1] Nevertheless, for all its freakishness, it is worthy of note as a rehearsal of the first Hague Conference nearly five hundred years later.

A trend parallel to that of small federations can be found in the growing resort to arbitration and mediation by contending princes during the later Middle Ages.[2] The number of authentic settlements by these means is enormous. In the thirteenth century there were a hundred cases in Italy alone. Usually the Pope was chosen as arbiter in virtue of Europe's spiritual affinities. When this was impossible one of his representatives (often an archbishop) served instead. The Emperor rarely acted in an arbitral capacity, for princes were jealous of their own temporal sovereignty. Edward I of England, Philip le Bel of France, the Emperors Henry III, Sigismund, and Maximilian, the Doge of Venice, the Republics of Venice and Switzerland, all submitted minor disputes and differences to the decision of disinterested third parties. In 1291 the Swiss Confederation even recognised the principle of obligatory arbitration. On one occasion the Parlement of Paris composed a dispute between an Emperor and a Pope (1244). Thus a growing federative sentiment can be traced, resulting, perhaps, not so much from the Church as from the Crusades, which Guizot hailed as "the first European Movement."

By 1500, then, there were in existence a number of articulate pronouncements regarding the future of the world; theories of war, doctrines of extreme pacifism, projects of world organisation from both the Papal and the Imperial standpoint, and arguments in praise of arbitration, federation, and popular sovereignty. There had been as yet, however, no mention of a specific High Court of Nations, and no attempts to frame a code of interstate law. The conception underlying most of

---

[1] R. L. Jones, *International Arbitration*, pp. 107–9.
[2] M. Novakovich, *L'Arbitrage International du 12e au 15e Siècle* (1905).

this medieval thought was that of Unity and Universality.
When, therefore, the sixteenth century ushered in the era of
individual Sovereign States and all hope of universality was
dispelled, the prophets took a new turn. Their aim after 1500
had to be to seek for unity in diversity. And this is true
internationalism.

(b) *To* 1815

(i) *The New Modern Conditions*

The sixteenth century opened a long period of chronic warfare, produced by a welter of conflicting causes. The discovery of the New World revealed vast fields for enterprise
which sharpened the rivalry of European monarchies already
sundered by the loss of a common language and by the concentrated ambitions of their ruling classes. Columbus was to
leave as legacy the African slave-trade and the American colour
question. The Renaissance and the Reformation proved dis-
ruptive forces. While Catholicism continued universal, Pro-
testantism, for lack of a "single authoritative religious centre,"
created State churches and aggravated sectarianism, with Calvin
as a lineal descendant of the medieval sects. At the same time
the Renaissance in Italy carried across the Alps a new diplomacy based on balance of power, and spread it throughout
Christendom, where it had barely reached its geographical
limits when the Peace of Westphalia put an end to wars of
religion and set the stage for wars of commerce and conquest,
justified by considerations of "vital interests." [1]

The nation States of post-Renaissance Europe throve and
developed in an atmosphere of war. Their conception of
state-craft turned on national sovereignty and a meticulous
balance of power, in the light of which the only justification for
war was *raison d'état*. The new state-craft had its apologists in
Machiavelli, Bodin, Hobbes, and Spinoza. Theorising on war
and peace had reference no longer to a Universal Unity, mani-
fested in the Church and co-extensive with Christendom itself,

---

[1] *Cf.* Luigi Sturzo, *The International Community*, p. 31 ; and C. L.
Lange, *La Doctrine Pacifique*, pp. 216–17.

but to the individual national State. Cosmopolitan unity was lost, even as a dream. Carried to their logical conclusion, Machiavellism and Hobbism led straight to Hegel and the conception of the State as an end in itself.

(ii) *The Sixteenth and Seventeenth Centuries*

Therefore, though pacifism remained permanent, being (as will be shown later) a dogmatic principle based on a fixed state of mind, international thought underwent a series of modifications after 1500 to meet changing conditions. Its bulk increased, with contributions from humanists, sovereigns, and statesmen, arguing variously from humanitarian, philosophical, and legal viewpoints. Many of their passages have become classics in literature and landmarks in history.

Among the Renaissance humanists Erasmus, the "greatest single influence north of the Alps," contributed most to the philosophy of war. More's *Utopia* furnishes occasional homilies on the vanity of war and the moral baseness of the spirit of conquest; Sebastian Franck taught the same lesson in his *Kriegbüchlin des Frides*; Rabelais and Montaigne noisily scoffed at warfare as an unintelligent extravagance; but Erasmus, in his *Laus Stultitiæ* (1510), elaborately condemned the whole concept of violence. War was wholesale homicide, albeit the Church condoned it. It was completely devoid of benefits; and it was morally unjustifiable. Even the Turk should be converted by persuasion and not by violence; for force could plead no certainty of success. Erasmus developed no plans for perpetual peace; but his *Praise of Folly* and his *Complaint of Peace* were both called forth by contemporary events. An endeavour had been made to induce universal peace by means of a conference at Cambrai between the Emperor Maximilian, Francis I of France, and Henry VIII of England. Its authors, William of Ciervia and John Sylvagius, worked out the details of the meeting; but the project came to nothing. In its place there came the "Universal Peace" of 1518, a landmark in that it was a diplomatic instrument ratified by the same three powerful monarchs—though the peace it proclaimed lasted barely four years.

The most famous of all the world's international projects is the *Grand Dessein* of 1603, conceived and drafted by Henry IV and his minister Sully. Inspired by the need for eradicating the Wars of Religion, the French King fashioned a panacea which he would have put into operation had he lived. Elizabeth was informed of it in a personal visit from Sully, and it even secured written approval in a treaty of 1596.[1] Its primary object was to overthrow the House of Austria and so remove the chief obstacle to lasting peace. This achieved, Europe was to be divided in equal proportions among fifteen Powers in order to extinguish any future uneven balance of power. The fifteen Powers were to be represented in a Great Council, whose members would be subject to re-election every three years: four representatives from each major and two from each minor Power—in all, about seventy members. The Council's expenses were to be furnished by proportional contributions from the member States, and its duty was to consist in dealing with common affairs as they arose and settling disputes between the States. No definitive provisions for the arbitration of disputes were formulated,[2] but precaution was taken against any flouting of a Council award by prescribing (the first proposal of its kind) an international army and navy to enforce compliance.

It is easy to exaggerate the merits of the *Great Design* by emphasising the earnestness and the political wisdom of its author, but the later significance of the plan can hardly be overestimated. Henry IV's conception offered the raw materials for every subsequent internationalist project; and in many cases his structure was adopted completely, with only trifling modifications. Its historical value lies in its conception of a federal partnership among Sovereign States, in its provision of machinery whereby different national influences could function in harmony, and in its resort to combined

---

[1] See *Grand Design*, ed. E. D. Mead (1909).
[2] *Cf.* W. E. Darby, *International Tribunals* (1904), p. 18.

sanctions of force to execute awards when good faith failed. The modern problem of sanctions has its first tentative solution here.

Twenty years later two further advances of tremendous significance were made with the publication of Emeric Crucé's *Nouveau Cynée*. The central theme was the same as that of Henry and Sully—a federation rather than a sovereign authority of the medieval type. A city was to be chosen (preferably Venice) to which all sovereigns were to send resident ambassadors who would form an assembly for the purpose of settling disputes. "Human society," said Crucé, "is a body all of whose members have a common sympathy, so that it is impossible for the sickness of one not to be communicated to the others. . . . The evil passions of princes are the real causes of wars. . . . Supposing that we could obtain a universal peace, the finest fruit of it would be the establishment of commerce. . . ." His plan therefore laid down rules for safeguarding free transit and exterminating piracy. Its two innovations, however, were, first, that the League of States should comprise non-Christian as well as Christian States (the invitations being issued by the King of France and the Pope respectively); and, secondly, that war should be entirely superseded by a regulated system of arbitration. This is the first distinct proposal for substituting organised international arbitration for war, and the first daring suggestion of a world federation. Sanctions also were to be there—a logical conclusion in that age—but they were only vaguely defined under the title of "satisfactory means" of bringing defaulters to reason.

The *Nouveau Cynée* was thus a mighty step forward in theory. So far, however, no pronouncements had been made as to the rules of conduct which were to determine the ordinary intercourse of nations as distinct from emergencies and crises. It was the work of the Dutchman, Hugo Grotius, to supply this need.[1] Grotius' work, *De Jure Belli ac Pacis*, published in 1625,

---

[1] Grotius was anticipated in some ways by several thinkers who cannot be studied here : notably Ayala, Suarez, Gentili, and Francis de Victoria.

sought to supersede contemporary canons of self-interest by an ethical principle of right. He was not a pacifist; indeed his thesis rests in part on the theory that war was both ineradicable and on occasion just. What he essayed to prove, starting from the "licentiousness in regard to war" which he observed everywhere around him, was that, just as each State enjoyed a system of law which served its own interests, so there was a higher law, divine in origin, established in the interests of all nations. It is unnecessary here to follow the argument in its analysis of *jus naturæ* and *jus gentium*. What matters for the present purpose is that, in addition to providing for a "Congress of Christian Powers" in which international disputes would be resolved by impartial outsiders, Grotius sketched a code of rules which were to be ratified by the Powers as laws determining their several relations, and so founded the modern science of international law; or, more precisely, he "divides the lay science of international law from the Church's tradition." [1]

Extreme pacifism, meanwhile, had developed with the sects which had renounced violence. While the organised Churches, Catholic and Protestant, found it vitally necessary to allow and even to use war as a means of self-preservation, and while Bellarmin and Calvin and Luther sanctioned war by their writings, the various Anabaptist sects uncompromisingly condemned resort to force in any circumstances. Their spokesmen, Memno Simons in Holland and Sozzini in Switzerland, extended the arguments of Erasmus and recognised resistance to oppression as purely subjective—a matter of conscience alone. Their cardinal rule was that of obedience and outward submission. How far they and their brethren obeyed it can be seen in the long list of martyrs—Mennonites, Simonians, Socinians, Moravians, Brownists—handed down from the sixteenth century.

Most of the sects expired. Their anti-militarist tradition was continued, however, by the Society of Friends. It was in 1660 that George Fox and eleven other Quakers issued their

---

[1] *See* W. Barry, in *Dublin Review*, vol. 160 (1917); and F. M. Stawell, *Growth of International Thought* (1929), p. 121 *seq.*

famous Declaration "against all sedition, plotters, and fighters in the world; for removing the ground of jealousy and suspicion from magistrates and people concerning wars and fightings." [1] Their position was triumphantly set forth in 1676 in the *Apology* of Robert Barclay. All their teaching followed conclusively from the fundamental belief that each man's life was guided by an "inner light" which transcended even the Bible, in virtue of which there could be no right to constrain men; wherefore non-resistance and pacifism were axiomatic. This belief, fortified by the Sermon on the Mount and by the precepts of the early Christian Fathers, categorically ruled out war as a species of human relationship so completely—even to the extent of discountenancing the right of self-defence—that no Toleration Acts could relieve Friends from suffering for their faith as late as 1914.

William Penn, the son of the founder of Jamaica, was the Quaker apologist on war and peace as conclusively as Barclay was the exponent of the Friends' general position. Penn advanced, in his *Plan for the Permanent Peace of Europe* (1694), a scheme for the future organising of the world which he claimed would create untold benefits. By averting wars he hoped to secure a saving of blood, a saving of money by princes and peoples, a strengthening of Christianity's threatened reputation, an increase in trade and commerce, a period of security from the nightmare of Turkish inroads, and—ironically—a possibility that princes might in future marry for love and not for power. The scheme propounded was a revival of the "Grand Design." A permanent International Tribunal was to be set up by the sovereigns of Europe. It was to consist of ninety representatives, chosen by a system of proportional representation, and meeting every year to discuss and settle all international differences which had not been successfully composed by diplomatic means. The tribunal was to give its decisions by means of a ballot, with a minimum majority of three-quarters of the votes. All business was to be done in Latin or French; records were to be kept and circulated to each sovereign; and quarrels over

[1] M. E. Hirst, *Quakers in Peace and War*, chap. v.

precedence were to be obviated by holding the annual assembly in a circular room containing many doors, through which at a given signal the delegates could enter simultaneously.

The scheme presents problems. Penn's tribunal had as one of its functions the establishment of "rules of justice"— which would endow it with judicial powers, and therefore seem to limit the sovereignty of the member States. Penn denied that national sovereignty would be thus restricted, since all the obligations undertaken were mutual compacts; the effect would be not to limit sovereignty, but to forge a situation in which "the great fish can no longer eat up the little ones." Again, he gave no decision as to the employment of force to constrain a recalcitrant State to abide by an arbitral award— which seems incompatible with Quaker principles. Here, indeed, was a sharp dilemma. To have provided sanctions would have been to forsake his faith; to forbid sanctions would have rendered his whole scheme futile—for every government that has ever existed, except one, has cherished the inalienable right to employ force.[1]

The exception was his own government. Penn's famous treaty with the Indians, concluded in 1682 in terms of complete fellowship, enabled him to set up the first and only unarmed government in the world. "We meet," he said, "on the broad pathway of good faith and good will. No advantage shall be taken on either side, but all shall be openness and love. . . . The friendship between me and you I will not compare to a chain, for that the rains may rust, or the falling tree may break. We are the same as if one man's body were to be divided into two parts; we are all one flesh and blood."[2] In pursuance of this he paid the Indians for the land his people settled, and settled all disputes with amazing success by an arbitral tribunal of six colonists and six Indians.

Penn's scheme for peace was echoed in England by John Bellers of Gloucester in 1710. In the interval other

---

[1] For an admirable discussion of this problem see F. M. Stawell, *Growth of International Thought* (1929), pp. 138–9.

[2] Cited at Frankfort Peace Congress (1850); see *Report*, p. 15.

condemnations of war occurred. Fénelon in France was the
first writer who condemned (on other grounds than religion)
all war except resistance to unprovoked aggression. Johannes
Comenius (Komensky), the Czech educationist, took up the
extreme position of non-resistance to evil, and sought to har-
monise nationality and international sentiment by promoting
the study of languages. His *Via Lucis* (1642) foreshadowed
the popularisation of a universal tongue. Leibnitz drafted a
Codex Juris Gentium Diplomaticus in 1693. Pufendorf followed
Grotius more completely in his *De Jure Naturæ et Gentium*
(1672), while Christian Wolff elaborated Leibnitz. Contributions came also from a Duke of Lorraine and a Landgrave of
Hesse-Rheinfels; and a continued resort to arbitration has
been read into Cromwell's French Treaty of Westminster
(1655) and the Treaty of Ryswick (1697).

(iii) *The Eighteenth Century*

A rough distinction can be drawn between the sixteenth and
seventeenth centuries—the age of ethical theories of war—and
the eighteenth century—the age of national theories of peace.
While Addison and Swift, Pascal and La Bruyère, continued the
Rabelaisian attack in a vein of ridicule, a more reasoned condemnation of war became apparent, particularly in Montes-
quieu, as a necessary evil. The French Encyclopédistes, led
by Diderot, even foresaw clearly the modern interdependence
of the whole world. At all times the opposition to war was
based on reason.

The work of Grotius was expanded by Emerich Vattel in
Switzerland. Vattel's *Law of Nations* (1758) conceived the
Society of Nations as a *natural* fact, and as functioning according to certain laws which ought to be codified. Arbitration
was declared to be "a very reasonable mode . . . of deciding
every dispute which does not concern the safety of the nation,"
though the national sovereignty of the members remained
intact and force was permissible in cases of extreme necessity.
But neither Grotius or Vattel actually furnished a Code of International Law. What they produced was rather a collection of

3

precedents and opinions—the work "not of legislators, but of scholars." [1] The fund of maxims was steadily enlarged as the century wore on—from Alberoni's scheme for a European Parliament (1735) to Chateaubriand's *Génie du Christianisme* (1802).

Four monumental works tower high above the rest, published (in order of time) by Saint-Pierre, Rousseau, Bentham, and Kant.

The Abbé de Saint-Pierre's *Project for Settling Perpetual Peace in Europe* (1713), prompted by the peace negotiations at Utrecht at the close of the War of the Spanish Succession, ranks as the greatest exposition of its kind up to that time. The sordid bargaining that went on at Utrecht convinced the Abbé of the need for an International Tribunal, to the discussion of which he devoted eleven "fundamental" and eight "important" articles. His work shows the inspiration of Henry IV. There was to be a League of Sovereign States enshrined in a permanent Congress of Representatives; a code of Articles of Commerce; provisions for arbitration of disputes by the permanent Senate; combined military sanctions against any State which flouted an arbitral award. Peace-time armies were to be reduced in all States to 6000; weights and measures and coinage were to be standardised throughout Europe; and efforts were to be made to create a similar self-contained Asiatic League. All these features were described in the most comprehensive manner, and the whole essay was rounded off with answers (in advance) to sixty-two objections. But despite its minuteness and its circumspection, there are two criticisms which could not be adequately met. First, it was too patently a scheme for a coalition of kings—"wolves to guard the sheep," as Comte put it. Secondly, it was too deeply rooted in, and dependent on, the contemporary *status quo*.[2]

Rousseau made Saint-Pierre's project the text of the *Judgment on a Plan for Perpetual Peace* which he published in 1761. He endorsed its principle, believing with the Abbé that war was

---

[1] *Cf.* Elihu Burritt at Brussels Peace Congress (1848); *Report*, p. 24.

[2] Spain, for instance, was to remain in the hands of the Bourbons.

a matter, not between nations, but between princes and cabinets; and he endeavoured to succeed (where Saint-Pierre had failed) in making it possible to set the international machine in motion by guaranteeing the existing *status quo* and rendering it subject to modification by arbitration only. He provided, further, for the drafting of a Code of International Law, and for its amendment by the unanimous vote of the Diet or Congress of Representatives. But his finished plan had two serious defects. The first—that the interests of princes would effectively postpone its realisation—he admitted. The other was more insidious, and left a legacy of dissension and bloodshed which endured far into the next century. This was the principle that sovereigns should be guaranteed against rebellions among their subjects—the principle that was made the cornerstone of the Holy Alliance in 1815.

At the same time the rationalistic conception of a world united by common ties was being vindicated on more concrete grounds—by economists like Adam Smith and David Hume, and the French Physiocrats under Quesnay and Turgot, and from the legal standpoint by Jeremy Bentham. The *Fragment of an Essay on International Law* occupied Bentham during the years 1786–89. He was completely cosmopolitan in sentiment. His view of the future, never quite explicit in his writings, resolved itself, among later thinkers, into the idea of a United States of Europe. He insisted on reciprocal rights and duties among civilised nations—the duty of abstaining from injury to others, and the right of expecting from them a like consideration. To avert war for the future he devised a plan which comprised four fundamentals: the reduction of armaments;[1] the establishment of a "Permanent Court of Judicature" with powers of arbitration backed by sanctions of force; the codification of International Law; and—a sidelight on the wars of the eighteenth century—the emancipation of all colonies.

But there had already occurred, through the revolt of one group of colonies, a shock to the prevailing conception of the

[1] In 1787 he projected a Franco-British treaty for the limitation of naval armaments. *Cf.* C. L. Lange, *Doctrine Pacifique* (1926), p. 335.

State, to which the French Revolution was to administer a death-blow. The French and American Revolutions together changed the connotation of the word State. International relations were to be the affairs no longer of dynastic princes but of whole nations. So apparent was the transformation and so strong the realisation of the growing interdependence of the nations that as early as 1793 a World State was being trumpeted by one Anacharsis Klootz.

The last of the eighteenth-century philosophers, Immanuel Kant, accepted the new theory of the nation State but rejected the headstrong logic that would enlarge the nation into a Cosmopolis. Kant's *Perpetual Peace* (*Zum Ewigen Frieden*) won him the reproach of being a Jacobin (1795). The book falls into two parts—an examination of certain reforms to be undertaken while war still existed, in order to create a public opinion favourable to the abolition of war, and a body of suggestions for the final organisation of perpetual peace. Kant firmly believed eternal peace to be an unrealisable ideal; therefore his suggestions were more properly concerned with seeking the right road and following it as far as was humanly possible. He agreed with Hobbes that man was by nature selfish and base, but he drew from history the lesson that mankind had risen to a high state of civilisation through the competition and "mutual antagonism" of individuals "in society," which not only had produced social chaos but also had brought out all man's latent powers, until the chaos had been resolved by the formation of the State. This argument he employed similarly to foreshadow an analogous development among States themselves, culminating in a "federation of free republics." By republic he meant any form of government which embodied the liberty and equality of its subjects ; and he favoured federation in preference to a World State, for the psychological reason that "law weakens as territory expands." Federation would involve "the surrender of a portion of power in return for participation in a wider, richer, and more secure life." In order to hasten this federation, and in order thereby to essay the path towards everlasting peace, Kant prescribed his series of "preliminary articles," concentrating on non-intervention and the gradual abolition of standing armies. He made no detailed provisions for an International Tribunal. What struck him most in the institution of war was the use of methods so diabolical and revolting to secure the ends of justice.

The criticism that is most usually offered as a retort to Kant's philosophy of Peace is that his analogy between individual and social evolution is not altogether true; that individuals have, and that States have not, the power to curtail an acute dispute by literally retreating out of the way; and that, therefore, disputes between States are "likely to reduce to questions of existence." [1] But Kant's enduring contribution to the theory and literature of his problem was not so much the foundations of his plan as the fact that he lifted the discussion of war and peace far above the level of politics—at which it had lain since the days of Pierre Dubois—and exalted it into a question of ethics and social conscience. Wherefore it was Kant alone who could do battle on their own plane with the high-priests of ethical war —Hegel, Schiller, and Treitschke.

(iv) *The Settlement of* 1815

The theories and projects that have been outlined in the preceding pages may be regarded as the body of scientific speculation from which the physicians of the first organised Peace Movements of the nineteenth century, when once they had realised that the abolition of war was a question of analysis and diagnosis as well as mere empirical awareness, drew their formulæ for nourishing a better world. But by 1815 the old world of Henry IV and Rousseau had undergone a serious operation, and during the recovery it became evident, by several ominous and characteristic symptoms, that its malady had not been cured. One symptom—"balance of power"—reappeared in a more chronic form than before; another—"legitimacy"—returned vigorously, though not for long; a third—"dynastic marriages"—showed itself occasionally, but

[1] *See* particularly Mary C. Smith's edition of Kant.

rarely with the strength of an outbreak. On the whole, Europe was only patched, though the patch held for forty years.

It is still fashionable to praise the Treaty of Vienna and the Concert of Europe because they kept Europe at peace till 1854. An equally attractive case might be made out for the thesis that Europe contrived to stay tranquil in spite of the Treaty and the Concert. Certainly the Vienna Settlement accentuated dangers and aggravated problems that were foreseen at the time, and ignored warnings that had long ago been borne across the Atlantic from the New World.

For two years Europe was ruled by an oligarchy—from the assembly of allied statesmen which drafted the Treaty of Toeplitz in September 1813 to that which signed the Second Treaty of Paris on 20th November 1815. During that period the oligarchy evolved the theory of the Concert of Europe, largely the work of the British Foreign Secretary, Viscount Castlereagh.[1] The settlement of Europe after the fall and exile of Napoleon, the Concert that was built up to maintain that settement, were both based on two principles which destroyed most of the value they might have had as instruments of international organisation.

One principle was that of Intervention, whereby the five great Powers (Austria, France, Great Britain, Prussia, and Russia) were free to interfere collectively in the internal concerns of any State whose condition seemed to them to threaten the peace of Europe. The underlying ideas were fear of revolutions like that of 1789 and reverence for the principle of legitimacy which had sent the Bourbons back to Paris. Intervention obtained its most extravagant formulation in the Declaration issued at the Conference of Troppau by Austria, Prussia, and Russia (9th November 1820), from which Castlereagh dissented. Two years later it was on the same issue that Canning severed England from co-operation with the Holy Alliance during the Congress of Verona.[2]

---

[1] See C. K. Webster, *Congress of Vienna* (1918), and *Foreign Policy of Castlereagh* (1925).
[2] See H. W. V. Temperley, *Foreign Policy of Canning* (1925), chap. iii.

The other principle was that of the Balance of Power, the contribution of Renaissance Italy to modern politics—than which there has been no greater obstacle to international thought down to the present day. Theoretically balance of power connoted equality of power and equilibrium. In practice it meant a struggle for preponderance and a destruction of equilibrium. "The armed State seeks first of all to be self-sufficient, and when this limit is reached to impose a hegemony on others. Yet for the same reason other States seek the same end, and thus the limit of force extends towards an instinctive balance of power, or towards the hegemonic dominion of one or more Powers." [1] The system involved secret diplomacy and made distrust the first lesson in statesmanship. Moreover, the name was merely conventional and idle. Statesmen neither discussed it openly nor knew how to measure it. Power was never apportioned, and at no time was there an exact balance. What the belief did was to perpetuate hatreds and fears, and foster effete monstrosities like the Austrian Empire.

The fears which underlay both principles were therefore only magnified as time went on. In one further respect also did they surround the globe with barriers. It was the constant dread of the three autocratic Powers (Austria, Prussia, and Russia) that some sudden revolutionary upheaval might liberate the Spanish colonies in Latin America. To prevent such a calamity a campaign of interference in the affairs of the American continent was opened through Madrid. The direct result, after the successful revolt of the colonies, was the promulgation by President Monroe of the Doctrine which has henceforth determined United States policy, and which cleft a line of demarcation between the two hemispheres.[2]

Nevertheless the Vienna Settlement shows evidences that the phrase "international government" was already beginning to have significance. The Vienna Final Act has indeed been called the first example of "deliberate international legislation." It contained provisions regarding the navigation of certain

[1] Luigi Sturzo, *The International Community* (1929), p. 85.
[2] *See* A. B. Hart, *Monroe Doctrine* (1916).

rivers, which led to the establishment of the first International Executive—the Danube Commission. It provided, further, a prohibition of the Slave Trade which ultimately rendered necessary the creation of some form of control (by right of search) to prevent infringements of the prohibition. In both decisions statesmen and diplomats had met expressly to regulate the vital interests of all nations. The whole settlement, moreover, can be regarded as a rudimentary form of international organisation rather than an alliance of the customary dimensions. Even intervention can be made to postulate (in theory) a conception of a society of nations. Actually the truth was far otherwise; diplomacy vacillated between desires of union and dominion. The Concert degenerated into a series of reunions, and very soon waned, to revive later in an altered form.

Finally, the Vienna Treaties formally annexed the principle of arbitration and made it an orthodox means of adjusting disputes among the nations—by resorting to it to settle four vexed questions of the time. These were the problems of the Rhine transit dues, the Netherlands public debt, the customs dues between Uri and Tessin (Swiss Cantons), and the succession to the Duchy of Bouillon.[1]

But besides the Concert of Europe, which became a six-Power responsibility when France was admitted in 1818, there existed the Holy Alliance of the three autocrats, conceived by the Tsar Alexander I in 1815 and enshrined in a tripartite declaration (issued on 26th September) which was thrown open to the whole of Christian Europe for adherence.[2] All sovereigns signed except two—the Pope and the British Prince Regent. Castlereagh dubbed the Alliance a "loud-sounding nothing." Its inspiration, in so far as it emanated from the Tsar, was partly Christian and partly mystical. Its text, embodied in the declaration, was "a fixed resolution" on the part of all three monarchs "to take for their sole guide the precepts of . . . Justice, Christian Charity, and Peace . . . as being the only

---

[1] J. Gennadius, *International Arbitration*, p. 56.
[2] Text in Eliz. York, *Leagues of Nations*, pp. 319–21.

means of consolidating human institutions and remedying
their imperfections." This was a magnificent declaration of
the Christian standard of international relations. Had it been
adhered to, the future might have turned out far different.
But the Holy Alliance was an association of autocratic sovereigns speaking (with divine sanctions) for their peoples; at
best, a theocratic despotism. In point of fact it speedily
showed itself at its worst—for instance, in the Troppau declaration. The autocrats forgot their Christian protestation. What
more natural, then, than that the first organised Peace Societies
should take a firm stand on that same declaration?

PART TWO

THE FIRST PEACE MOVEMENT: 1815–67

If people would but understand that they are not the sons of some fatherland or other, nor of Governments, but are sons of God, and can therefore be neither slaves nor enemies one to another. . . .
LEO TOLSTOY

Not that I love my country less, but Humanity more
CHARLES SUMNER

CHAPTER III

THE FIRST PEACE SOCIETIES: 1815–43

(a) *Foundation, Principles, Environment*

ORGANISED pacifism may be regarded as one manifestation of
the humanitarian movement which was quickened into action
by the Napoleonic Wars. The list of the early heroes of Peace
includes names more famous in other directions—in prison
reform, in temperance reform, in industrial reform, in anti-
slavery. All these causes were linked together in the tempera-
ment of the humanitarian evangelist, and of the Quaker. The
Peace Movement, like its contemporary reformist agitations,
was largely Quaker in origin. It was born just before the end
of the Napoleonic Wars, prompted, not by the Vienna Settlement, but by the dreary protraction of the war itself; and it
began, quite independently, in two continents simultaneously.

The antecedents in America cover ten years. It was in 1805
that David Low Dodge, a New York merchant of Non-Resistant
principles, published a pamphlet entitled *The Mediator's
Kingdom not of this World*, in which he denounced all warfare
as contrary to Christianity. A vigorous reply to it induced him
to consider the possibility of forming a society to preach the
blessings of universal peace; but his plans were interrupted
by the Anglo-American War of 1812, and he published nothing
more until 1815. Then, on the basis of a second pamphlet,
War Inconsistent with the Religion of Jesus Christ, he founded
the world's first Peace Society on 14th August 1815. Meanwhile there had appeared in Massachusetts, on Christmas Day
1814, a pamphlet by one Dr. Noah Worcester, *The Solemn
Review of the Custom of War*, later the most widely distributed
of all Peace literature. Worcester was not a Non-Resistant,

45

and he knew nothing as yet of Dodge's writings ; but his arguments against war were identical with those of Dodge. God, he said further, could put an end to war as thoroughly as He had put an end to British slavery, and by the same means. Man's part would consist in devising schemes to organise the world into a Confederacy of Nations, strengthened by a "High Court of Equity." To achieve this end it was necessary to found Peace Societies.

By the close of 1815 three such societies had been founded in the United States—by Dodge in New York, by Worcester in Massachusetts on 28th December, and by two Friends in Ohio on 2nd December. Each was formed in ignorance of the other two.

Simultaneously the same movement began in England, again quite independently. The earliest traces appear in an anonymous letter in the *Monthly Magazine* during 1811 urging the establishment of a "National Court of Arbitration." [1] Two years later Dr. Bogue, the head of the Gosport Missionary Society, called attention to the problem of war and peace in a sermon which was widely discussed. It cannot be proved, however, that this sermon was known to the founder of the British Peace Movement, William Allen, who gathered his friends round him on 6th June 1814, at his house in Lombard Street, to consider measures "for the promotion of Permanent and Universal Peace." Out of this meeting, attended entirely by Quakers, and renewed a year later with an attendance of only three, emerged the Peace Society, founded on 14th June 1816. [2] And as the three American societies were later fused into the American Peace Society, the British "Society for the Promotion of Permanent and Universal Peace" has always claimed to be the oldest in the world.

The organisation of the new movements on both sides of the Atlantic consisted in annual meetings for the discussion of principles and the review of progress, supplemented by vigorous and intensive campaigns of propaganda and publicity.

[1] Vol. xxxi, p. 526.
[2] Full account in *H. of P.* (1819), pp. 2-3.

All the societies were non-sectarian and open to all Christians. Membership and life-membership were procurable at graded fees.

In America there was not an entire unanimity of sentiment among the founders. Dodge was a Non-Resister, Worcester was not. William Ellery Channing, a co-founder of the Massachusetts Peace Society, did not dogmatise his faith until later. But there was no lack of unanimity in action, since questions of fundamental principle did not emerge until the time came to incorporate the American societies into one body. In England, from the moment of its foundation, the Peace Society stood resolutely against all forms of war, without exception; and never once has it wavered. Non-Resistance was an article of its faith. Based on the inspiration of the Scriptures, and realising how in time of war the political fate of one's country counted for more than the moral and religious life of the people, the Quaker pacifist creed contained a single proposition—that war was incompatible with Christianity.[1] Even defensive war was denied justification. Killing in self-defence amounted to taking life in order to avoid a *risk* rather than a *certainty* of death. Secondly, denial of the right of suicide precluded the taking of the lives of others. Thirdly, resistance would only provoke further aggression and violence. Lastly, counter-arguments based on the *instinctiveness* of self-preservation were declared false, as instinct could not be pleaded as vindication for any action controlled by reason or religion. To allow defensive war would be either inconsistent or disingenuous. Accordingly the London Society advised pacifists who could not accept Non-Resistance to form auxiliary societies of their own which could pursue the same goal of universal peace from a different standpoint. Nevertheless there is conclusive evidence that many remained outside the Society on the sole ground of its opposition to defensive war. Many

---

[1] This belief was not based on any text in Scripture, but many texts were constantly cited to support it : notably Matthew v. 38–48 ; John xviii. 36 ; James iv. ; Romans xii. 20 ; Galatians v. 14, 22 ; 2 Corinthians x. 4 ; 1 Peter ii. 20, 24. And *cf.* G. W. Knowles, *Quakers and War*, p. 3.

of these abstainers, moreover, were ministers of the gospel. Here, therefore, is one reason why the Peace Society was ever loud in protest against the lack of support which it received from the Churches.

Propaganda in both countries was organised on careful and comprehensive lines. The object in view was "to effect a change in public opinion on the subject of war, and to persuade men to examine it by the light of the Gospel. . . ." The societies were to form a medium of correspondence between the friends of peace all over the world; to eschew party politics since their cause was religious and not political; and to propagate ideas of the peaceful organisation of the world. All this was to be done by printing and circulating tracts. There was at first no project for travelling lecture-tours, though it was realised that much valuable work could be done by particular denominations of Christians—Methodists, Baptists, Moravians —and by the Societies' members in their own districts. References were frequently made to the Bible Societies and the schools of Lancaster and Bell. Nor were there, for some years, any proposals put forward for Peace machinery on the lines discussed in the last chapter. Noah Worcester's *Solemn Review* remained for long the single classic of the movements.

When practical schemes did begin to be formulated, the Peace Societies could find encouragement in three precedents furnished by diplomacy during the preceding thirty years. The first was the United States Constitution of 1787, wherein thirteen Sovereign States had renounced their right to declare war independently, and had clothed a Supreme Court with "affirmative jurisdiction" over all interstate disputes, backed only by a moral sanction—the first real International Tribunal in history. The second was the Anglo-American Treaty of 1794, the famous Jay Treaty of Arbitration. This document enshrined Benjamin Franklin's prayer for "the discovery of a plan that would induce and oblige nations to settle their disputes without first cutting one another's throats." Its enduring value lies in that it was the first diplomatic instrument in history which provided for arbitration on a large scale. The

third precedent resulted from the Anglo-American War of
1812–14, when, under the terms of the Treaty of Ghent, the
frontier between the United States and Canada was delimited
and entrusted (along its whole length) to the guard of one
steamer.

(b) *The First Years:* 1816–30

Under such auspices the Anglo-American Peace Movement
began its work—two simultaneous and independent groups.
Of the twelve leaders in England the most influential were
William Allen himself, the brothers John and Thomas Clarkson,
William Crawford, and Joseph Tregelles Price. They were all
members of the Peace Society's committee, and all were Friends.
The Clarksons were already well known to the public for their
labours during the Anti-Slavery campaign. Tregelles Price
was a master mariner, whose pacific opinions had been divested
to practical ends ever since the occasion when, during the
Napoleonic Wars, his ship had been pursued and the boarders
had been dumbfounded at finding that he carried no guns.

The official organ of the Peace Society was a monthly journal
of twenty-four pages, called the *Herald of Peace*, first issued in
January 1819 at twopence per copy. It is still in existence.
Its first number bore in its preface the following astounding
assertion: "A theme of such paramount importance . . .
requires only the aid of its natural ally and powerful auxiliary,
the Press, to evince its pretensions and ensure its success."
Side by side with the *Herald*, pamphlets and tracts were issued
regularly to subscribers and for general distribution. In the
first year a total of thirty-two thousand copies of four tracts
was reached, and four thousand addresses were delivered in
various parts of England; while by 1818 a "regular channel of
communication" had been opened up with America. Auxiliary
branch societies were formed wherever an average of forty
members could be recruited—by 1819 in ten towns. Most of
the funds of the Society accrued, however, from the sale of
tracts, though after 1824 special tracts were issued for distribution free among the poor. All the nine pamphlets of the

4

first fifteen years were exclusively religious in attitude. As time went on propaganda widened. District meetings were held by each branch in surrounding villages; essays on peace found their way into the local Press; public libraries were presented with files of the *Herald*; and translators were kept busy in London copying the tracts into French, German, Spanish, and later into Italian, for propagation among the Maltese. Bound sets were carried to statesmen and crowned heads—to Lord Sidmouth in 1818, by Clarkson to the Tsar Alexander at the Congress of Aix-la-Chapelle, and by Bowring (the Foreign Secretary of the Society) to the King of Spain in 1822; while the *Herald* went off regularly to every member of the British Diplomatic Service.

The effect of all this was, of course, imperceptible for many years, apart from the small increase in actual membership. Publicity in the Press, also, was on the smallest local scale. In 1828 only four journals accorded the Society even the briefest notice; and of these, the most influential, was the now forgotten *Record*. One lengthy criticism alone had appeared, a scurrilous attack in the *Northumberland Monthly Magazine* in 1819. It is worth quoting as typical of the attitude of the Press down to the Crimean War. "It is not likely that all the world, at one time, can be brought to agree upon the abolition of war; and whatever nation began first to lay aside the means of self-defence would soon become a prey to the rest. . . . The Peace Society begin their work at the wrong end, when they would persuade men to lay aside war before they have laid aside their crimes. . . . They are for inspiring an abhorrence of war from religious motives; but such motives cannot be expected to influence any except the civilised part of the world. And by what means are we to restrain the ravages of barbarous nations? Will holding out the idea that war is inconsistent with Christianity restrain the Turks, the pirates of Algiers, or the savage Indians of North America? Nothing would be more gratifying to Turkish and heathen nations than to hear that Christians had abolished war; in this case every European kingdom would soon be deluged with blood, and every Christian community exterminated. . . . Can any Peace Society [moreover] persuade us that it is a sin for the magistrate to use the sword? And if a magistrate has a right to use the sword against one robber, why not against thousands, when assembled for the avowed purpose of plunder and devastation? . . ." [1]

Such criticism had a strong positive value, however. It revealed the need for practical suggestions from the Peace Society to enhance the force of its doctrines. This need became apparent from another angle as early as 1825, for in that year the London Society found occasion for the first time to note with regret a slackening in the increase in membership. Its income fell seriously, and from Bristol and Bath there came importunate comments on "the distressing apathy that seems to prevail upon this interesting question." The need was arising for a *programme* of Peace.

The greatest advance that the Society achieved before 1830 consisted in the foundation of the Birmingham auxiliary by Joseph Sturge on 3rd December 1827 with forty-one members. Sturge, a Quaker, ranks among the three greatest leaders of the British Peace Movements. He recruited the auxiliary largely from among the members of the Birmingham Anti-Slavery Society in response to a plea in the *Birmingham Chronicle* on 7th December 1826. Until his death as President of the Peace Society in 1859 his auxiliary was the most active in the country. Meanwhile members of his fraternity, led by Daniel Wheeler, had settled in Russia at the invitation of the Tsar Alexander I (1818) to reclaim the swamps around Petersburg and to spread the Friends' message of goodwill—in the fulfilment of which commission they spent fourteen useful years.[2]

In the meantime the American Societies had been fused into one. Of the groups founded in 1815 Worcester's adherents in New England were the most thriving, articulate in the columns of the *Friend of Peace*, which Worcester edited until his retirement in 1828. He aimed high from the outset by

---

[1] Reprinted in *H. of P.* (1819), pp. 289 *seq.*
[2] M. E. Hirst, *Quakers in Peace and War*, pp. 460–1.

inviting both President Jefferson and President Adams to become members; but these aspirations failed. The Society quadrupled its sale of tracts in the first four years, some even finding their way to Bombay and Ceylon, where they were spread inland by Baptist ministers. By 1820 there were thirty-three societies in the United States; three times the number in England. And whereas Allen was unable to enlist many Christian ministers in England, several denominational branches in America either offered the Peace Movement the support of pulpits and parish magazines, or themselves formed Peace Societies.[1]

The summer of 1823, however, saw the emergence of an influence that was to knit all this individual effort into one national crusade. That influence was a New Hampshire sea-captain, William Ladd. He had been educated at Harvard, whence he had gone to sea. When he first heard of the existence of Peace Societies, in 1819, he was forty-six years old; but from 1823 until his death in 1841 he was the greatest link between the Movement in the two hemispheres. Finding that its principles were in complete harmony with ideas he had often evolved in private contemplation, he began in July 1823 a series of articles on Peace in the columns of the Portland (Maine) *Christian Mirror*. At first he did not denounce uncompromisingly all forms of war. But later he realised that to discriminate between lawful (defensive) and unlawful war would leave him without either a principle or an inflexible standard of values. His articles and his public speeches (begun at Portland in 1824) won him a high local reputation. He entered the Maine Peace Society, began to correspond regularly with Bowring in London, and urged the consolidation of all the American societies. In 1826, by which time Dodge's Society in New York had become moribund, the Peace Society of Maine decided to form a national organisation ministering to the whole of the United States. Within two years the ground had been surveyed.

---

[1] *See* E. L. Whitney, *American Peace Society* (1928), pp. 15, 16. Canada had twelve societies by 1826; *see* M. E. Curti, *American Peace Crusade* (1929), p. 36.

Ladd drafted a constitution in February 1828, and on 8th May following the "American Peace Society" came into being, in New York, with a monthly organ, the *Harbinger of Peace*, edited by Ladd himself.

The basis of the Society was religious. "If peace," said Ladd, " be not an enterprise strictly evangelical, its principles a part of the Gospel, its duties an element of our religion essential to the full and perfect development of Christian character, we are prepared to abandon it forthwith for work more appropriate to our high and holy calling." Under the terms of the new constitution, the object of the Society was "to diffuse the light respecting the evils of war and the best means for effecting its abolition." This was to be essayed by the tested methods of printed tracts, auxiliary societies, and contact with fellow-workers abroad. Members paid an annual subscription, in return for which they were supplied with all literature issued by the Society. Ladd expressed a hope that, once a "healthy public opinion" had been created, their goal of universal peace could be reached along lines already more or less definitely conceived. This is important. "We hope," he declared in a circular letter issued immediately after the consolidation of the Society, "to increase and promote the practice already begun of submitting national differences to amicable discussion and arbitration; and finally of settling all national controversies by an appeal to reason, as becomes rational creatures . . . and that this shall be done by a Congress of Nations, whose decrees shall be enforced by public opinion that rules the world. . . . Then wars shall cease." [1] Thus the American Peace Society began its existence with the essentials of a programme organised on a religious and non-sectarian basis.

But here a striking distinction must be noticed between the British and American Movements. Though both Peace Societies were preponderatingly religious and took their inspiration from Scripture, the American Society was from the start precise in aim, while the British Society was not. Arbitra-

[1] Constitution in full in E. L. Whitney, *American Peace Society*, pp. 20-21.

tion and a Congress of Nations figured in the American programme some four years before they were endorsed as vital means in England. Indeed, the first notices of the American campaign towards these two ends to appear in the *Herald of Peace*, while strong in approval, contained no suggestion that the cause might be advanced by collateral effort in Europe.

In England the one notable contribution to Peace literature during the first fifteen years was a philosophy rather than a programme. *The Enquiry into the Accordance of War with the Principles of Christianity*, by Jonathan Dymond of the Exeter Peace Auxiliary (1823), did no more than present in an admirable form the orthodox Quaker standpoint. The precepts of Jesus had expressly forbidden war; the practice of the Apostles and the Early Fathers had borne out his testimony; and Providence had foretold the banishment of violence from the earth. For a Christian, the final duty in time of war was Non-Resistance. The only constructive Peace scheme of the period, James Mill's *Law of Nations*, came from outside the Peace Movement. In America, on the contrary, it was to this question of a Congress of Nations that the energies of both theorists and preachers were directed from 1828 onwards, as will be seen later.

Further pacifist activity had in the meantime begun on the mainland in Europe. One manifestation, a Christian Brotherhood founded in Holland in 1817 by one Dirk Valk, lived barely ten years, as its advocacy of Platonic communism brought on it rapid suppression by the Government.[1] But in France and Switzerland the Peace Movement took firm root.

As early as 1815 Joseph Garnier had published articles on war and peace. On 20th December 1821 the *Société des Amis de la Morale Chrétienne* was inaugurated in Paris by the Duc de Rochefoucauld-Liancourt. This society, the backbone of the Liberal Movement in 1830, was not strictly an organisation directed towards promoting peace. But S. V. S. Wilder, of the Massachusetts Peace Society, was among its founders, and it very soon opened up a regular

[1] It lived till 1833. See its story in *H. of P.* (1847), pp. 245–7.

correspondence also with the Peace Society in London. Its object was "to recall continually to the human mind the principles of Christianity." To this end works on the improvement of the moral and physical condition of man were to be collected and their ideas expounded in a periodical. But the Society did not condemn all war, and could thus open its doors to Catholics. By 1825 also it enjoyed patronage in high places —from the Dauphin and the Duchesse de Berry; though Charles X and the Duc de Broglie eyed it askance. Seven years later it became definitely a Peace Society. "It corresponds with those of London and Geneva; it professes the same principles [this was not so]; it aims at the same ameliorations; it endeavours, like them, to influence public opinion. . . ." [1]

The Geneva Society here mentioned was the last national organisation founded before the end of 1830; the last, indeed, before 1867. It was the creation of the Comte de Sellon, founded expressly to co-operate with the other existing societies. What was most remarkable about the Comte de Sellon was his eminent practicality. In addition to launching at once a fourth Peace periodical, *Les Archives de la Société de Genève*, he offered a prize of a gold medal for an essay outlining practical suggestions for realising the *Grand Design* of Henry IV. His watchword was publicity. [2]

Until 1867 the history of these four societies—in Great Britain, the United States, France, and Switzerland—is a record of expansion and definition, helped by co-operation from outside by other reformist movements, rendered more articulate by means of resolutions introduced in the Parliaments of two continents, but not productive of any fresh crystallisation of pacifist sentiments elsewhere. No further national Peace Societies were formed for thirty-seven years.

[1] *See* the Society's *Journal*, viii, pp. 358–69 ; and (1832), No. 5.
[2] Account in *H. of P.* (1831), pp. 3, 4, 34.

(c) A "Congress of Nations": 1830–43

The one access of strength which the Movement received before 1843, an alliance which, indeed, enabled it in that year to inaugurate a series of Peace Congresses, came from Free Trade. Object-lessons for the future were seen, no doubt, in the four successful arbitrations which were effected under the terms of the Jay Treaty[1] and in Bolivar's Pan-American Congress of 1826 (though Pan-America was a dream not realised until 1890). But by far the most potent encouragement came, however, from the outburst of economic speculation which, about 1830, began to evolve more or less coherent theories of free trade and *laissez-faire*. Stimulated by the French and Belgian Revolutions, the "Third Estate" throughout Europe began to raise its voice in a cry for the reduction of tariff barriers as one means among many for confounding clerical conservation. The Industrial Revolution and the speedy revolutionisation in means of transport had opened new horizons and created a new social problem—the "division of labour in an international world." Cobden and Bright in England, Frederic Bastiat in France, and William Ellery Channing in America were the protagonists of the international questions prompted by this new and boundless outlook. They were not of one mind regarding either method or object. Channing was a pacifist before everything, and a Free Trader solely as a means to peace. Bastiat rejoiced in an inexorable logic which envisaged peace as the inevitable consequence of destroying tariff walls. Cobden began his political career primarily as a Free Trader, and died in 1865 the founder of present-day internationalism. He was never a pacifist. Bright altogether declined to dogmatise on war.

"The plain duty and plain interest of the human race," said Channing in 1836, "is to level all barriers to free exchange, to cut up the system of restriction root and branch, to open every port on the earth to every product."[2] Cobden's letters and

---

[1] Details in W. E. Darby, *International Tribunals* (1904), p. 775.
[2] W. E. Channing, *Lectures on War*, ed. E. D. Mead, p. 50.

speeches thundered the same burden. But Cobden probed the
international system of his day to its very roots, and so deduced
from Free Trade a logical theory, vehemently expressed, of
world organisation. Free Trade and Non-Intervention became
to him the means whereby the fetish of Balance of Power might
be cast aside and an era of stable peace inaugurated. His
central principle was "the harmony of men, irrespective of
political, racial, or linguistic barriers, by means of organised
mutual aid. . . . This free human co-operation, transcending
the limits of nationality and race, was the positive force, intellectual and emotional, of which non-intervention was the negative
condition. . . . Enlightened self-interest, operating through
free contract or free competition, was the true instrument of
individual progress and social harmony."[1] Not that Cobden
was antipatriotic: his letters to Sumner during the American
Civil War clear him of such a charge. Nor was he altogether
democratic: it was ever his belief that to enfranchise the agri-
cultural labourer would weaken the middle class by strengthening the upholders of political and economic privilege, since the
middle class was hated equally by aristocracy and labour. But
he contended that the time was ripe for the welding of a new
international order. "The Equilibrium of Europe," he once
said, "was a phrase of some significance when the whole world
was in Europe. It has lost its meaning now." Foreign policy
had to adjust itself to the task of equating a world equilibrium
tempered by non-intervention and free exchange. Bright
agreed with him in principle, but could rarely be induced to
condemn the institution of war in the light thereof. True,
Bright denounced all the wars of his lifetime, except the Turkish
War of 1876; but he judged each on its merits. "I advise you,"
he said in a letter written late in life, "not to trouble yourself
with the abstract principle. The practical question is the one
which presses, and when we have settled that, there will remain
very little of the mischief to contend about or to get rid of."[2]

[1] J. A. Hobson, *Richard Cobden the International Man* (1918),
pp. 20–22, 330, 394.
[2] John Bright, *Public Letters*, p. 238.

"I have never advocated the extreme non-resistance principle," he wrote to Sturge in 1857; "I don't know whether I would logically maintain it."

It was not, however, until after 1840 that definite co-operation began between the Peace and the Free Trade Movements. During the ten years of unco-ordinated effort, the Peace Societies were occupied in speculating as to the form their promised world authority should take, and in tinkering at the mechanism which would enable it to function when constructed. These were, respectively, a "Congress of Nations" and Arbitration. In both England and America the years 1830–42 saw the rise of a persistent endeavour to get the virtues of arbitration aired in parliaments and recognised by ministers. Beyond this, the American Movement concentrated on elaborating a device for a Congress of Nations, while in England most of the Peace Society's funds were devoted to an extended publicity campaign throughout the Parliamentary constituencies.

The details of all this propaganda recorded in the *Herald of Peace* are apt to give an exaggerated impression of the Society's progress. For though James Hargreaves, the Home Secretary of the Society, carried out annual pilgrimages of the whole of England from 1832 onwards, and organised lecture tours were begun six years later, the local propaganda attracted hardly any public notice whatever. Stephen Rigaud alone, who gave up his post of Sunday School visitor in 1839 to travel for the Society, stands out above the agents who honeycombed England. Within a year of his appointment Rigaud sent up the circulation of tracts to a quarter of a million; at the end of four years he crossed to Brussels for the first of a series of Continental tours that were to plant more branches in France (his mother's home) than existed in England. At the same time there was some hope for the future spread of the Movement, by reason of the prominent Quaker families which either founded or patronised its branches. Some of these—the Gurneys of Norwich, the Sturges of Birmingham, the Dymonds of Exeter—were names well known about the country. Joseph Sturge had the ear of anti-slavery members of Parliament; Samuel Gurney had gone to Geneva in 1834 to establish links with Sellon. And in this way, by contact with individual members of Parliament, an innovation appeared in 1842 with the first presentation of a Peace Society petition to both Houses. The Prime Minister, Peel, had been sent a memorial during the China War a year earlier, but the first general petition, presented in the Commons by Joseph Brotherton and in the Lords by Lord Brougham, condemned not only the current events in China and Afghanistan but all war without exception. This event was the first articulation of organised pacifism in the British Parliament.[1] At the time, the Peace Society numbered among its members only four other M.P.s: Edward Baines (the Staffordshire mill-owner), Charles Hindley (later President of the Society), Joseph Hume (the human advertisement of all the reform movements), and James Silk Buckingham. Of these, Baines was the most influential, for he controlled the *Leeds Mercury* and the *Staffordshire Mecury*.

Across the Atlantic, meanwhile, Ladd had launched the practical idea of a Congress of Nations, not only in the columns of the *Harbinger* but also in the Senate of Massachusetts, where, on its second introduction in February 1837, his petition was adopted and passed by both Houses—by the Lower House unanimously; and both Houses forthwith invited the President to open negotiations with foreign Governments on the lines Ladd suggested. These were the establishment of a "Court of Nations" for the settlement of *all* international disputes by means of arbitration.[2] The year 1837 was thus a first triumph for the American Peace Movement, of more significance than the success in 1842 in England.

Five months later, in May 1837, the constitution of the American Peace Society was revised. A firm stand was now taken "on the principle that *all* war is contrary to the spirit of the Gospel." From Hartford the offices were moved to Boston.

---

[1] See *H. of P.* (1842), p. 143.
[2] *Calumet* (1835), pp. 203–4; *A. of P.* (1838), pp. 68–70. A precedent for memorials to Congress had already been set in the Privateering question; *see* M. E. Curti, *American Peace Crusade*, p. 29.

Ladd was elected first President, and George C. Beckwith Secretary. The *Harbinger* became the *Advocate of Peace*.

The new constitution, however, must not be construed as endorsing the extreme principle of Non-Resistance. The very fact that it did not do so precipitated a serious disagreement among the Society's leaders within a year, as a result of which the Society as a whole could never quite rid itself of the suspicion held by many well-wishers that it was non-resistant and antipatriotic. The important facts are as follows. Ladd himself was by 1837 a Non-Resistant. "I do *not* believe," he wrote in 1838, "that a Christian has the right to take life in self-defence." " I ought not to fight in defence of life, liberty, or religion, much less for property; but to leave vengeance to God, to whom it belongs." Many other members of the American Peace Society were solidly with him: chief among them, Beckwith and Henry Clarke Wright. But Ladd and Beckwith were in favour of keeping the membership as comprehensive as possible —to which end the Society had consistently avoided pronouncing on the question of defensive war. Wright, however, toured New England in 1838 preaching Non-Resistance. He received enthusiastic support from the leader of the American Anti-Slavery Movement, William Lloyd Garrison, who had already opened his journal, the *Liberator*, to Non-Resistant arguments. Elsewhere, in the pages of the *Calumet*, the wrongfulness of defensive war had been vehemently argued by Thomas S. Grimké of South Carolina for two years continuously. When one Elijah Lovejoy of Illinois was murdered in 1837 while repelling burglars, Ladd declared in the *Harbinger of Peace* that he had not been justified in resisting.[1] But at a Peace Convention held in Boston on 18th September 1838, called by Non-resistants to organise a campaign against defensive war, Ladd, acting for the Society, supported an amendment to a motion put forward in the most uncompromising terms by Wright. The result was that Garrison and Wright with a large following seceded from the Society and founded the New England Non-Resistance Society, avowing that "We

[1] *See* Hemmenway, *William Ladd*, pp. 66–9, 71, 76.

register our testimony not only against all wars, whether offensive or defensive, but all preparations for war. . . . But while we shall adhere to the doctrine of non-resistance and passive submission to enemies, we purpose, in a moral and spiritual sense, to speak and act boldly in the cause of God." Early in 1839 Garrison launched a new bi-weekly, the *Non-Resistant*. Beckwith, believing in a maximum of comprehension, declined to leave the American Peace Society, which declared the new organisation to be too extreme. Garrison retorted that he was doing no more than carrying to its logical conclusion the Peace Society's denunciation of all war in the constitution of 1837. Nevertheless he was repudiated by the Peace Society of New York, and condemned even in religious journals like the *Christian Examiner* and the *Universalist*. Prominent Non-Resistants in England similarly held aloof from him. Of these there were three who were active—Joseph Sturge of Birmingham, George Thompson, and John Scoble. The New England Non-Resistance Society endured only for ten years.[1]

Apart from this schism the main interest of the years 1830–43 centres on the Prize Essay competitions organised in all four countries. This idea was first exploited by the French Society of Christian Morals in 1824, and imitated by Sellon at Geneva in 1830. Sellon offered a second prize four years later for the best essay on *The Evils of War and the Best Means of securing a General and Permanent Peace*—ultimately sent in by Professor Sartorius of Zurich. When the London Society followed suit in 1838, however, the theme selected was an old one—*The Principles of the Peace Society*; and the English competition achieved only one success, by bringing into the Movement Dr. Henry Macnamara of the Temple (the winner), later one of the leading figures during the years of Congresses. Nor did the fifth competition, in France in 1841, produce a programme. Its subject was eminently practical (*The Means of*

[1] For the whole question see M. E. Curti in *New England Quarterly* for January 1929. The bible of Non-Resistance is Adin Ballou's *Christian Non-Resistance* (1846).

obtaining the Benefits of a Permanent and Universal Peace), but the winning entries did little more than lay down principles. It was the American *Prize Essays on a Congress of Nations*, published in 1842, that at last furnished the Movement with a definite goal.

The superiority of the American prize essays over the European awards was the result of the difference in object. The aim in America was, and in Europe was not, to provide a complete programme for the Peace Movement. This the prize essay volume succeeded in doing; so completely indeed that it "anticipated every essential principle embodied in the Hague conferences and the international court more than half a century later."[1] Most famous of all was Ladd's *Essay on a Congress of Nations*, which was included in the volume as a supplement. Ladd's own summary of his proposals is the best: "First.—A congress of ambassadors from all those Christian and civilised nations who should choose to send them, for the purpose of settling the principles of international law by compact and agreement, of the nature of a mutual treaty, and also of devising and promoting plans for the preservation of peace, and meliorating the condition of man. Second.—A court of nations, composed of the most able civilians in the world, to arbitrate or judge such cases as should be brought before it, by the mutual consent of two or more contending nations." That is to say, a Congress to prepare a code of international law, and a Court of Nations to administer it. Ladd was not explicit as to procedure. There were to be two judges from each country, paid either by their own Government or by the Congress; but the only rules laid down in the essay as fundamental to the satisfactory working of the Court were that both sides should be heard in every dispute, that the judges should enjoy diplomatic immunity, and that they should promulgate awards by a majority vote on the basis of existing laws and treaties. Behind this proposed system was the principle that no nation would be justified in resorting to war if there were in being an international opinion and an impartial tribunal to try its case. A

[1] E. L. Whitney, *American Peace Society*, pp. 53-4.

second principle must also be borne in mind. The executive or diplomatic function of world organisation must be kept separate from the judicial function. This was Ladd's one original contribution to his subject; and it has never been more a reality than at the present time, for it is one of the principles which have determined the attitude of the United States towards the League of Nations.

Simultaneously there appeared Judge William Jay's *War and Peace : the Evils of the First and a Plan for preserving the Last*, in which a powerful case was made out for the insertion of a "compromissory [arbitration] clause" in future treaties, and for the arbitration of all disputes arising specifically from the interpretation of treaties. During the next decade the American Peace Society was to concentrate its propaganda along precisely these lines. A beginning had already been made—in memorials to the President in 1833 and a campaign for petitions in 1837— during the settlement of outstanding questions with Mexico. The British Society adopted the expedient of arbitration much later, and less enthusiastically. Its first resolution, even in its own annual meetings, did not occur until 1834, nor its first petition to Parliament for arbitration until 1836. During a tense moment in the Anglo-American boundary dispute in 1839 (finally resolved by the Webster-Ashburton Treaty) both societies co-operated for the first time, at Beckwith's instigation, in airing the idea of a Congress of Nations in the two Parliaments.[1]

This last event is of special importance as being the first step towards the Peace Movement's new aim of startling the world by means of a General Peace Convention in London. Links had been steadily increasing—in Sellon's circulation of articles to the journals of the British and American societies after 1834, in visits of Sturge and Gurney to Geneva, in an address from the American Peace Society to King William IV in 1837, in Gurney's visit to America in 1839, and in Stephen Rigaud's projected continental tours. The formal proposal for a Peace Convention in London was made at a meeting of

[1] *H. of P.* (1839), Annual Report, and pp. 319–21.

the American Peace Society early in 1841. Joseph Sturge, who was present, carried the suggestion home with him to England, where, in the wake of circulars of invitation sent out to the whole of Europe and America, delegates arrived in London in 1843 to inaugurate ten years of united pacifist effort.

Ladd did not survive to give his blessing. He had died at Hartford on 9th April 1841, exhausted by his last tour. In 1837 and 1838 alone he had travelled 5500 miles and delivered 208 lectures. Other pioneers also were gone. Noah Worcester died in 1837, Channing in the spring of 1843. In England, William Allen and John Clarkson were dead, and Bevan and Marsden. The period of Peace Congresses was to be organised by Hindley, Brotherton, and Macnamara in England; by Beckwith in America; and by Rochefoucauld-Liancourt in France. In Switzerland, Sellon had died in 1839.

(d) *Summary*

The year 1843 thus put an end to the parochial isolation which had characterised the early years of the Peace Movements. Activities which had begun in 1815–16 under a common principle and towards a common ideal were henceforth to be continued along a common path of endeavour. Until 1843 the emphasis had been on principle in England and on method in America. Dymond and Macnamara stood to Jay and Ladd in the relation of end to means. The Peace Society in London had followed the precepts of its Master in appealing to the poor and humble, until reminded by Boston that, in the existing distribution of political power, better results were to be expected from an appeal to monarchs and parliaments. How far the local propaganda had prevailed in either country—through Ladd or through Rigaud—it is impossible to say. Certainly the conditions were more favourable in America, where sturdy support from churches and individual ministers was forthcoming to a far greater extent than in England. In both countries, until 1843, Press support was practically negligible. The positive achievement of the Movement consisted so far in a few classics of pacifist literature, a body of practical suggestions that could be extracted from several series of Prize Essays, a number of petitions to Congress and Parliament, and the successful passage of a Peace resolution through one State legislature in America. Little active propaganda was going on in France and Switzerland.

As yet the Peace Movement had weathered no crisis, and its only test had been that of Non-Resistance in America. Events in the current of world politics had pointed the various arguments advanced in favour of arbitration; statesmen had cordially acknowledged the receipt of pacifist memorials; other democratic and humanitarian movements—Abolition and Temperance—had lent the Peace Societies an increased personnel. During the next ten years momentum in the cause of Peace was to come primarily from three additional sources—Free Traders, Parliamentarians and Congressmen, and publicity in the Press.

CHAPTER IV

THE PEACE CONGRESSES : 1843–53

(a) *First General Peace Convention:* 1843

AMONG the many manifestos issued before 1843 is one which admirably expounds the programme adopted by the first Universal Peace Congress. "The object . . . is to procure the abolition of the custom of war, in the proper sense of the term, as existing between independent nations. The custom of war is wrong . . . is tantamount to duelling in principle, and incalculably worse in its consequences. . . . The plan for the overthrow of this custom is, not to induce one nation to surrender its rights to another for the purpose of preserving peace, but to induce the various nations to act on the common-sense principle of referring to arbitration such disputes as they cannot amicably adjust between themselves. We do not wait, in our management of the case, for the evil to begin. We meet it on the threshold. [Our] International Tribunal the Society does *not* propose to have invested with power to enforce its decisions, but to have the efficacy of those decisions depend solely on their justice and the honour of nations." [1]

In the programme itself the object was stated simply: "To deliberate upon the best means, under the Divine blessing, to show the world the evil and the inexpediency of the spirit and practice of war, and to promote permanent and universal peace." The gathering, calling itself the First General Peace Convention, met in the Freemason's Hall, London, on 22nd June 1843, under the Presidency of Charles Hindley, M.P.,

[1] New York Peace Society, 10th Annual Meeting ; cited in *H. of P.* (1839), pp. 260 *seq.*

66

President of the British Peace Society. Altogether there were 324 delegates—292 from the United Kingdom; 26 who had crossed from America under the leadership of Beckwith; and 6 from the continent of Europe, led by Rochefoucauld-Lian-court. Most of the British delegates were persons nominated by Peace Society branches, religious bodies, and public meet-ings. They sat for three days, listening to papers read by the leaders of the cause and passing optimistic resolutions. The Rev. John Burnet of London expatiated on "The Essential Sinfulness of War." Macnamara, the Prize Essayist, followed him next day on "The Best Means of carrying out" the principles he had laid down. Beckwith stirred the assembly with a tirade against the maxim *Si vis pacem para bellum*. But the resolutions at least were practical. Beyond two declarations of theory—Jay's principle of arbitration and Ladd's conception of a Congress of Nations—they all dealt with propaganda, along the channels already explored, of tract and pulpit, petition and protest. The one new note was a plea for the formation of "associations among the working classes." In its stride the Convention also denounced military education, and stressed the value of Temperance in facilitating "reasonableness" in times of crisis.

The proceedings were rounded off in a public meeting held in Exeter Hall on 26th June, attended by two thousand people. Further letters were read from notables who had been un-avoidably absent from the Convention, and a "Peace Congress Committee" was set up to carry into effect the several resolu-tions. For the next few months the record of the Committee's diligence is astonishing. An address had been drawn up in the Convention for transmission to "the governments of the civilised world." The Committee had it presented by Bowring to the Prime Minister, Peel, to Leopold I, King of the Belgians, at Buckingham Palace, and to Louis Philippe in Paris through Guizot, while Beckwith took home a copy for the President of the United States. Accounts of all this were sent to twenty-two leading British newspapers; nineteen other sovereigns were approached through their diplomatic representatives in

London; and a further consignment of memorials went off to twenty-eight Governments at the end of the year.

For the time being no more could be done. The gesture had been made, all the forces of the Peace Movement had been marshalled, and the problem was now, after an interval, to repeat and emphasise the impression produced. But to judge from Press comment that impression was meagre. Religious papers and journals controlled by Peace Auxiliaries were ecstatic.[1] But only two London papers noticed the Convention, and both, regarding it in its contemporary setting, condemned it. "We have often commented," said the *Times*, "on the fanaticism of association as a distinguishing characteristic of modern times; but of all the developments of this disease which it has been our lot to handle, there is not one that can bear an instant's comparison with the vagaries and delusions of those unhappy individuals who have just been figuring before the public (in our columns) under the title of 'The Universal Peace Convention.' Whether formed on the model of the Society for the Prevention of Cruelty to Animals, or on that of the Association for the Relief of Small Debtors, . . . the Convention professes no less than the total abolition, throughout the terrestrial globe, of war; whereby we understand to be meant not only international but civil warfare, and not only open conflict upon equal terms, but all physical compulsion on the part of any civil power or authority whatsoever; all capital punishments, all revolutions attended with violence and bloodshed, and, lastly, all duels. For these evils it is proposed to substitute a judicious and well-regulated system of 'arbitration.' . . . And how do our readers suppose that it is all to be brought about? By uniting into a society some half-dozen Whig members of Parliament, a score or two of Quakers, a few hundred less prominent Englishmen, and a scattering of not very influential foreigners. . . ."

[1] E.g. *Friend, British Friend, Peace Advocate and Correspondent* (Newcastle), and *Bath and Cheltenham Gazette* : see *H. of P.* (1843), pp. 451 *seq.*

(b) *Between the Congresses:* 1843–48

After 1842 pacifism and Free Trade went hand in hand in England. "Unrestricted intercourse among nations," declared the Manchester Auxiliary in a resolution in May 1842, "would powerfully tend to preserve peace by preparing the way for civilisation and Christianity; obliterating the recollections of national enmity; diminishing local and national prejudices; and rendering countries reciprocally dependent upon each other." Cobden himself, now with Bright at the head of the Manchester Anti-Corn Law League, began to speak of Peace and Free Trade as "one and the same cause. It has often been to me a matter of the greatest surprise that the Friends have not taken up the question of Free Trade as the means—and I believe the only human means—of effectual peace." [1]

The Peace Society itself seized every available opportunity for publicity, sending its petitions to Parliament henceforth in a long stream rather than all at once. In March 1844, for instance, Hindley rounded off a six weeks' campaign by delivering a final batch of forty-three. And during the intensified propaganda that was put forward in the Tahiti question and the Jamaica revolt of 1845 the man appeared who was in a few years to become the undisputed leader of the British Peace Movement—Henry Richard. His place in the history of Peace will be considered later. Here it must be noticed that his forty years' service opened with a single lecture, delivered under the auspices of the Peace Society in the Hall of Commerce in London early in 1845. In the same year the Society carried to Parliament its first formal petition for the insertion of an arbitration *clause* in all future treaties. [2] On the Continent Rigaud was still busy creating. When Eugénie Niboyet began in Paris a fortnightly periodical called *La Paix des Deux Mondes* in February 1844, he hurried to the capital and founded a "Société de la Paix de Paris," started it off by opening a Prize Competition, and bore on his way to the south of France.

---

[1] Morley, *Cobden*, i, p. 230 ; J. A. Hobson, *Cobden*, p. 37.
[2] *H. of P.* (1845), p. 305.

Three years later there began the practice of "International Friendly Addresses" between the societies of both countries.

The method in all this proselytism was undoubtedly circumspect enough, but it was futile to hope for mighty results. Six men only were touring Britain and the Continent, rarely with success and often with much discomfort. At Carmarthen in 1843 Rigaud "attempted to read, but found it impossible, and was several times annoyed by persons coming into the parlour, staring rudely at me, and then going back to their companions, saying, 'Old spectacles is there,' and bursting into a loud laugh; two of the men came in drunk—one in his shirt sleeves, with his nightcap on—lighting his pipe and without ceremony sat on the sofa beside me, and began to smoke; after they went out, another came to the door with a gun in his hand, and demanded of me who I was, where I came from, and what was my business, and at last went away saying, 'I suppose you are some —— Methodist parson '." [1]

Similar tours were undertaken in America by Beckwith, aided by several Methodist and Congregational ministers. The need for propaganda here was especially urgent for financial reasons. Ladd's death put an end to the grants he had been in the habit of bestowing on the American Peace Society, and even his final bequest left the Society over two thousand dollars in debt. But two champions appeared at this very moment to strengthen its prestige. One was Charles Sumner, in whom a personal enthusiasm for Peace had recently been stimulated by his researches into the laws of war. He later became the friend of Cobden and Bright, and one of America's leading international prophets. Cobden said of him that he "never subordinated his conscientious convictions to the ordinary ambitions of the politician." Other critics have revered him for "calling us away from all purely *subjective* points of view in our dealing with the problem of war." In his championship of Free Trade and of "enlightened self-interest" he was the Cobden of America. But, above all, he was a constitutionalist. Though he sympathised, for instance, with Garrison's "Aboli-

[1] *H. of P.* (1843), p. 470.

Elliott & Fry

HENRY RICHARD

ELIHU BURRITT

tionist" campaign in 1841, he held aloof from it; for the Abolitionists' refusal to vote under the American Constitution seemed to him to be subversive of all government. "The conscience of every right-minded man," he declared, "proclaims that it is contrary to the Golden Rule of justice. How, then, can we sustain it?" This attitude of constitutional criticism later decided his conduct during the American Civil War. Sumner's *True Grandeur of Nations*, printed from an address which he delivered at Boston on 4th July 1845, has become a classic in American literature. Its argument took the American Constitution as a proof that war not only should be, but could be, outlawed as an international institution. "In the light of reason and religion there can be but one law of war —the great law which pronounces it unwise, unchristian, unjust, and forbids it for ever as a crime." Defensive war— resistance to foreign aggression—he defended; similarly he allowed the right of all governments to maintain their authority at home by means of militia and police. At the same time, however, he believed that civilisation had reached a point at which "strictly defensive war is impossible." [1]

The other champion was Ladd's successor, Elihu Burritt, the greatest name in the history of American pacifism. Burritt was a Connecticut blacksmith who had returned to his forge after an unsuccessful venture as commercial traveller and merchant. Until his writings on Peace and Anti-Slavery made him a public figure, he had never heard of Ladd or of the American Peace Movement. But the fame of his weekly paper—the *Christian Citizen* (1844)—carried him inside the Society at the age of thirty-five, to begin a period of twenty-four years' superhuman labour for the cause. The *Christian Citizen* became the most powerful organ of American pacifism until 1851.

[1] *See* Pierce, *Sumner*, ii, p. 191 *seq.*; J. A. Hobson, *Cobden*, p. 223; C. C. Morrison, *Outlawry of War*, p. 84; M. E. Curti, *American Peace Crusade*, p. 147. In 1847 the *True Grandeur* had a circulation in 1200 towns in England and America.

But Burritt's official career opened during a crisis which nearly shattered the American Peace Society. The Mexican War of 1846-48 (the first war undertaken by the United States since 1815) reopened in an acute form the half-healed sore of Non-Resistance. Burritt insisted that "the foundation principle of the Constitution of the American Peace Society asserts the entire uncompromising opposition of *all* war to Christianity. . . . We could not keep rank for a moment with Peace advocates of defensive wars." But a substitute resolution was passed, evading the issue and confining the work of the Society to "international war." Burritt therefore resigned his Secretaryship in June, together with S. E. Coues, the President, and Joshua P. Blanchard, the Treasurer. The Society, cleared of Non-Resistants, sought to redraft its Constitution; but the idea was abandoned as being likely to mislead adherents. Beckwith resumed control.[1] His petitions and memorials to President Polk were reinforced from London, where the Peace Society also approached the Mexican Government and besought the British Prime Minister (Lord Russell) to proffer mediation. But the war ran its course, until finally ended by the Treaty of Guadeloupe-Hidalgo in February 1848.

This treaty was subsequently claimed by certain pacifists in America to mark a resounding triumph for the Peace Movement, for Article 21 provided that, for the future, certain disputes between the United States and Mexico should be submitted to arbitration. But the claim is misleading. Article 21 was the cause rather than the result of Peace agitation. At the time little was made of it by the American Peace Society; and there is no evidence in the diaries of President Polk, nor in the memoirs of N. P. Trist, the United States Commissioner, to show that petitions were sent in for "stipulated arbitration." The proposal for Article 21 emanated from the Mexican side. In the United States preliminary draft treaty there was no

[1] This schism has been examined in an unpublished thesis, *The Early History of the Peace Movement in the United States*, by Miss Katharine A. Frederic, to whom I am indebted for allowing me access to her work. *See also* E. L. Whitney, *American Peace Society*, pp. 80-2, and *A. of P.* (1846), p. 275.

mention of arbitration.[1] The increased agitation in America after 1848 was due partly to this article, partly to the renewal of the Peace Congresses, and partly to the fact that on 24th February 1848 the American Peace Society was incorporated by an Act of the Massachusetts Legislature, entitling it to hold property.

In the meantime the Anglo-American Oregon boundary dispute had reached a crisis and passed. There was never any real danger of war, but two impassioned speeches by President Polk and Sir Robert Peel created a tense situation in 1846. In America some credit for the final adjustment of the dispute is certainly due to Burritt, whose articles in a new paper, the *Bond of Brotherhood*, stimulated Daniel Webster, the man most responsible for averting friction. In England the agitation of the pacifists is chiefly remarkable for its coincidence in time with a change of attitude in certain sections of the Press. The *Times* and the *Edinburgh Review* both counselled arbitration as a sane way out of the crisis.

Burritt sailed soon afterwards for England, to recoup his health. The visit has left us, among other things, a description of a tour of England which, all too little known, is worthy to rank with Cobbett and Borrow. His immediate object, however, was to revive the co-operation which had preceded the Convention of 1843 and had lapsed afterwards. His method was the creation, in London, of a "League of Universal Brotherhood," to function not only in England along the approved lines, but to spread itself throughout Europe and America and link up with the older societies by means of International Friendly Addresses.[2] This League is peculiarly interesting as a complete precedent for the War Resisters' International of to-day. That is to say, each of the ten thousand members who were recruited in its first year signed a personal pledge never to join any army or navy, never to assist any preparations for war, but to work unceasingly for its abolition. The element of personal

[1] See an article by M. E. Curti in *American Historical Review*, April 1928. Text of treaty in Martens, *Recueil des Traités*, xiv, p. 32.
[2] Branches grew up in America (1847) and France (1848).

responsibility in the Peace Movement was thus accentuated. And Burritt used the League's organ—the *Bond of Brotherhood* —to propagate one of his ancillary schemes for an Ocean Penny Postage.

During his stay in England the "invasion panic" of 1846 flared up between Great Britain and France, at the very moment when shortage of funds compelled the Peace Society to reduce its agents to three, dismissing even Rigaud, and when Cobden was returning to London after a tour of six European countries. He forbore to preach Free Trade, for Europe was suspicious of England, and the only result of his doing so would have been to fortify Continental Protectionists. He preferred to let England's example point its own moral in course of time. And now on his return the bond between Free Trade and Peace became incomparably stronger: Cobden in the Commons was the Peace Society's most valuable asset. But before the International Congresses were resumed, a leader had emerged who was to be for England what Ladd and Burritt together were for America.

Henry Richard, the son of a Calvinistic minister of Tregaron, became Secretary of the Peace Society on 23rd May 1848. He had been minister of the Marlborough Chapel, London, since 1835. Ten years later he had begun active work for the Society as a lecturer in the annual series held in the Hall of Commerce. He became Secretary at the age of thirty-six. He died as Secretary just under forty years later, as well known as any man in England, with a record of achievement—written, spoken, and Parliamentary—greater than that of any other patriot and pacifist the world has ever seen.

His accession coincided with the resumption of the Peace Congresses, which the 1843 Convention had intended should be held annually. Preoccupation on both sides of the Atlantic had made their continuation impracticable, to the chagrin of Burritt, whose watchword was *Organise*, and of Beckwith, who in 1844 had proposed the establishment in London of a World Peace Society for the whole world.[1] For five years the unity

---

[1] Details in *A. of P.* (1844), pp. 193–203.

existing throughout the Peace Movement had been demonstrated only in the exchange of friendly addresses between Great Britain, America, and the Continent, and in Burritt's League of Universal Brotherhood and Cobden's tour. The summer of the Year of Revolutions was a particularly opportune moment for organising a second gesture to the world. If the Peace Societies were rashly optimistic in thinking that they had convinced Governments of a moral as well as a national obligation in all dealings with other Governments, or that already the English-speaking world was becoming more averse to war and less complacent at the prospect of being called upon to volunteer as cannon-fodder, it was an undoubted fact that commercial intercourse was making for interdependence among the nations. And the realisation of this fact pointed to "stipulated arbitration" as the theme to be laboured during the next few years; while the theory of a united world was expounded from a new standpoint by Mazzini.

Though Mazzini never joined a Peace Society, and though his influence for peace was small, he represented, through the *Liberty, Equality, and Humanity* of Young Italy's flag, the positive contribution which Nationalism could—and can—make to world peace. He saw no contradiction between Nationalism and Cosmopolitanism. Man, the servant of humanity, in virtue of his innate law of duty, could attempt his appalling task only by uniting into nations; wherefore the nation was "a divinely appointed instrument for the welfare of the race"—"countries are the workshops of humanity." Patriotism, therefore, must have regard to the moral no less than the material greatness of the Fatherland; love of country involved a negative duty of non-intervention, and a positive duty of friendly co-operation, outside the frontiers. Democracy and Nationality would together produce a world of large, evenly balanced nations, in which "all excuse of war would disappear, and in its place [would] arise a spirit of brotherhood and peaceful emulation on the road of progress." [1] This is, perhaps, the noblest ideal which the modern State system has produced.

[1] Cited in Bolton King, *Mazzini*, chap. xvii.

It is to be carefully distinguished from the "enlightened self-interest" of the Free Trade internationalist, and from the counsel of despair which, in our own day, tells us that, unless we exterminate war, war will exterminate us.

(c) The Peace Congresses: 1848–53

The invitations to the new Universal Peace Congress were issued from London by Burritt, who crossed in August to Paris, where the demonstration was to be held. But as Paris was in a state of high excitement arising out of the July Revolution and fear of Italy, the plans were hastily changed. The Congress opened instead at Brussels, on 20th September.

Procedure here, and throughout the next four years, was identical with that of 1843, save that men outside the Movement attended and spoke—notably Edmund Fry and J. S. Buckingham—and that younger Peace advocates came forward who were from this time onwards to lead the Movement in their own countries. From France there came Francisque Bouvet; from Belgium, Adolphe Visschers, the President of the Congress; from Spain, Ramon de la Sagra. Burritt and Richard dominated the gathering. In all, seven countries were represented, by a total of about 300 delegates.

Only one fresh note was struck—a resolution recommending Great Britain and the United States to lead the world in disarmament. It was during the debate on this resolution that one Roussel, a Belgian delegate, was inspired to exclaim that the time for disarmament was already at hand; and that "the greatest tactician is nothing better than a clever executioner!" The Peace Congress Committee was now supplemented by national committees set up in America and England, in order expressly to find a common platform which could include not only the Peace Societies but persons whose pacifism did not extend to a denunciation of *defensive* war.

But the Press was not hopeful. Charles Dickens, in the London *Daily News*, was the only leading journalist who took up the question of armaments and argued it in the way taken by

the Congress.   Praise was forthcoming from religious quarters
and from Leeds and Manchester, but the general attitude of the
British and Continental Press is fairly represented by the
London *Times*—"the most formidable of our assailants."
Justice, said the *Times*, searching for a fallacy in the Peace
arguments, was no less important than Peace; while if the word
Peace were deleted from the speeches of the Congress, the plans
there advanced would resolve into "nothing else than harmony,
mutual consideration, and deference to judicious advice"—
which, far from being a new discovery, had been for centuries
the creed of kings and statesmen.   As to a Congress of Nations
and an International Code, "we have these things already;
the first in our system of embassies and consular establishments,
the second in certain books and precedents of universal
authority." [1]   What mattered most in all this was not so much
the reception as the mere fact of publicity.   For the Peace
Societies had entered on a course of intensified world propaganda which, by 1854, was to raise them by a series of waves to
a crest which they never again succeeded in reaching until the
end of the century.   As early as January 1849 communications
were opened for the next Congress to be held in Paris in the
following summer.

The interval was spent in bearding Parliaments.   Bouvet in
the French Chamber, and Amos Tuck in the United States House
of Representatives, moved resolutions in January: the first for
a Congress of Nations, the second for "stipulated arbitration"
in future treaties.   Both of course failed, through the force of
arguments on the unsettled state of the world.   But the third
Parliamentary attack, though it failed to secure a majority, was
an epoch-marking event.   This was Cobden's famous motion
of 1849.   The way having been prepared in England by over
a hundred petitions to Parliament from monster meetings,
Cobden moved in the Commons, on 12th June, that the time was
ripe for the Government to enter into communications with
foreign Governments for the establishment of a *system* of

---

[1] Full citations in *H. of P.* (1848), September–December.   The
American Press naturally made few references to the Congress.

arbitration throughout the world. This was more comprehensive than any resolution hitherto aired in any chamber. The initiative lay partly with Joseph Sturge. Ewart, Gibson, Roebuck, and Hume vigorously supported it in a memorable debate ; the first time that any Parliament had been asked to commit itself to a full policy of arbitration. The champions, wisely avoiding arguments from Christianity which might have been used by opponents to stigmatise them as dreamers, urged that arbitration was eminently practicable (witness 1794), and that the duty of introducing it to the world lay, if anywhere, with Great Britain, in virtue of her prestige and her declared pacific sentiments. "In fact," said Cobden, "I merely wish to bind [nations] to do that before a war which nations always virtually do after it." But the Commons decided otherwise. Palmerston and Russell contended that arbitration was not applicable to the existing state of Europe, and that its effects would injure the position of Britain. The motion was defeated by 176 votes to 79. Nevertheless, its effect was phenomenal. The number of petitions in its favour rose to a thousand; and the Peace Society started a fund of £5000 which was all but subscribed by the end of the year. The division list, indeed, represented three million people against the motion but over four millions in its favour. Before April was out, Richard and Burritt went to Paris to arrange for the coming Peace Congress, which a committee of ten Frenchmen and eight foreigners already had in hand.

The Paris Congress, which sat in August 1849, was in every way the most stupendous of the whole series. Great Britain alone sent 670 delegates in special trains; the rest of the world about 170.[1] The French Government accorded them all an official welcome, and dispensed with an examination of their passports and luggage. The prospects, moreover, were unprecedentedly high. Lamartine and De Tocqueville had received Burritt and Richard beforehand, advising them not to

---

[1] They were : France about 100, Belgium 21, U.S.A. 20, other countries about 30. Burritt feared that a preponderance of British delegates would rob the Congress of its universality.

jeopardise the cause by recruiting too many Free Trade adherents. Louis Napoleon had been similarly approached. The one distressing difficulty was that of ecclesiastical jealousies, which provoked many evangelical pastors to hold aloof from the gathering. Under the presidency of Victor Hugo himself the multitude of harbingers of peace astonished and dazzled the world for three days, consummating their deliberations in a *soirée* given by the Foreign Minister, De Tocqueville, on the evening of the last day.

Hugo's inaugural address was a marvel of erudition, delivered as only Hugo could deliver it. "A day will come when you, France—you, Russia—you, Italy—you, England—you, Germany—all of you, nations of the Continent, will, without losing your distinctive qualities and your glorious individuality, be blended into a superior unity, and constitute a European fraternity, just as Normandy, Brittany, Burgundy, Lorraine have been blended into France. A day will come when the only battlefield will be the market opened to commerce, and the mind opening to new ideas. A day will come when bullets and bombshells will be replaced by votes, by the universal suffrage of nations, by the venerable arbitration of a great sovereign senate, which will be to Europe what the Parliament is to England, what the Diet is to Germany, what the Legislative Assembly is to France!" In that day, added Hugo, a cannon would be a museum exhibit, and the world would have learnt better than to spend £128,000,000 on armaments in thirty-four years. The future lay in the federation of Sovereign States united by a bond of brotherhood. This theme was to be developed by Continental pacifists during the next two decades —the United States of Europe. Pacifism in Europe was already broadening out beyond the religious limits of the Anglo-American Movement.

In the resolutions, again, there were points that had not been stressed before—resolutions for the improvement of communications between nations and against the raising of loans and taxes for "wars of ambition and conquest." Sturge laconically moved the omission of the last four words in this latter resolution, but was out-voted. One other question which would have been strenuously debated by Cobden and the French economists—that of the reform of international tariffs—was wisely neglected.[1]

Even without it the Paris Press found ample material for satire. The *Journal des Débats* cried aloud, "In our great and turbulent city . . . behold the delegates from all parts of the world, who come to open a pacific Congress. . . . Happy are those who possess faith!" *Le Crédit* and *L'Univers* were openly satirical; the latter dubbed the Peace party "infidels" and Jacobins. *Charivari* (the Paris *Punch*) good-humouredly caricatured the leaders. British and American comment, however, was reserved. The London *Quarterly Review* saw fit to print a wild picture of the Congress, led by nonentities, including "an unknown Elihu out of the Old Testament." [2] But Elihu and his fellow-prophets, elated, went with Hugo to bestow a copy of their resolutions on the French President, Louis Napoleon.

In the following spring, while preparations for the third Congress were being made in England by Sturge and Richard, Burritt returned to America to instigate petitions for a Government vessel to convey the American delegates to Europe. The petitions failed, but the delegates crossed nevertheless; Burritt and Richard going on ahead to Frankfort, where the assembly finally opened on the anniversary of the Paris Congress.

Apart from its oratory, the Frankfort Congress produced two developments important for the future of the Movement. The first was the setting of a precedent against discussing current political questions. An attempt was made by a German, Dr. Bodenstedt, to induce the Congress to offer mediation in the Schleswig-Holstein dispute raging in Germany; but he was reluctantly ruled out of order. Burritt and Sturge subsequently went to Schleswig-Holstein to try to compose the dispute, but purely as private individuals. Their discussions actually

---

[1] E. Potonié Pierre, *Mouvement Pacifique* (1899), p. 15. The problem was later raised at the Edinburgh Congress in 1853.

[2] *Q.R.* (September 1849), pp. 452–74.

resulted in unofficial negotiations being opened between the Duchies and Denmark, but the Great Powers raised obstacles to settlement, and the war went on.[1] One other legacy was left by the visit—a short-lived Peace Society founded in Königsberg (immediately suppressed by the police).

The second significant development occurred in the open debate on disarmament, which became extremely heated. The crux lay in how far the Christian principle should be stressed. Garnier declared that, of all the causes of wars, the prime cause of the future would be Nationality. Cobden pressed the need for disarmament chiefly on the grounds of expense and taxation. Dr. Hitchcock of America raised the issue to the level of the Sixth Commandment, and stolidly held it there. In the end Cobden prevailed: the resolution urged the preparation by Governments of a "system of international disarmament, without prejudice to such measures as may be considered necessary for the maintenance of the security of their citizens," in consideration solely of the fact that "the standing armaments with which the Governments of Europe menace one another impose intolerable burdens and inflict grievous moral and social evils upon their respective communities." This was a phraseology very different from that of Hindley's original draft; and the passage of the resolution in this form was a victory of the internationalists present over the pacifists. In the existing condition of international relations, however, the change in wording, savouring though it did of apostasy on the part of the Peace Societies, was likely to render the resolution less unpalatable to the various national news-writers. In point of fact Press comment this time, though not materially different from the previous year, was far more widespread.[2]

And this time again, during the months that elapsed before the next Conference, Parliaments were attacked once more. The result in England was negligible, for 1850 was the year of the Kaffir War and of Don Pacifico, and of the second French

---

[1] *See* Miall, *Henry Richard*, pp. 81-3. During the Danish crisis the London *Times* was pacific.

[2] Citations in *H. of P.* (1850), *passim*.

invasion panic. Palmerston condescended to discuss arbitration in his written reply to an appeal by Richard,[1] but he quashed Cobden's second disarmament motion in the Commons by a resounding appeal to national pride (17th June). In America the emphasis was rather on "stipulated arbitration," which was by now being popularised in thousands of "Olive Leaves" distributed by Burritt's agents in railway-cars and public places. The American Peace Society had begun to petition Congress regularly every year. At this point a committee was actually set up by Congress to study the petition. But though the report was entirely favourable, recommending to the President an arbitration clause in future treaties "wherever practicable," a resolution of Senator Foote introduced to the same effect in February 1851 met with a laconic "Let it lay over"—as it has done to this day. Such has been the fate of literally hundreds of pacific resolutions at the hands of the United States Senate, whose dread powers of obstruction were to be felt much more severely by the Peace Movement towards the close of the century.

The fourth Peace Congress eventually opened in London on 22nd July 1851, during the Great Exhibition. This coincidence in time (deliberately planned) has rendered it doubtful whether the claims subsequently put forward by the Peace Societies that they had taken the world by storm were really justified, and whether the four thousand people who filled Exeter Hall for three days do not represent the reflected glory of the Prince Consort's Exhibition rather than a world-gesture of international friendship. Certainly the Congress, despite its sixty American delegates and its official representatives from ten other countries, was overwhelmingly British. Of the twelve hundred delegates over a thousand were nominated within the British Isles. The shining lights of the gathering were the same as in former years—Cobden, Beckwith, Hindley, Visschers, Burritt, and Richard—aided this time by new leaders who had risen during the campaign and by old friends who had not attended all the earlier Congresses—Bright, Brotherton,

[1] J. A. Hobson, *Cobden*, pp. 64–5.

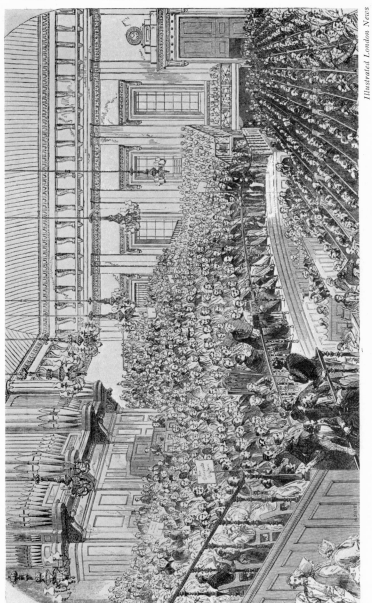

LONDON PEACE CONGRESS, 1851

and William Ewart. Twelve working men from Paris attended, creating a deep impression when they solemnly entered the assembly on the third day.

In one direction the impression created was indeed profound. Press comment in England and on the Continent was for the first time voluminous. Though neither the *Times* nor the *Daily News* uttered anything constructive, every London daily had reports of each day's proceedings. The *Morning Chronicle* and the *Sun* were frankly antagonistic, declaring (the former) that no amount of olive branches would hasten the season of Peace, and (the latter) that "a self-sufficiency so enormous, an assumption of moral superiority so contemptible," had never before been witnessed in Exeter Hall, the "Hall of Humbugs," where the self-elected apostles of arbitration had just been "at it again." The *Manchester Guardian* (in staggering contrast to its attitude in later years) regarded the Congress as positively harmful, since "arguments brought in support of a self-evident truth weaken its impression." Of these, the *Sun* had the widest public, in the coffee-houses of the time. On the other side, the most influential supporter of the Congress was the *Weekly Dispatch*, which enjoyed an extensive middle-class and working-class circulation. Its tenor was echoed in the *Morning Advertiser* and the *Economist*, the *Athenæum* and the religious Press. Among periodicals, three reviews were friendly: the *Westminster*, the *North British*, and the *Eclectic* (the latter two were already printing articles by Sir David Brewster). The *Quarterly* did not relax its earlier attitude—but the very fact of its noticing the Peace campaign may be taken as an index of the social heights to which the Movement had sent echoes. *Punch* showed a frivolous but not unkind interest. In the provinces eight prominent newspapers reported the Congress—all in its favour.[1] On the Continent the longest and most favourable notices appeared in the *Köln Zeitung*, the *Journal des Economistes*, and *La Presse* (Paris).

But Exeter Hall was the last of the truly international Congresses. Plans for a fifth assembly in 1852 were curtailed at

[1] Full citations in *H. of P.*, pp. 211 *seq.*

the London Peace Sociey's annual meeting on 17th May, in view of the alarmed condition of the European Governments in face of one another's swelling armaments, and in view of the hostile tone of the more influential Press. The decision, judged by later events, was lamentable; but nothing more could be done. The psychological panic created by Louis Napoleon's *coup d'état* was sublimated into the Militia Act of 1852, which Peace Society deputations to Lord Aberdeen and similar protests from four thousand London merchants and bankers were impotent to avert. This agitation constituted the background of the two final Congresses, both British, at Manchester and Edinburgh in 1853. At Manchester the general feeling was hopeful, for the new Ministry contained one man, Gladstone, who was known to be pacific. But there soon began the diplomatic tangle that was to end in the Crimean War. European Balance of Power asserted itself by refusing to suffer the Ottoman inheritance, so valuable since it lay scattered round a strategic Constantinople, to fall into the hands of the Russian Menshikov. Richard took up his pen in July, during the days which produced the Vienna Note, to inveigh against "the prostitution of the Holy Name of Christ in connection with this most miserable business." When the Tsar declared that Russia had advanced too far in her demands to draw back, Richard flung at him that stipulated arbitration would never have allowed him to get so fatally far.[1] The *Herald of Peace* anticipated all the arguments that the Press would use to induce British intervention in the Near East—our "ancient ally" the Turk, balance of power against Russia, the principle of large Powers bullying small Powers, and fear of what might happen to India. In September the scare died down ; but by the beginning of October it had returned in a wilder form still. The Friends of Peace thereupon called a special Conference at Edinburgh. Cobden bitterly criticised the manner in which the Press was lashing the country into a fury and the impudence with which all hatred of France had suddenly been transformed into admiration. Bright championed disarma-

[1] *H. of P.* (1853), pp. 239 *seq.*

ment and non-intervention. On this occasion he broached an argument that was to become the chief of all arguments when the second era of peacemakers began in 1867—that wars were financed by a class (the working-class) which stood to lose most by them.

How the agitation fared during the last weeks before the outbreak of the Crimean War must be reserved till later. It is necessary here to pause and estimate the Peace Movements which, after the London Congress of 1851, went into decline. No more International Peace Congresses were to be held until twenty years had elapsed; no further *series* of Congresses until a further sixteen years had passed. The first Peace Movements reached their apex in 1851 and their crisis in 1853. The leaders lived on and nursed their societies into a renewed vigour. But the second Peace Crusade, though it overlapped the first in personnel, was fundamentally different.

(d) *Criticism*

The fact which emerges most arrestingly from a close study of the first forty years of the Peace Movements is just the fact that is least likely to be appreciated fully by later generations—namely, that between 1848 and 1854 the disciples of Allen and Dodge did command the attention of two Continents. In contemporary histories they figure only occasionally, in isolated sentences. In later histories they have been neglected altogether, until their protagonists have become totally forgotten, unless, like Sumner and Cobden, they were representatives also of crusades which captured the attention of historians more enduringly. But without mention of the Peace Societies no picture of the political world of 1848–54 is strictly complete; for the evidence of the newspaper Press in America during the Mexican War, and in Europe during the Peace Congress era and the Crimean War, is sufficient to show that the phrase " Peace Society," whether quoted literally or paraphrased ironically as "doves," was a household expression. This fact is of supreme importance in any attempt to estimate the Movement

and judge it in its contemporary setting.   No other judgment,
of course, is pertinent.   The Friends of Peace have to be
visualised in the age which they strove to lead towards paths
of righteousness, and not merely to be praised or condemned
by the inflexible standards with which their work began.   For
the same reason their own cry of triumph in later years of *post
hoc propter hoc* has to be scrutinised at all times, and frequently
discounted.

In solid achievement the record of Peace after 1830 had been
prodigious.   Sellon had struck the first practical note in his
prize essays and his programme.   London and Boston had
rapidly followed suit—the former to preach a gospel through
Hargreaves and Rigaud, the latter to translate the same gospel
into rules of conduct through Ladd.[1]   Both Movements were
essentially popular and evangelical, even after the American
Peace advocates took the lead in acting on a new realisation—
that the people can act only through its representatives, and
that appeals to Governments were equally as important as local
propaganda.[2]   A long list of petitions to Parliament and
Congress testified to the virtues of a Congress of Nations and
of Arbitration.   Until 1843 the emphasis was on the first of
these;   from thence onwards to 1853 it was on the second.[3]
Simultaneously the theme of Peace had endeared itself to
reformers whose opportunities as Members of Parliament or
Congress made them invaluable assets for the Peace Movement
itself.   Whether they were primarily Abolitionists, or Temperance Reformers, or Free Traders, or even Freethinkers, they
were at hand—and willing—to canvass arbitration within the
walls of parliaments, and to present the accumulated evidence
of a wider outlook contained in local and national petitions.
The climax of this development so far had been reached in
the Massachusetts resolution of 1837, the American Congress
report on the Peace Society's petition of 1850, and Cobden's

[1] Sellon, 1830; England, 1832 onwards; America, 1834 onwards.
[2] America, 1830 onwards ; England, 1836 onwards.
[3] Congress of Nations—America, 1830 onwards; England, 1839
onwards.   Arbitration—America, 1833 ; England, 1836.

motion of 1849. When Sumner entered the United States Senate in 1853 hopes soared higher still.

The effects of all this concerted agitation, part Utopian as it was and part practical, are to be measured by the changed attitude of the Press by the time the Peace Congresses ceased. Criticism at first had been delivered in tones of complete astonishment and hysterical contempt; it was outrageous that a few fanatics should hope to eradicate an evil deeply rooted in human nature by means solely of amiable sermons. Christianity was a futile principle to advocate among pirates and non-Christians; moral sanctions were useless to keep down murderers and footpads. This argument, though it betrays the still fashionable error of ignoring the efficacy of personal and national ethics and of convention, contained an important measure of truth (as will be seen later) despite the offensive tones in which it was uttered. As the activities of the Peacemongers grew, the offensiveness increased proportionally, though nothing was added to the material argument until the opening of the Congresses. Then the burden of comment changed, for both the national Peace Movements were now airing a *programme* of reforms for immediate action. Banter and sarcasm still continued in the Press—a fact which by its very existence proves that the propaganda had become sufficiently noticeable to prompt remark in high places; but there also emerged after 1848 an annual series of reasoned comments, of which the burden was no longer that the Friends of Peace were very exceptional saints, but that the self-evident truths and benefits which they were popularising were impossible of realisation for centuries to come on account of obstacles at that moment insurmountable (which was perfectly true). The remarkable admission had been made in Liberal organs in both Continents that armaments were no longer vitally necessary for external relations, though they must ever be maintained (in the form of police) to preserve order within the State. The extent of the change is shown best by an extract from a British quarterly journal in 1853: "The principles of the Peace Society, fanatical as they are, have unquestionably gained

ground among us; statesmen shrink from war now, not only
on account of its risks, its cost, its possible unpopularity, but
from a new-born sense of the tremendous moral responsibility
which lies upon those who, directly or indirectly, bring upon
humanity such an awful curse." [1]

This quotation at once measures an effect and reveals a
weakness. It was in some ways most unfortunate that all
peace propaganda was apt to be judged exclusively by the
principles advanced by the Peace Societies themselves. Though
the religious side of the crusade was definitely on the wane
before 1853, and though Free Trade and Internationalism were
fast becoming the major themes, *all* peace efforts were popularly
tarred with the brush of religious fanaticism in time of peace
and with that of personal cowardice in time of war. Thus the
stigma which had fallen on the pioneer Peace Societies ham-
pered the Movement of later and more practical endeavours. It
was not even beyond question that Christianity did forbid war.
The precepts of Justin the Martyr and Martin of Tours were
contradicted by those of other Christian Fathers, notably
Ambrose and Athanasius. The record of the early and medieval Church, moreover, was read by critics of the Peace Societies
as betraying a career of "blood-stained conquest and repressive
bureaucracy," militant and ruthless in its conversion of the
barbarian. Nor did the Peace Societies refute such a charge
against themselves until 1872, when a pamphlet widely circulated in England declared that "the mistake lies in supposing that the Gospel *as hitherto preached by Christians*" was that
preached by Henry Richard. [2] Within the religious principle,
further, there was no unanimity. The Friends insisted on
complete Non-Resistance as a fundamental belief of their
fraternity; the British Peace Society stood resolutely against
all war, whether defensive or otherwise, without too much
repetition of the personal Non-Resistance in which its members
also believed; the American Peace Society, aiming at compre-

[1] Cited in *H. of P.* (1853), p. 228. The *Manchester Examiner*
particularly was thirty years ahead of its time in foresight.

[2] London Peace Society pamphlet (1872), pp. 56-7.

hension and flexibility, had already been rent by two critical disputes—one over Non-Resistance, the other over defensive war; and in France the programme of the Society of Christian Morals forbore to dogmatise in any way.

Above all, no dogmatic Christian principle could hope to become the sole basis of universal peace. Christianity was a pacifist argument that could not be made to prevail outside Christendom. A religious basis for peace was not enough when propounded in terms of one religion only. To this extent the bizarre criticism of 1819 was just. The Peace Societies claimed that they were broad-based and non-sectarian. But their very Christianity rendered them sectarian when viewed from the standpoint of the whole world (whose permanent pacification was their declared end). They forgot the Moslem and the Mongolian. And this is all the more significant when we reflect that most of the major wars of the nineteenth century came from the East, and that on one occasion the prime ostensible motive was that very Christianity on which the Peace Societies took their stand.

Apart from this, and at a much lower level, the first Peace Movement committed errors of both omission and commission. Until the years of Congresses were well advanced the leaders displayed an optimism that may have been stimulating to themselves but was exasperating to their detractors. Ladd had stood safely above undue excitement, as Richard was to do later. "Some may ask," said Ladd modestly, "of what use it is to address crowned heads. We expect little from them; but, as they are so elevated, may it not be wise to use them as a flagstaff on which to hoist our colours?" [1] Even by 1843, when the elaboration of the means to be sought had revealed the many difficulties which lay ahead, a tendency to over-simplify the problem was evident in the speeches of the first Peace Convention. "Upon the results of the Convention this is not the time to speak; but it may safely be affirmed that a greater degree of attention has been gained to the principle upon which the Peace Societies are founded than it has ever received before,

[1] Cited in Hemmenway, *Life of Ladd*, p. 87.

whilst the deliberate opinions which the Convention has recorded as to the means of diffusing and carrying out that principle cannot fail to produce discussion, always favourable to truth, if they should not have the immediate effect of interposing a check to the councils of war and strengthening the friendly alliances of nations."[1] This optimism expressed itself not only in firebrand speeches during the Congresses, as when Roussel cried out at Brussels in 1848 that the time for disarmament was at hand, but also in lack of restraint in matters of detail. In December 1850 circulars were issued describing a forthcoming "Bazaar of Brotherhood." Cobden earnestly advised its promoters to change the name, to avoid bringing on themselves odium and ridicule and a charge of Red Republicanism.

The conception of Brotherhood advanced was itself too simple and limited. The Peace advocates without exception regarded the State as little more than an aggregation of individuals. Even as late as the end of the century this belief—natural enough in 1850—was still made the foundation of false arguments in favour of peace. "Respect for the human person is the only basis of all justice; it is the rule among individuals; it cannot be a mistake among social groups. Transport the principles of natural right and justice to International Law and their nature is not changed."[2] "The principle of right and morality for nations is identical with that of right and morality for individuals. As no one has the right to exact justice for himself, [so] no State has the power to declare war on another."[3] Cobden had declared, on the night of his motion in 1849, that "the intercourse between countries is nothing but the intercourse between individuals in the aggregate." The idea of the State as an organism had not yet intruded itself into the political thought of the Peacemakers. They did not appreciate that the supreme law among nations in 1850 was the law of self-preservation, and that a Government's internal and external aspects were

[1] Peace Convention Report (1843), ed. J. Jefferson, p. 1.
[2] M. Revon, Arbitrage International (1892).
[3] Universal Peace Congress, Rome (1891).

not identical; that National Sovereignty and Balance of Power meant the law of the jungle, tempered only by a tendency to association, alliance, and arbitration. Thus it was that speakers at the Peace Congresses so often laboured an analogy between private war and the duel, and prescribed the same simple remedy for the former as for the latter.

Tactical miscalculations too were inevitable with evangelists whose predominant rule of progress was that truth needed nothing for its ultimate triumph so much as advertisement. Cobden realised the danger here also. "I have always endeavoured," he wrote to Richard in November 1851, when the Peace Society's public meetings in England were being made debating-grounds for Non-Intervention and Non-Resistance, "to avoid being brought into collision with the Friends' principle. . . . If the agitation is to be based exclusively on the non-resistance principle, it will cease to occupy its present position in the domain of practical politics."[1] On several occasions, indeed, agitations were undertaken at ill-timed moments—never more so than in 1854 in England, when protests continued long after the Crimean War had broken out and the "Stop the War" Movement was scorned as defeatist and antipatriotic.

For the rest, the recrudescence of warfare in Europe after 1850 was to prove too strong for the protests of the Friends of Peace, while in America pacifist endeavour was to be deflected along the path of Abolition. Anti-Slavery speakers in the south and west of the United States were already beginning to steal the audiences—and the collections—of Burritt's henchmen. Burritt himself, after 1856, devoted himself more and more to the Slavery question at the expense of his Peace activities proper.[2] In the one hemisphere the growing danger of civil war and the cry of "Young America" were paralleled by "invasion panics" and the dawn of Imperialism in the other.

None the less by 1853 the Peace Movement had both gained a hearing and concocted remedies for the evils it perceived. The

[1] Cited in J. A. Hobson, *Cobden* (1918), p. 97.
[2] M. E. Curti, *American Peace Crusade* (1929), pp. 219-20.

most hopeful sign as yet had been the broadening of the Peace
programme after 1848. While Beckwith urged the American
Society to confine its attention to international war, so limiting
the end in view, Sumner had added to the means towards that
end the powerful weapon of Free Trade. In England a
resolution passed at the annual meeting of the Peace Society in
1853 declared, after reciting the Christian principle, that the
Society "deems it to be no less the right and duty of the Friends
of Peace to employ, as auxiliaries to that Christian argument,
all considerations drawn from the manifold social, commercial,
and economic evils which the war system has inflicted, and is
inflicting, on the world."[1] This was nothing less than Cobden
had been preaching since his first alignment with the Peace
Society. Bastiat and Garnier similarly had been thundering
the same lesson in France (where, however, the Socialist
economists remained outside the Peace Movement). There
was, too, a third cry already articulate in England and America
—the appeal to class consciousness. As an argument against
war, this last development owed nothing to Marx and Engels.
Its appearance in America in 1846 preceded the Communist
Manifesto by two years. Burritt elaborated it in a pamphlet
in 1855, demanding "an organised strike of the working-men of
Christendom against war." Bright toyed with it in England in
1853.[2] It was to become the battle-cry of the second great
Peace crusade in the years 1867–70.

The significance of this broader basis of 1850 onwards lay in
that the pacifist thenceforward would be using arguments far
more urgent and immediate than religious dogmatism. The
appeal was in future to the common sense of the many rather
than to the moral integrity of the few. Nevertheless other
reformist ideals proved stronger still.

Encouragement came also from the fact that the normal
course of international diplomacy was steadily providing—
albeit very slowly—fresh precedents to reinforce the Peace

---

[1] 17th May 1853 : *H. of P.* (1853), p. 231. Resolution moved
by Charles Stoval.
[2] M. E. Curti, *American Peace Crusade* (1929), pp. 114, 150.

propaganda. Between 1794 and 1840 there had been twenty-three disputes between States submitted to arbitration and satisfactorily settled. None of the awards had been rejected. By 1854 the number had increased to about fifty.[1] The same gratifying trust could be pointed to in the treaty of 1838, in which—backed by nothing but the good faith of the Great Powers—a future of perpetual neutrality had been guaranteed to Belgium. The Great Exhibition of 1851, further, had prompted lively speculation as to the future economic inter-dependence of nations.

The obstacles to be surmounted, however, before a healthy public opinion could be created were overwhelming. The Press itself could ruin months of intensive lecturing and neutralise dozens of petitions in a moment. Public opinion was always something manufactured, and always strongest in moments of crisis and panic. And it was precisely at such moments that a newspaper Press which thrived by pandering to sensations and emotions was most likely to think of sales rather than of responsibility, and to heighten the scares that ignorance had already produced among the population.[2] Lord Aberdeen firmly believed that such was the agency which forced the British Government into the Crimean War. As a safeguard William Ellery Channing had urged the establishment in America of a national newspaper which might "give to upright and honourable men an opportunity of making known their opinions on matters of general interest, however opposed to the opinions and passions of the day."[3] The *Morning Star* was founded in England in 1854 with precisely the same intention, when hints of the repeal of the Paper Duty prompted schemes also of vigorous local neswpapers, directed to keeping the public adequately informed on matters of foreign policy. But, save in times of crisis, the public is notoriously apathetic.

There was also the problem of the Churches—the bitterest problem which the religious pacifists had to solve. Channing's

[1] List in H. La Fontaine, *Hist. des Arbitrages Internationaux* (1902).
[2] *Cf.* G. L. Dickinson, *The International Anarchy* (1927), pp. 40 seq.
[3] E. D. Mead, *W. E. Channing*, p. xii.

work in America, indeed, has been summed up as an attempt at "the conversion of the Christian Church to Christian principles." The Peace Societies' grievance was admirably summarised many years later by W. Evans Darby, Richard's successor. "They, as Churches, do not come into account. . . . Only the Society of Friends, and probably the Moravians, have a clear and consistent record as regards the Christian doctrine of Peace, which they rightly hold to be fundamental and essential. . . . Ministers are, individually, all for Peace in a way, for it is Christian to be so; but many of them are careful to explain that they are 'not for peace at any price,' which simply means that they reserve to themselves the liberty to go in for the next war favoured by their political party or personal predilection, and to support it blindly."[1] "The Church of Christ, the Lamb's wife," said Ladd, in a not too happy metaphor, "sits still with arms folded, as though her children were only at play, and does not lift a finger to reprove them."[2] Bright, at the end of his life, broke out bitterly that "it proves the indestructible quality there is in the Christian faith that it should so long have survived the treason of those who pretend to teach it!"[3] Behind the sting and disappointment in all these words was the conviction, not only that it was the duty of every Christian Church to refuse to sanction war henceforward and to refuse to allow itself to be used as an agency in the support of war, but also that such a categorical declaration would remove the stigma of fanaticism which still clung to the Peace Societies, and materially lighten their labours. It is true that the advocates of Peace never entered deeply into the question of Church and State relations, nor asked themselves how far the disestablishment of the Church of England, for instance, might have facilitated a definite stand on the part of the State Churches against war; but they did realise the anomalous situation of official Christianity. Only the Society of Friends and a few minor sects in America could point to an

---

[1] W. E. Darby, in a paper on *Sanctions* (1900), pp. 11–15.
[2] In 1830; Hemmenway, *Ladd*, p. 57.
[3] Cited in M. E. Hirst, *Quakers in Peace and War*, p. 301.

uncompromising ruling on the subject of war and peace. The Church of England still held to its Articles of 1562, of which the thirty-seventh article laid down that "it is lawful for Christian men, at the command of the magistrates, to wear weapons and serve in the wars." The Catholic Church similarly failed when looked to for a definite pronouncement, though it was possible to infer that "from the standard of Catholic morality . . . war is almost an impossibility." [1]

Domestic weaknesses inside the Societies finally made decline inevitable. The Peace leaders in America were rapidly ageing, with few youthful enthusiasts to carry on their task. Burritt was becoming preoccupied with Abolition; Beckwith lost favour in 1851 when his financial integrity in keeping the accounts of the Society was only barely vindicated against charges levied at the annual meeting.[2] Financial strength waned as the older members died off. Tregelles Price (one of the British founders) died in 1854; Samuel Gurney in 1856. Internal difficulties sapped the vitality of the Societies in both countries at a time when Slavery and the Crimean War were obliterating the impression made on an inert world by the international congresses. Even without its later trials, however, the Movement could hardly have hoped to endure. It showed a fundamental weakness. "There is no more persistent error in the calculations of reformers than the attempt to reduce a complex situation to a single formula and then apply that formula in its absolute fullness to varying conditions and stages of culture."[3]

[1] *See* F. Stratmann, *The Church and War : a Catholic Study* (1929), pp. 42, 65, 73, 111–12. Article 37 was made the subject of a Prize Essay competition by the British Peace Society in 1861. See *H. of P.* (1861), p. 174, and (1862), p. 60.

[2] Details in M. E. Curti, *American Peace Crusade* (1929), pp. 150–1.

[3] J. T. Shotwell, *War as an Instrument of National Policy* (1929), p. 16.

CHAPTER V

TRIALS AND DECLINE: 1853–67

(a) *Europe from 1853–60 : The Crimea and India*

It is noteworthy that the final impassioned attempt to avert the Crimean War was made, not in the name of any Peace Society, but in that of the Society of Friends. Joseph Sturge, mindful of the Tsar's friendship for the Quakers which had endured throughout the fifteen years of Daniel Wheeler's sojourn among the Russian marshes, set out from England on 20th January 1854 to see the Tsar in person. Accompanied by two Quaker friends he arrived in Petersburg on 2nd February. A week later he was admitted in audience, and with mixed feelings heard Nicholas I declare in the same breath that, while he abhorred war, he would make it his business to insist on his rights under the Treaty of Adrianople, which had concluded the Russo-Turkish war of 1829. Sturge's letters show that for some days the three emissaries saw grounds for hope. But by 15th February, when they were received by the Duchess of Leuchtenberg, all cordiality towards them had evaporated, for the English mails had arrived with accounts of warlike speeches at the opening of Parliament. The mission failed. Sturge returned to meet a storm of ridicule and misrepresentation in the Press; and these comments, when reported in due course in Russia, only aggravated the situation. War was declared on 27th February, while he was on his way home.[1]

Richard in London redoubled his efforts. He filled the

---

[1] For the mission see M. E. Hirst, *Quakers in Peace and War*, chap. x; M. H. P., *Life of Pease*, pp. 44–67 ; Peckover, *Joseph Sturge*, p. 112 ; H. Richard, *Memoir of Joseph Sturge*, pp. 480 *seq.*; *Times* of 23rd January and 21st February 1854.

Herald of Peace with denunciations against the war on political as well as religious grounds, confounding its protagonists by quoting them against one another—citing Sidney Herbert as denying that Great Britain had any real sympathy for the Turks; Aberdeen as rejecting the myth of "our ancient ally"; Clarendon as proving that the desire to preserve Ottoman integrity could never be realised; Palmerston as exploding the fear of Russian aggrandisement. A long array of Eastern travellers—from Lamartine to Lord Stratford de Redcliffe—were made to prove that the Sick Man was undoubtedly expiring; wherefore the war might be expected to provoke rebellions among the subject populations of the Porte, which would be imitated by national minorities on the Continent, at a time when the Concert of Europe was already wrecked.

Urgent appeals were made by the Peace Society for funds, while a circular sent out to every Christian minister exhorted the Churches to preach against the war. Bright delivered an inflammatory speech in the Commons, condemning the war as "contrary to the national interests and the principles professed and avowed by the nation." A few days later, such was the panic rife in England, he was burnt in effigy in his own city of Manchester. Cobden meanwhile sought to restrain excessive Peace propaganda now that the war had begun, since it was futile to "set up our standard and begin preaching for peace while the bells are ringing for victory." [1] But the Peace Society continued its crusade, refusing to adjust itself to the condition of public opinion; and in Christian England the reproach attaching to the epithet "pacifist" became more bitter than ever before.

The British Press stood solid. In 1854 criticisms against the war were confined to two only of the more prominent London journals—the *Nonconformist* and the *Empire*—while the *Times* and the *Spectator* vigorously supported the Crimean expedition. In the provinces pacifism was sometimes articulate in the leading newspapers of Hull, Preston, and Manchester,

---

[1] *H. of P.* (1854), p. 58; Miall, *Henry Richard*, p. 100; J. A. Hobson, *Cobden*, chap. vi.

and *Punch* occasionally waxed sardonic as the campaign advanced.   But until the launching of a special journal by the Peace Party itself the only consistently anti-war utterances came from the *Household Words* of Charles Dickens.   In the United States, where a more detached view was possible, criticism was more discriminating.   The *New York Tribune*, for instance, noticed ironically that in the Crimea a Protestant Power was in league with a Catholic and a Mohammedan against another Christian Power.   Comment in the *Advocate of Peace*, though regular, was at first restrained.   In France little activity in favour of peace is traceable beyond a series of letters from Bastiat to the *Manchester Times*.   The most significant reaction in Europe against the war was an organised movement founded in Sweden by Miss Frederika Bremer, on Midsummer Day 1854, to promote an alliance of Christian women throughout the world for the care of the wounded and prisoners.

In the meantime the American Peace advocates had been enlisted.   Richard had written to Sumner in March 1854 imploring assistance to prevent the war.   In December both Houses of Congress discussed the feasibility of American mediation.   Burritt at the same time interviewed President Pierce.   But the project failed; for not only was there a fear lest American mediation in Europe should justify an attempt from Europe to mediate between the United States and Cuba, but the American Peace Society itself neglected to canvass the two resolutions.

But so obdurate were the Peace Party in England that they deprecated all purely humanitarian expedients.   The Peace Congress Committee resolutely declined to contribute to the patriotic fund opened for the relief of Crimean widows and orphans, since to help the fund would be to condone the war system by which they had been bereaved.   Yet in spite of the obloquy which he called down on the Society by such fanatical consistency, Henry Richard detected a subtle change in British public opinion by the end of the year.   It cannot be established that the six tours organised by the Peace Society as a "Stop the War" agitation, led by Edmund Fry and by

CHARLES SUMNER

RICHARD COBDEN

Elliott & Fry

Arthur O'Neill of Birmingham, were directly responsible for this reaction. Certainly the agents raised between them a total of 150 meetings, but the memorial to Parliament which resulted bore only 1100 signatures, and the Movement was badly handicapped by lack of newspaper publicity. When the war ended, therefore, an attempt was made to remedy the defect by founding a special newspaper, pledged to furnish a sane interpretation of foreign affairs and so avoid repetitions of the fateful Crimean scare.

The need for such an organ was urgent, since even the religious Press could not be relied on in times of crisis. "The present generation of Christians," wrote Richard, "seem to have no faith whatever in the vitality of the gospel, except as it is placed under the shelter of the sword." Not that the new paper was dominantly religious in outlook. Though the initiative for it lay with Joseph Sturge, and though Richard was its first editor, the *Morning Star* had Cobden as chief adviser through the medium of his regular correspondence with Richard; and Cobden insisted that, in order to build up and maintain a wide circulation, it must be primarily a *news*paper and not a second *Herald of Peace*. It must postpone much of its cherished messages to mankind, and use the "wisdom of the serpent" to promote the "harmlessness of the dove." "We must guard ourselves against being a party aiming at peace by any means, and at any price, and without any care for national character, or what some people call honour." The aim was undoubtedly to be the moral reform of public opinion, but "the audiences must be taught without their knowing it." Thus at the close of the war Cobden contrived to impose his own shrewd moderation upon his allies. The *Morning Star* functioned under Richard's editorship until an attempt was made to restrict its scope and its appeal for Peace, when Richard resigned from it.[1]

Simultaneously with its foundation the Peace Society took

---

[1] *See* J. A. Hobson, *Cobden*, pp. 159, 231 ; Miall, *Henry Richard*, pp. 113–7 ; the later editors were Lucas (till 1864), M'Carthy (till 1868), and Morley (till 1869)—when it was merged with other papers. *Cf.* the later work of W. T. Stead.

a step which was to achieve the greatest triumph yet secured
to the cause. A deputation was sent to the Peace Conference
in Paris, taking advantage of the fact that, as the business of the
Conference was to restore the shattered Concert of Europe, no
more opportune moment could have been looked for. The
deputation, headed by Cobden, carried a commission to urge
on the delegates of the Powers, individually and collectively,
"the importance of proposing at the conference then sitting
some system of international arbitration which may bring the
greatest interests of nations within the cognisance of certain
fixed rules of justice and right." To secure this would be a
monumental triumph for the Peace efforts of the preceding
ten years. The deputation, having received an encouraging
reply from Palmerston in London, chose Richard, Sturge, and
Hindley to cross to Paris. Arrived in April, the three interviewed the delegates in turn, bringing special pressure to bear
on Lord Clarendon, whom they persuaded that stipulated
arbitration would facilitate an impartial enquiry *before* disputes
could produce irritation and before the Press could inflame
public opinion. Clarendon brought the memorial before the
Congress, and it finally secured a place in the Treaty of Paris
as Protocol 23—a sorry shadow of itself, but none the less
a landmark in the history of Peace in so far as it was the
first clause of its kind to be inserted in a multilateral treaty.
The protocol expressed a wish only, and it was confined to the
question of mediation. "The Plenipotentiaries do not hesitate
to express, in the name of their Governments, the desire that
States between which any serious misunderstanding may arise
should, before appealing to arms, have recourse, so far as
circumstances might allow, to the good offices of a friendly
Power. The Plenipotentiaries hope that the Governments
not represented at the Congress will unite in the sentiment
which has inspired the desire recorded in the Protocol." The
wording was manifestly cautious; but, at the least, the protocol
rendered it impossible for an offer of mediation to be reasonably
interpreted (as hitherto it had sometimes been interpreted) as an
unfriendly act. Recourse has been had to it three times—

during the Turko-Greek conflict of 1869, by Great Britain on the outbreak of the Franco-Prussian War in 1870, and at the Hague Conference of 1899—as a precedent for recommending arbitration.[1] Gladstone spoke of the occasion as "the first time that representatives of the principal nations of Europe have given an emphatic utterance to sentiments which contain at least a qualified disapproval of the results of war, and asserted the supremacy of reason, of justice, humanity, and religion." The *Times* foresaw that it would make "all Europe one court of appeal."

Protocol 23 was a political gesture. Parallel with it there ranks the legal gesture of the famous Declaration of Paris (16th April), an equally momentous landmark in the history of International Law, which was in time ratified by all the European Governments except that of Spain. The Declaration abolished privateering, pronounced all enemy property in time of war (save contraband) to be safe from capture if under a neutral flag, and nullified paper blockades by stipulating that for the future a blockade, to be respected, must be effective. This was the first attempt to harden into law the customs and rules of naval warfare which had persisted as mere customs since the time of Grotius. As such it marks an epoch: though no later development of the principle down to 1920 could surmount the difficulty of finding an agreed body to enact International Law and interpret it, for the ultimate claim of one Power on another lay in treaties and not in statutes.

Nearly half a century was to elapse before the Powers began seriously to build on the foundation provided by the Declaration and the Protocol. The immediate future was to be clouded with wars, rebellions, and nationalist upheavals. By the spring of 1857 the British Peace Society was bewailing two fresh outbreaks which seemed to be converting China and Persia into free zones for "British imperialism." Richard dilated on the ludicrousness of being at war (in China) with "an Empire of 350,000,000 of the human race." But if the Press was

---

[1] *See* Miall, *Henry Richard*, pp. 107-8 ; Howard Evans, *Sir Randal Cremer*, p. 65 (for text) ; and Lange, *Doctrine Pacifique*, p. 387.

on the whole pacific, the Peace Party lost ground heavily in the General Election of 1857, which gave a mandate to Palmerston. Bright and Cobden were both unseated in Manchester and Huddersfield; and about the same time Burritt's League of Universal Brotherhood in London collapsed and was merged into the London Peace Society. The "Olive Leaves" lived on only in America. Two months later (August) the Indian Mutiny broke out, and Richard parcelled out the land among his agents, to bequeath to the future a lurid account of British rule in India as one long story of "seizure on a basis of might," and to found a Peace and Arbitration Society in Manchester. Cobden laboured the impossibility of assimilation in India as an insurmountable obstacle to future peace under British rule: even Penn, he said, would have failed in India. But the activity of the Peace Society was interrupted by the death of Hindley, its President. Sturge, who succeeded him, followed him to the grave within sixteen months, after fighting for Peace and Abolition for thirty years.

Nevertheless, by 1860 British pacifism had learnt a lesson. The moral conviction was at last strong that Cobden's tactics were the wisest. "It now seems accepted as a maxim which it is almost disloyalty to call in question," said the Peace Society's annual report for 1861, "that whenever England has become involved in a quarrel in any part of the world, the justice or injustice of the quarrel is a matter of no moment compared with the assertion of British supremacy and the maintenance of our military prestige." There were to be no more futile "Stop the War" Movements till 1900.

At this point also an event of enormous significance occurred in France. A circular written in three languages was issued in the winter of 1858–59 by one Edmond Potonié-Pierre (as a result of a sojourn in Germany with the scientist Virchow) advocating a resumption of the Peace Conferences of the years 1848–51. Though this object was not achieved, the document is a landmark in the history of the European Peace Movements, for its author was to raise on its foundation a "*Ligue du Bien Public*" which forms a link between the Anglo-

American crusade which was now declining and the Continental crusade which was to begin in 1865. His aim, which he purposed to realise partly by means of a polyglot monthly journal, *Le Cosmopolite*, read as follows: "To secure, what conquerors have never secured by the force of arms, nor legislators by the force of law, nor the founders of religion by the power of dogma . . . the inauguration of that universal republic in which all men, all peoples, must one day unite." [1]

The beginnings were modest; for the year 1860 opened with a recurrence of the invasion scares which had punctuated Anglo-French relations since Napoleon's enterprise of 1803. Lord Derby could speak of those relations at the Lord Mayor's dinner as standing on a "perfectly friendly footing," but Great Britain's armaments bill (£22,000,000) had exactly doubled itself since 1835. There can be no doubt that the British Government wished earnestly to avoid friction, or that it realised with Earl Russell that wars were still being precipitated by "some particular feeling of insult or animosity, sedulously encouraged, and aggravated into that feeling of pride which belongs to a great nation, until trifling occurrences have produced war which under other circumstances would have been passed over or explained away by diplomatic correspondence." But the panic persisted until the end of the year. Cobden sought to quell it at the outset, when the Orsini question was inflaming passions on both sides of the Channel, and when the Treaty of Villafranca had strengthened in England the fear of French designs in Italy, by crossing to France to negotiate a commercial treaty.

The Cobden Treaty of 23rd January 1860 had its origin in a letter of Henry Richard to the *Times* and a suggestion by Bright in the House of Commons during the winter of 1859. It was not easy to negotiate, though Cobden arrived in France with a sympathetic backing from Palmerston (the Prime Minister), Russell (the Foreign Secretary), and Gladstone (Chancellor of the Exchequer). And even during the negotiations with the French Minister of Commerce proposals were

[1] E. Potonié-Pierre, *Mouvement Pacifique* (1899), pp. 82-3, 91.

discussed in London for augmenting British armaments (July) and the *Times* feared that Cobden was being "bubbled." The treaty provided for a mutual reduction of duties on each other's imports — on French wines and British coal and iron. In France it served to heighten the distrust in which business men held the Emperor's free-trade predilections. In England it did little to allay suspicion of France. The most charitable appreciation of it came from Gladstone. "Nothing was given to France which was of any value to us. On the other hand, nothing was received from France except a measure by which that country conferred a benefit upon itself. At a small loss of revenue we had gained a great extension of trade."[1] Richard organised meetings in this strain in twenty manufacturing towns in England. Cobden and Bright together endeavoured to get the treaty supplemented by a Disarmament Convention between the two Governments, while the Peace Society got up Addresses to the People of France which were printed in full in the *Journal des Débats* and ten other Paris journals. But Palmerston took no action; and Cobden's pamphlet on *The Three Panics* (of 1848, 1853, and 1860–61), which appeared in the following year, could only hope to prepare England for a peaceful future after Palmerston had ceased to guide her. Henry Richard's diary reveals that the fleet of some seventy flat-bottomed boats alleged at the time to be about to invade England were in reality nothing more formidable than coal-barges intended for the canals of France.[2]

(b) *America from* 1853–65: *The Civil War*

While they merely scotched the Peace Movement in Europe the years 1853–65 all but killed it in America. The Civil War, more complex than the simple international issues rife in Italy and athwart the English Channel, cleft the American continent with a blow which first dumbfounded and then sundered the American Peace Society.

[1] Cited in J. A. Hobson, *Cobden*, p. 254.
[2] Miall, *Henry Richard*, pp. 138–9 ; J. A. Hobson, *Cobden*, pp. 279, 298 ; M. E. Hirst, *Quakers in Peace and War*, p. 288.

By 1861 the Peace crusade in the United States had been waning for some years. Between the Peace of Paris and the outbreak of the Civil War there were only three petitions presented to Congress on international questions. Pacifist activity became gradually confined to three States—Maine, Ohio, and New York; and the earlier vital co-operation with Peace workers became slowly a matter of history only. The American Peace Society chose to see, in the arbitration clauses inserted in treaties with Great Britain in the summer of 1854, a tribute to five years' agitation for stipulated arbitration.[1] But Burritt's preoccupation with the growing Slavery issue, the death of Jay in 1858, and the Society's shaken faith in Beckwith, left no leader who could meet the test of civil war squarely when it came. The last effective demonstration of the Anglo-American Peace Movement is to be found in the series of addresses which crossed the Atlantic in 1856 during the Crampton question. These efforts the *New York Herald* ranked very high in assessing the influences which averted a crisis.

When the American Peace Society passed its first resolutions for the "simultaneous disarmament of all nations" (May 1859) the likelihood of civil war was already strong. The fatal significance of Slavery for the Peace Movement lay in that the champions of Peace were also the prophets of Abolition. A conflict of loyalties arose which could not but wreck at least one of the causes, unless plausible sophistries could be invented that would simplify the issue and facilitate a decision one way or the other without affronting conscience. Thus, in America Abolition triumphed over Peace on the easy assumption that the conflict was a rebellion (not an international war) and outside the orbit of the Peace Society; while in England Peace triumphed over Abolition on the Non-Resistant argument that *all* war was unchristian and anathema. The result was disastrous alike for the prestige of the American Peace Society and for amicable relations between the Peace advocates of both hemispheres.

As early as 1856 William Lloyd Garrison had given out that

[1] Whitney, *American Peace Society*, p. 102.

in the last resort he would countenance war as a means of eradicating Slavery from the United States. "Peace or war," he declared, "is a secondary consideration in view of our present perils. Slavery must be conquered—peaceably if we can, forcibly if we must."[1] Burritt, though uneasy, was more sanguine. He believed that peaceful abolition was still possible; for it needed not an agreement among all nations for its eradication, as would be necessary for the final passing of war, but merely the consent of a single population bound by nearly three centuries of common inheritance. Nor had Slavery suborned to its glorification the most brilliant literature of all ages, as war had done from Homer to Tennyson.[2] But early in 1861 the war came: legally, in so far as it affected the Constitution of 1787, a rebellion.

Until the outbreak the American Peace Society pleaded earnestly for Peace. But the attitude adopted by the *Advocate of Peace* was, *selon* Beckwith himself, that the conflict was a rebellion calculated to subvert the Union, and that the South must be put down at all costs. "We cannot for a moment countenance or tolerate rebellion. . . . The cause of peace was never meant to meet such a crisis as is now upon us. It belongs not to peace, but to government alone; and all that can be required of us is that we prove ourselves loyal citizens. . . . It is not strictly war, but a legitimate effort by government for the enforcement of its laws." This standpoint was reasserted at the close of the war in the annual report for 1865. "The sole question agitated through all these years of blood has been whether our laws should be enforced against those who violate them." The American Quakers alone stood firm and refused to fight, for which they underwent untold sufferings. In the North Lincoln sympathised with them and avoided persecution. He had been a friend of the Gurneys. In the Southern Confederate States, partly because the need for men was more urgent in the South, they were mercilessly harassed.[3]

---

[1] *W. L. Garrison*, ed. Tolstoy, p. 150.
[2] *Cf.* Burritt's introduction to Hemmenway's *Ladd*, pp. 6–7.
[3] Details in M. E. Hirst, *Quakers in Peace and War*, pp. 416–51.

Richard in London was bitterly chagrined at the position taken by the American Peace Society. "This evasion is so utterly weak and preposterous, and so flagrantly at variance with the doctrines taught in the American Peace Society's own publications, that we cannot bring ourselves to believe that such strong and clear-minded men . . . can possibly have practised such delusion upon their own judgment and conscience by so pitiful a sophism." He conceded that it was his privilege to take a detached view from a safe distance, free from the excitement rife in Boston. But though he declined to argue the vital constitutional question whether the United States were a federation of Sovereign States or one homogeneous commonwealth, no legal argument could have affected the view he took, which was founded on the Christian principle of 1815— "Infinite as is the iniquity of Slavery, the attempt to abolish it by war is only an attempt to cast out devils by Beelzebub the prince of devils." In a word, "we must say candidly we are not prepared to buy the freedom of the slaves at so tremendous a cost." He was not even persuaded that Abolition, and not the preservation of the Union, was the essential cause of the war.[1] But that fact, which reconciled Sumner to four years of conflict, was considered immaterial by the London Peace Society. Bright's letters to Whittier betray a gloomy acquiescence in the inevitability of the war. "The war was, and is, the only way out of the desperate difficulty of your country, and, fearful as the path is, it cannot be escaped."[2]

Late in 1861 Amasa Walker wrote from Boston to ask advice of the Peace Society in England. He inquired what Richard would have done if the southern counties of England, disappointed at a General Election, had thrown off their allegiance and seized arsenals and dockyards. The reply was delayed for five months. When he received it he found in it little consolation and no guidance; but it was an honest reply. Richard

[1] *H. of P.*, June 1861, pp. 198–201; July 1861, p. 209; November 1862, p. 131. Nevertheless Richard supported the British Government's recognition of the Southern States as belligerents.

[2] 27th February 1863 : cited in M. E. Hirst, *Quakers in Peace and War*, p. 290.

shrank from stating with certainty how the Peace Society would meet an outbreak of rebellion in England, but he was confident of where its duty would lie; for Christian principles were applicable to civil war even more than to international war, and a Society founded as that of 1816 must unwaveringly "begin to familiarise the public mind . . . with the idea of some friendly mediation."

These exchanges only served to embitter the relations between the two Societies. At the same time a growing tension became apparent between their respective Governments, arising at first from American resentment at the comments and disinterested advice offered by the British Press, then later aggravated by the *Trent* dispute and southern privateering in general, until finally perpetuated by the Manchester cotton famine consequent on the Northern blockade. The *Trent* affair undoubtedly went near to provoking war by the end of 1861. In England the stoppage of the vessel by a Northern warship for the purpose of arresting the two Southern Commissioners on board was greeted by an outburst of fury. The Peace Society at once clamoured for the dispute to be submitted to arbitration. Richard and Samuel Gurney carried a memorial to Palmerston. The regular lectures deluged Russell with local petitions. Pressure was brought to bear further on the Government by petitions, not only from the Society of Friends, but from the Congregational Board and the Baptist Board as well. In America Sumner harangued the Senate on 9th January 1862 in a brilliant address which insisted that "the question involved in the controversy is strictly a question of law, precisely like a case of trespass between two neighbours," and that it was therefore clearly arbitrable. Cobden initiated two debates in the House of Commons and held the same burden. Ultimately the dispute was settled by a tactful suggestion of the Prince Consort. It might easily have lingered for months, for the plea for arbitration was met in the Press by significant queries as to the enforcement of arbitral awards and the loss of national dignity that would be entailed by arbitrating an insult so palpable. Richard held afterwards that the Press in both countries had kept a course leading straight to war.[1]

Before the year was out indignation had risen anew on account of the depredations of the *Alabama*, which had left Birkenhead and begun a career of lightning raids on Northern shipping which were to last until she was sunk in June 1864. The settlement of the *Alabama* claims belongs to later years. What was of most significance during the months of her furtive existence was the emergence (at a protest meeting held in London in 1863) of William Randal Cremer, destined later to become the leader of the revived Peace Movement in England. During the same year (1863) Henry Ward Beecher crossed from the United States to England to dispel misunderstandings by lecturing on the principles involved in the Civil War; but he was at cross-purposes with his would-be allies from the outset. Richard deplored the "total absence of any Christian element" in his speeches. "The principles and motives on which he founded his justification of the war were wholly pagan. . . . He has never once disclaimed the doctrine of the utter extermination of the people of the South, if necessary to the preservation of the Union. . . . Those who encourage Mr. Beecher and his party should distinctly understand what it is they commit themselves to. It is nothing less than the approval of a most murderous, ruthless, internecine conflict." [2]

When that conflict ended and Abolition was secured the American Peace Society took stock of its position. Many members, led by Amasa Walker and by the Non-Resistant Adin Ballou, were disgruntled at the Society's record during the war and outraged by its official attitude, which was re-asserted at the annual meeting in 1865. These malcontents seceded to form a separate society, the Universal Peace Union, in Boston (May 1866). For a time they continued to criticise the older Society, though later the two bodies co-operated in harmony. The new Union at once opened up regular

---

[1] *H. of P.* (1862), pp. 7, 62–3, 37 ; T. L. Harris, *The Trent Affair*, (1896).

[2] Richard's article was sold in thousands at 2s. per hundred copies.

communications with the movement which was beginning simultaneously in Europe.[1] The American Friends at the same time founded a Peace Association in Baltimore. The parent Society itself continued under Beckwith as Secretary until 1870. Its first series of resolutions after the war (1865) revived the project of Ladd and Jay for a Congress and High Court of Nations.

(c) *Cross-Currents*, 1860–67: *Nationalism, Disarmament, Labour*

Detached observers might have gathered grains of comfort from the international situation during the years of the American Civil War, despite the recrudescence of militant nationalism which was rending the Balkans and North Germany. The word *international* was beginning to connote a reality. Common bonds among Governments and interests which cut across frontiers were slowly coming to receive more than mere lip-service. London housed an International Industrial Exhibition during the spring of 1862. Geneva saw the birth, in 1864, of the Red Cross Convention to ameliorate the condition of the wounded in time of war—an enduring monument to the eloquence of Tolstoy and Henry Dunant; and in the same year Marx raised the voice of organised labour for the first time in the First International.

Nevertheless the years 1860–70 were, in Continental Europe, the crowning years of emergent Nationalism, which was denounced by the Peace Societies as irrational, oppressive, and anarchic. "This idea of nationality is a poor, low, selfish, unchristian idea, at variance with the very principle of an advanced civilisation; and must, so long as it is cherished and pursued with the headstrong and passionate zeal which its advocates now display, prove fatal not only to peace but to all progress in liberty and good government." So wrote Henry Richard on the outbreak of the Schleswig-Holstein War early

[1] *H. of P.* (1866), p. 137; (1869), p. 213; London *Star*, 27th May 1869; E. L. Whitney, *American Peace Society*, p. 116.

in 1864. Six months later his clamour for strict British non-intervention in the Polish insurrection was raised in the name of Russian dominion rather than Polish independence. But it was found impracticable for the Peace Societies to parade a massed front on the lines of the four Congresses; for in 1867, when the occasion of the Paris Industrial Exhibition was seized in order to convene a second Paris Peace Congress like the first of 1849, the French Government unaccountably withdrew its permission.

The disappointment was severe. Much had been hoped from Napoleon III, whose internationalist sentiments were already the bane of his ministers and the diversion of the rest of Europe, especially on the question of disarmament. An unprecedented concern for the burden of armaments had been growing apparent in both Europe and America since 1860. The American Peace Society had passed its first resolution in favour of "the simultaneous disarmament of all nations" in May 1859. The London Peace Society, taking its cue from a *Times* article, had circulated by thousands Cobden's pamphlet on *The Three Panics*. Napoleon III startled the diplomatic world late in 1863 by projecting an International Disarmament Conference to be convened forthwith. He warned the Chambers of the peril of armaments, "a peril so much the more formidable that the improvements brought about by the civilisation which has bound nations among themselves through the solidarity of material interests render war more destructive than ever." All Europe except Great Britain applauded the initiative. All Europe without exception neglected to act on it. Nor was the gesture better received when it was repeated in 1870.[1] In the interval disarmament won its first recognition in a formal Government proposal, when Lord Clarendon suggested an Armaments Conference as a means of settling the Schleswig-Holstein question (1866). This proposal, abandoned in default of Austrian support, was abortively revived in 1869, by which time the problem could boast a small literature of its

[1] *See* P. Guedalla, *Second Empire*, pp. 259, 325, 353 ; full details in *H. of P.* (1863), p. 284 ; (1864), pp. 8–10.

own. The American jurist, David Dudley Field, famous later
for his International Code, read a paper on disarmament at
Manchester in 1866 simultaneously with Burritt's resolution
at the annual meeting of the London Peace Society in favour
of progressive reduction of armaments among the Powers. In
the next year a masterly proposition on similar lines was contributed from France by Emile de Girardin.[1]

These years, unproductive of results for the American Peace
men, were a period of intense propaganda in England, tempered
by differences among the leaders of the cause. On more than
one occasion during the insurrections of 1863–66 Richard
was to be found alongside Palmerston and Russell, in defence
of Authority: opposed, that is, to Cobden and Bright. Richard's
Memoir of Joseph Sturge appeared in June 1864, when the Peace
Society became further articulate in the lectures of Leone
Levi, Professor of Commercial Law in the University of
London. Manchester was the scene of animated conferences
on arbitration which brought into public view men like Joseph
Rowntree and Marriage Wallis, renowned later as patriotic
pacifists. At the General Election of 1865 Richard canvassed
huge numbers of candidates on all the salient Peace questions,
with especial reference to the *Alabama* claims. He stood
himself for Aberystwyth, but retired before the polling-day in
order to ensure a Liberal victory. So that by the end of the
year, when Cobden and Palmerston had both been laid in the
grave, Parliament had lost its greatest internationalist without
yet gaining its greatest pacifist. The world, when it thought
at all, could still think with Ruskin that "war is the foundation
of all the high virtues and faculties of man." [2]

It was not from the older Peace organisations that hope was
to be expected now. Free Trade and Evangelical Christianity
were never again to capture the world's unwilling attention as
they had done after 1848. A new cause was rising which
could command a far wider appeal: to the masses whom the

---

[1] H. M. Field, *David Dudley Field* (1898), p. 221 ; *H. of P.* (1866),
p. 60 ; (1867), pp. 162–4.
[2] Ruskin, *Crown of Wild Olive* (1866).

Peace Societies seldom had reached. It was a cause more vitally international, if European and not inter-continental. It had two aspects. Within the frontier it spoke in terms of extended franchise and liberal education; across the frontier it condemned war in the interests of the class of humanity which (in all countries) suffered most from the effects of war. The organised labour movements of 1865–67 were, in their international aspects, the articulate emergence of the cry which had been stifled among other more anxious cries when first uttered by Burritt and Bright in 1849. In England they centred on the Reform League.

To some extent the foundation of the Reform League in London was fortuitous. The League came into being as a result of Garibaldi's visit to England in April 1864. It was formed after a demonstration at Primrose Hill against the Government's precautionary measure of hurrying the Italian patriot out of the country after a short three weeks. Its importance lies not in its programme, which was not primarily international, but in its personnel; for among the leaders of the Reform League were men who soon were to take over unbidden the charge of the Peace Society. The President, Edmond Beales, an Evangelical churchman of East Anglia, was already a man of some standing. Bradlaugh the atheist and Odger the agitator sat with him on the committee, whose records were kept by a bricklayer Secretary. The latent strength of the League lay chiefly, however, in William Randal Cremer, a carpenter who had established himself in London in 1852 after a childhood spent in extreme hardship. Cremer in 1864 was unknown. When he died in 1908, Member of Parliament, Knight, and winner of the Nobel Peace Prize, he left a record equal to that of any other man who has ever striven for Peace in an unheeding world. Edmond Beales confined himself to the domestic concerns of the Reform League; but Cremer used his position as co-founder to link the cause of labour in England with its parallel manifestations on the Continent.[1]

[1] For Reform League see Howard Evans, *Sir Randal Cremer* (1909), pp. 42–4.

8

The League's first public action proved to be the notorious Hyde Park riot of 23rd July 1866.

Within a year of the foundation Cremer and Odger inaugurated the International Working-Men's Association in Soho (September 1865). The theme of Odger's presidential address was taken from Mazzini: "No rights without duties, no duties without rights." In amplifying it he insisted on the truly international aspects of labour questions, and on the retardation of progress as a result of miserable conditions in "less intelligent countries." During its first year the Association did little but contract a debt on current expenses, and its continental branch fared hardly better. Its one sure gain consisted in bringing together kindred spirits on both sides of the Channel: Cremer and Odger, and Tolain, Limousin, and Hermann Jung.[1]

The republican Potonié-Pierre meanwhile was striving in France to realise ambitious dreams of propaganda. He had founded the *Ligue du Bien Public* on his return to Paris from Germany, and had the satisfaction, by 1864, of seeing its documents translated into nine European and American tongues. In November 1863 he recruited an ally who was soon to succeed him as the leader of the French Peace Movement until 1912—Frederic Passy. Passy and Potonié began to issue from London a journal in English and French entitled *Le Courier International*. Potonié himself still projected the foundation of a polyglot monthly *Cosmopolite* which should popularise his scheme for a world republic. During 1865 the three men discussed an elaborate draft project for a Supreme Court of Nations, sent to the *Ligue* by John Noble of Brighton. The draft is strongly reminiscent of its predecessors from Henry IV to William Jay. There was nothing new in it, and no point that was not better dealt with in the draft projects beginning at that time to be published in England by eminent jurists. Of more consequence was the exhortation conveyed to the *Ligue du Bien Public* in a letter from a pacifist named

[1] Howard Evans, *Sir Randal Cremer* (1909), pp. 31–4. The Association died in 1874, but left vigorous offspring.

Ernest Dapples at Berne at the close of 1865—a letter which
at once fired the leaders anew and revealed the colossal financial
problem they would have to solve. Dapples' scheme of propaganda read as follows: "Posez une question, par exemple
celle de l'abolition des armées permanentes, à laquelle se
rattacherait comme corollaire la suppression des douanes ou
bien toute autre question; mais posez-la d'une manière
impérieuse, et ne quittez le champ de bataille que lorsqu'elle
sera résolue. Provoquez une discussion générale dans la
presse, provoquez des écrits spéciaux sur la matière, répandez-
les par millions d'exemplaires, . . . provoquez des *meetings*,
provoquez un pétitionnement universel, convoquez des
congrés, installez des comités généraux et des sous-comités;
créez, s'il le faut, un organe spécial; en un mot, travaillez
l'opinion publique sans relâche." This was written on
Christmas Day. Within a year Potonié had founded six
branches.[1]

Within another year the future of the Peace Movement in
Europe was to be assured, on a basis wider than that of the
pioneer societies. But the difficulties were as insurmountable
as ever. Not only was there a universal resentment against
the assumed moral superiority of the older Peace Societies;
there were also the interest which certain classes took in maintaining the War System, the subtle and incalculable influence
of history and literature, and the dull apathy of public
opinion when asked to "call in question or oppose that
which is customary." Above all, the new organisations
that were to multiply during 1867 were faced with the same
financial hardships that had dogged the Peace Societies since
1815.

The British and American Peace Societies had now seen their
best days. The era of Ladd, Burritt, Jay, and Richard was to
be superseded by a half-century dominated by the Frenchman
Frederic Passy. Richard lived on until 1885 as a link between
the old Movement and the new. His successor, W. Evans

[1] E. Potonié-Pierre, *Mouvement Pacifique* (1899), pp. 100-1, 107;
H. of P. (1864), p. 57 ; (1866), p. 128.

Darby, was to continue the fellowship right down to the Great War.   The Peace Societies contrived a continuity and a survival by merging, along with the new organisations of 1867, into the world-wide Peace Movement that was to be established during the next twenty years.

Part Three

THE EXPANSION OF THE PEACE MOVEMENT
1867–89

Si nous voulons atteindre notre but final qui est la paix et le désarmement, il faut que nous soyons écoutés et suivis par les gouvernements sans lesquels nous ne pouvons rien.—J. Duplessix

CHAPTER VI

THE NEW ORGANISATIONS FOR PEACE: 1867-70

A LETTER of Frederic Passy in the Paris *Temps* of 26th April 1867, suggesting the formation of a French League of Peace, marks the active beginning of the second great Peace crusade, which within six years was to permeate the whole of Western Europe and penetrate legislatures. That the second crusade gathered momentum, as it did, is all the more remarkable when it is considered that the crusaders had neither a common objective nor a united programme. Peace propaganda emanated from three centres—Paris, Geneva, and London—at the bidding of three separate inspirations. Fusion was impossible. But the tactics adopted by the several organisations coincided sufficiently to allow of concerted and simultaneous action in the two directions of disarmament and arbitration.

Passy's letter created a revived Peace Movement in France, where the pacifism of the Society of Christian Morals had long been dormant. On 21st May 1867 a *Ligue de la Paix* was founded in Paris by Passy himself, under the presidency of Jean Dollfus. Its principles, as far as they reflected the aims of the founders, were similar to those of Potonié's *Ligue du Bien Public*, save that Passy laid emphasis more on Peace and less on Republicanism. For some months the most fruitful soil for propaganda was the *Temps*, which published the League's first manifestos—a series of addresses from the workmen of many French towns to the workmen of cities in Germany. But publicity in France was handicapped by the restrictions laid on the French Press, which necessitated a Government scrutiny of every new periodical that wished to obtain the licence of a *timbre impérial*.[1] The League flourished nevertheless. Twice it changed its name: in 1872 it became the Society of the Friends of Peace, in 1883 the Arbitration Society. Simultaneously during the spring of 1867 a *Union de la Paix* was founded at Le Havre by Ferdinand Santallier, to co-operate with Passy and with the Peace Society in England. Santallier, as editor of the *Journal du Havre*, put his paper to immediate use. Within a year he had recruited seven thousand members, distributed throughout Western Europe. The veteran Charles Lemonnier at the same time corresponded both with him and with Passy in an endeavour to organise an International Peace Congress in Paris during the summer. But the Government's permission was withdrawn.

Lemonnier therefore held his Conference in Geneva four months later (9th to 12th September). It resulted in the second great foundation of the year—the *Ligue Internationale de la Paix et de la Liberté*. This was an organisation fundamentally different from both Passy's League of Peace and Santallier's Peace Union, for it proclaimed political and social ambitions which far transcended the single aim of universal peace. Its leader was Lemonnier. The constitution which he drafted envisaged three lines of progress: to examine the basis of permanent peace and discover how far the existing social and religious situations favoured its realisation; to promote discussion of international problems; and to educate public opinion, among all classes, towards peace. An early step was taken to induce Passy to allow the two Leagues to coalesce; but Paris remained aloof from Geneva. Passy confessed to a single aim—war on war; he repudiated what he termed the "ulterior motives" of Lemonnier. These ulterior motives were certainly extreme. The "bases of permanent peace" examined by the League of Peace and Liberty resolved themselves into a substitution of democracy for monarchy everywhere, a separation of Church and State in all countries, and the formation of a United States of Europe as a consummation of Hugo's dream of

[1] *See* F. Passy, *Pour la Paix* (1909), pp. 14–19 ; *Travailleur* for 8th May 1879 ; *H. of P.* (1867), pp. 217–20, 227.

1849. Both Passy and Henry Richard were chagrined at the
prominence thus given to political schemes.   Richard, who had
not been the friend of Cobden for nothing, realised the doubtful
wisdom of appealing to the *masses* in Europe, and of parading
Garibaldi at the inaugural meeting.   But by the beginning of
November the Geneva League was aggressive in a fortnightly
organ significantly entitled *Les États-Unis de l'Europe*, which
was later issued from Berne as a monthly.[1]

The trenchant difference between the two bodies was
admirably defined by Santallier in a letter to Richard on 10th
November.   Both Leagues were consecrated to peace and
liberty; but Paris (and Havre) believed liberty to be unattainable without peace, and therefore stood resolutely against
war, whereas Geneva preached liberty as a prior condition of
peace, and might therefore be willing to secure liberty by means
of war.   Thus there could never be a complete understanding
either between Geneva and Paris or between Geneva and
London.

Passy's League of Peace increased rapidly.   At its first
annual meeting, on 8th June 1868, were gathered the founders
themselves, with Richard and Pease from England, Visschers
from Belgium, and the Grand Rabbi of France.   Means were
discussed of initiating in France a popular movement to counter
the growing diplomatic tension between Napoleon III and
Bismarck.   In the autumn the League crossed the Alps, when
a Committee of Peace affiliated to it was founded in Italy.   This,
the birth of the Italian Peace Movement, was sponsored by five
members of the Italian Parliament, one of whom, Senator
Mancini, Professor of International Law, was later to be the
Richard and Ladd of Italy.   Passy began the year 1869 by
opening a Prize Essay competition on the theme *Le Crime de la
Guerre dénoncé à l'Humanité*.

Lemonnier, by reason of his wider and more immediate
appeal, progressed still more rapidly.   At the first annual

---

[1] E. Potonié-Pierre, *Mouvement Pacifique* (1899), p. 111 ; F. Passy,
Pour la Paix (1909), pp. 24–5 ; *H. of P.* (September 1867), *passim* ;
Paris Congress (1878), *Report*, p. 22.

meeting of the Geneva League thirteen countries were represented. War was declared to be "justifiable only for legitimate defence" (a purely relative restriction). Standing armaments were "an absolute obstacle to the peace and liberty of peoples " and should be abolished, means being taken, however, to form an "army of peace" internationally controlled, as a sanction against aggressor States. The problem of disarmament was deliberately shelved as being impossible of solution until the United States of Europe should have become a reality.[1] In London the Peace Society strongly deprecated the advocacy of military sanctions on two grounds: that disarmament would remove the *power* to commit acts of aggression and thus render sanctions unnecessary, and that in any case "the army of peace must be a moral and not a military organisation." The Geneva programme, however, only became more flamboyant as time went on. The second annual meeting reiterated its goal of a United States of Europe on a uniform republican basis, and, in startling contrast to its earlier plan for an international army, proclaimed the right of every nation to decide its own questions of peace and war. Marie Goegg, the League's Treasurer, meanwhile was aspiring to loftier ideals. She urged (in *Les États-Unis de l'Europe*) the formation of an International Peace League of Women. It was not the first proposal of its kind; but it did not bear fruit. Twenty-seven years were to pass before the first Women's Peace League was founded (in 1895), and another twenty years before the Great War brought into existence the second.[2]

In England, outside the Peace Society, which was before all else a pacifist body, there was from the outset a strong likelihood that the cry of Geneva would be taken up. The Council of the Reform League, through its President, Beales, issued in June 1867 an "Address to the Peoples of Europe" which was sufficiently precise in principle and vague in method to delight Lemonnier. "Freedom," it ran, "is the birthright of no particular nation or race—it ought to be the universal inheritance

---

[1] Text in *H. of P.* (1868), pp. 127–8.
[2] See *Year Book of Inter-Parliamentary Bureau* (1924), p. 65.

of all. Despotism and arbitrary power are detestable in whatever shape they appear. . . . Our interest is one and the same; peace, concord, and harmony are equally precious to us all. We can have no interest in injuring each other. . . . War is the mad and wicked game played by Emperors and Kings with the lives and wealth of the people; place it under your ban. If you refuse to furnish the men and the means, if you refuse to sacrifice yourselves and immolate others, the bloody game must cease. . . . It is for you to say it shall not be. . . . How taxation would be minimised; how much of suffering and misery would be banished from the earth; how much of sorrow and anguish from our homes; how the power of the tyrant and the despot would be paralysed; how trade and commerce would spring forth with fresh elasticity. . . . All this rests with you." Accordingly, when Cremer founded a branch of the League of Peace and Liberty in London on 13th December, Beales became its President, and began by sending a deputation to inform Adams (the United States Minister in London) that war at any time between the English-speaking peoples would be a blasphemy and a catastrophe. Yet at the same time there was close co-operation between the Reform League and the Peace Society. Peace Society lecturers addressed Reform League branches; for even after the foundation of the Geneva branch Beales and Cremer did not subscribe actively to the federative and ecclesiastical endeavours of Lemonnier. Their appeal, though primarily to the masses, was limited to " War on War!" Thus, when the third International Working-Men's Congress was held in Brussels in September 1868, its deliberations on the attitude of the working-classes towards war produced nothing more offensive to Richard than the suggestion of a general strike, which was to be popularised in a periodical.

Such were the foundations of 1867, which, with Potonié's *Ligue du Bien Public*, were now ranged in full vigour alongside the Societies of 1815. The Peace Society in England had meanwhile organised its lecture tours into a regular routine by 1865. Between the annual reports of 1866 and 1869 the Society recorded well over 600 lectures. It had managed to reinforce the *Herald of Peace* by securing frequent notice in 43 London and 141 provincial newspapers. It had distributed an average of over 50,000 pamphlets each year—some of which had travelled to private agents as far afield as Spain and Russia. Much of this activity was directed towards mitigating the situation in Abyssinia at the end of 1867. In the following autumn Richard stood for Parliament again, and was returned for Merthyr Tydvil by a majority of 6000. The Peace Society had at last entered Parliament—where its voice was heard for the first time during the debate on the Irish Church Bill on 22nd March 1869. When the next autumn recess arrived Richard went off on a Continental tour.[1] In Belgium he met the future founder of a national Peace Movement, Couvreur; at Berlin he interviewed Virchow, who had shared with Potonié the inspiration which had produced the *Ligue du Bien Public*; at Vienna he saw Dr. Meyerhoffer, a prominent member of the Reichsrath. On his way home he was fêted in Paris by the League of Peace. And within two months of his return to England he had the satisfaction of knowing that his visits and his cajolings had inspired motions in favour of disarmament in eight European Parliaments.

The interest in disarmament begun towards 1863 had not died away. Napoleon III's proposal had been taken up in the Press of St. Petersburg, where the suggestion was made in June 1867 that a lead from Great Britain or France in reducing expenditure on armaments might prove a better earnest than the Emperor's empty behest.[2] Lord Clarendon repeated in 1869, while Foreign Secretary under Gladstone, the proposal he had made three years previously.[3] The motions prompted by Richard's tour all took place during the winter of 1869–70. By far the most famous of them was that of Virchow (of the Progressive Party) in the Prussian Chamber of Deputies on 5th November. Virchow appealed to the North German

[1] L. Appleton, *Henry Richard* (1889), pp. 100–2.
[2] *Journal de St. Petersbourg* and *The Voice*: cited in *H. of P.* (1867), p. 244.
[3] L. Appleton, *Fifty Years of Disarmament*, p. 2. France applauded, Prussia declined.

Confederation to give a lead to Europe in the matter of disarmament. His motion was lost (though it secured ninety-nine votes) through the opposition of the National Liberal Party, whose leader declared the moment inopportune in view of the condition of Europe. A similar motion introduced shortly afterwards in the Dresden Chamber of Deputies met a like fate. Couvreur aired the subject in the Belgian Chamber in December. Early in the new year a motion was actually carried in the Saxon Diet. Simultaneously the Netherlands and Bavarian Chambers were being harangued. Passy in Paris was stoutly supported by the Père Hyacinthe (who was summarily expelled from his Order in consequence). Meyerhoffer in Vienna later tabled a motion in the Austrian Lower House during the debate on the Budget. It managed to secure a division, but was lost by sixty-four votes to fifty-three. Napoleon III had meanwhile addressed his second plea for a Disarmament Conference to the Governments of the Powers (January); and the British Peace Society was bombarding the leading statesmen in Europe with free copies of Larroque's new book on *Standing Armies*—which estimated Europe's armaments bill for 1870 at £125,000,000 sterling.

It was, of course, futile to hope for any positive result whatever from these efforts. The motions did but serve the same purpose as the earliest Peace Society propaganda in America and England before 1830—to proclaim a world malady in terms that he who ran might read. The years 1868–70, indeed, were the most unhappy time possible for inaugurating a Peace crusade on the Continent, where Franco-Prussian tension over Luxemburg and Belgium had already become extremely acute; so much so, that the European Press comments on the growing disarmament agitation are surprisingly tolerant. The Virchow motion received world-wide notice. The bulk of the German Press, however, reported the debate without comment.[1]

In other directions better results were forthcoming to encourage the Peace advocates. Two men in particular were

[1] Details (with dates) in *H. of P.* (1869), pp. 277 *seq.*

working quietly to sound purpose.   In the summer of 1868 an Englishman, Sir John Bowring, negotiated successfully six treaties between foreign Governments, all of which contained clauses providing for certain specified kinds of disputes in future to be referred to arbitration.   The first treaty, between Siam and Sweden-Norway, served as a model for the other five (18th May 1868).[1]   At the same time a national Peace pioneer was coming to the fore in Spain in the person of Senator Arturo de Marcoartu, who scored his first triumph in 1870 when his eloquence secured the insertion of an arbitration clause in a treaty concluded by Spain with the Republic of Uruguay.   Instances of stipulated arbitration continued to multiply steadily; and the consciousness of common ties and responsibilities which Governments had seemed to recognise in the Declaration of Paris in 1856 found expression again in a conference held in St. Petersburg in December 1868 at the Tsar's invitation.   Its orbit as yet lay outside politics.   Even arbitration clauses were still a novelty and a risk.   The International System was still based on nothing wider than private treaties.   The Tsar's conference purposed to carry the legal bonds created in 1856 into the humanitarian field by regulating the means of warfare.   Its result was a Convention, signed by seventeen Governments, laying down rules for the use of explosives in war time.[2]

To the older Peace Societies this was a sheer mockery.   For the dreams of Ladd and Jay and Macnamara had extended far beyond the mere regulation of the customs of war; they had brought up at a point at which the War System disappeared altogether, giving place to an International Community functioning through a Congress of Nations and a Supreme Court, an organisation in which war and the means of war would automatically decay.   Since 1842 little had been written on the subject of a Congress of Nations; but between 1865 and 1870 three schemes were propounded in Europe which created

---

[1] *See* K. P. Arnoldson, *Pax Mundi*, p. 19.
[2] 11th December 1868 : see *H. of P.* (1869), p. 236 ; C. L. Lange, *Doctrine Pacifique*, p. 397.   A second Conference was held in 1874.

a fresh interest in the theory of international relations and penetrated right to the fundamental problems of Federation, a World State, and Sanctions.

The first plan, that of John Noble of Brighton, has already been noticed. The second, in order of time, was a paper by Professor James Lorimer of Edinburgh on *The Application of the Principle of Relative or Proportional Equality to International Organisation*. Lorimer's primary object was to establish the bases on which a permanent Congress of Nations or International Parliament might be brought into existence. The greatest merit of his exposition lies in that he realised the folly, in planning a future world organisation, of assuming that the existing political *status quo* would persist for ever. Every past scheme for world peace, he demonstrated, had committed the error of expecting too much from a mere reconstruction of the political map. He himself made caution his watchword. He pleaded for the future peace of the world, not on the basis of a Confederation of States—for all Confederations betrayed a weakness in attempting to balance centrifugal and centripetal forces—but under the loosest bonds possible. The looser the bond between States, the less risk of a sudden rupture in their intercourse. His International Parliament was to be empowered to decide whether questions submitted to it were international or domestic, but its jurisdiction was restricted to the former. International justice within this limit was to be dispensed by a Judicial Tribunal, appointed by the Congress of Nations, to whom a final appeal from the Tribunal could be taken. The sanction behind the awards, finally, was to be an international army similarly maintained.

There was a familiar ring about Lorimer's plan, for all the freshness of its elasticity. The third contribution, that of Santallier of Havre, was diametrically opposed to it and to Noble's. While Santallier agreed in full with Lorimer's refutation of earlier Peace plans—that they aspired to no loftier means of pacification than "manipulating political geography"—his pamphlet contained none of the customary details of an International Parliament and sanctions. Santallier believed that the organised efforts for Peace since 1815 had been directed too much towards securing the co-operation of *Governments*. The intervention of Governments and the fashioning of an International Parliament would be the last step rather than the first.   The right approach was for the advocates of Peace to continue their agitation in the Press and the pulpit until they should have created, if not a majority of pacifists in the world, at least a strong public opinion in all countries, and *then* agitate on new lines for a council of jurisconsults to draft an international code and devise a body to apply it.   So firm was Santallier in this conviction that he opposed all attempts to centralise the Peace Movement unless and until every other society had eliminated from its programme the primary appeal to Governments.

The two theories show clearly that the end in view could be sought in two opposite directions: one by taking as raw material the inert and apathetic mass of public opinion and inspiring it with a will to peace which must at last command recognition by the world's Governments—a task of the most colossal proportions; the other by acting on the Governments themselves in such a way as to induce them to reorganise the world on a living international basis which would deliver peoples from a bondage they had not the energy to denounce.   The one line meant delivery at the will of the slaves—from within; the other implied delivery from without as a gift of the master.   The Anglo-American Peace Movement of 1815 had begun with the first, to leave it later for the second.   The Continental Peace Movement of 1867, born and nourished in an environment which starved the political aspirations of peoples to a degree far beyond that of England and the United States, adopted the second line from the outset.   The years after 1867 are rich in schemes of world-peace based on Henry IV and Ladd.   Their annals bulge with resolutions in Parliaments and petitions to ministers.   And while in England and America local propaganda went on unabated, since effect was there sought on a public which regarded its Government as "an instrument of the public will," the emphasis on the Continent was on concerted offensives inside legislative chambers, with detailed schemes ready at hand when the time should come.

Thus the expansion of membership was held on the Continent to be less imperative than it was in English-speaking lands. Santallier's Congress of Freemasons, held in Havre in September 1868 to discover how Freemasons could best "oppose the idea of war, which is the negation of human fraternity," found few parallels within the next few years. The British Peace Society, on the other hand, had already founded its first over-seas branch in September 1864, in New South Wales. Others followed.

By 1870, then, the pacific forces at work in the world had undergone rapid expansion and definition. The first twenty years had been consecrated to the single principle of the Christianity of the pre-Constantine era. After 1840 this had been preached in close alliance with economic Free Trade and, to a much less extent, economic French Socialism. The foundations of 1867 had added two conflicting political forces— one humanitarian and internationalist, emanating from Paris ; the other internationalist but based on class interest, emanat-ing from Geneva. The earlier Movement, religious and economic, had looked to a Congress of Nations as its ultimate goal. The later Movement, as far as it was influenced by Geneva, prophesied the narrower geographical ideal of the United States of Europe—the germ of the Pan-Continental theory of to-day. In short, the Peace Movement was bifurcating as it grew; and the chances of its centralisation seemed remote.

9

CHAPTER VII

ARBITRATION, LAW, AND DISARMAMENT IN THE CONCERT OF EUROPE: 1870–78

IN 1870 internationalism at last became a world problem, under conditions at once illogical and fatal. The condition of the world after the Franco-Prussian War has been brilliantly summed up in two books—one an explanation of a historical evolution, the other a diagnosis of a world-wide malady.[1] The core of the disease lay in imperialism and nationalism, which together made inevitable a future of protection, economic isolation, militarism, and permanent alliances among the Powers. Imperialism was encircling India and partitioning Africa; nationalism achieved consolidation within the State, and independence based on self-sufficiency. As a result, financial and economic interests drove national policies into "isolationist" channels, while militarism and the "Armed Peace" gave living shape to the theories of State elaborated by Hegel and Steinmetz. Militarism in turn produced insecurity, which could best be cured by means of alliances. And these, once established and neutralised by counter "reinsurances," were to bear the world along in a vicious circle down to 1914. Yet at the same time, in almost all the aspects of their relations which were not political, the Powers were being forced to recognise a mutual interdependence, reflected already in international conferences like that of St. Petersburg in 1868, and confirmed later in conventions like the Postal Union of 1874. The political organisation of the world was running counter to its economic and social organisation. Political frontiers

[1] C. L. Lange, *Doctrine Pacifique* (1926), pp. 389–94 ; G. L. Dickinson, *The International Anarchy* (1927).

130

were hardening as geographical frontiers decayed. Prejudice was ignoring Aristotle's maxim of the things which make men alike. The result was a sharpened problem of internationalism.

(a) *The Franco-Prussian War:* 1870–71

Nationalism had first to record its two crowning mercies. It did so in the summer of 1870, when the last link was added to a chain of German unification reaching back to Napoleon, and when the Kingdom of Italy chose its final capital.

Faced with a crisis in July 1870 the pacifists of four countries moved heaven and earth to avert war. Potonié-Pierre made an urgent appeal to the Prussian Government as early as 18th June in the name of the *Ligue du Bien Public*. On 9th July Passy sent a protest against the war scare to the editor of every important newspaper in France, following it up with letters from the International League of Peace to the King and Queen of Prussia (6th September). In England Richard rushed off appeals to the Continental societies and to the British Government. Gladstone deplored that neither belligerent would set any store by London's offer of mediation under the protocol of 1856. The International Working-Men's Association, from its own standpoint, called for an exhibition of working-class solidarity to stop the war from spreading. Above the signature of Marx and Odger and others the hostilities were denounced as absurd, in that while two national armies were rending each other, the workmen of both nations were even now exchanging friendly addresses. From the United States, also, there issued in August a series of nine resolutions by the American Peace Society condemning all standing armies and armaments in the light of the present struggle. In co-operation with the British Peace Society Beckwith undertook a campaign of vigorous protests and memorials to the belligerents, to neutrals, and to prominent individual statesmen.[1]

---

[1] *See* E. Potonié-Pierre, *Mouvement Pacifique* (1899), pp. 91–3 ; F. Passy, *Pour la Paix* (1909), pp. 42–50 ; *H. of P.* (1870), pp. 95, 101–2, 118, 156 ; E. L. Whitney, *American Peace Society* (1928), p. 121.

Of greater value for the future than any of these manifestos, however, was the step taken in London by Cremer on 25th July, when he founded the Workmen's Peace Committee from among fifty members of the Reform League. He planted a foot in both pacifist camps. His Committee adopted the programme of the Geneva League of Peace and Liberty—though with only an ultimate faith in the United States of Europe; and it ranged itself in action alongside the Committee of the London Peace Society, by which it was subsidised during its early months. Edmond Beales became President until succeeded by Thomas Burt, M.P. Among the first leaders was Samuel Morley, a survivor from the agitation of 1848. Later on the Committee recruited the Cadbury brothers and Andrew Carnegie. By 1875 it was forging ahead on its own resources, with an annual income of £500.

But the folly of 1854—of attempting to stop the war after it had well begun—was not repeated. "It would be easy for us," said Richard, "to write a volume on the subject; but we feel that, as advocates of Peace, it is our plain duty to observe a certain reticence, so that we may not contribute in any dangerous measure to swell the feeling of partisanship as regards the one or the other of the belligerent Powers, which might easily find expression in language likely to provoke hostility between our own country and theirs. . . . " [1] This, from an editorial in the *Herald of Peace*, sums up the attitude of the Peace Party in England. On the Continent, where Press censorship was strict and popular feeling was in a frenzy, still greater caution was necessary.

There was one Power in Europe, however, which could raise its hand in warning and offer itself as a mediator. Pope Pius IX offered papal mediation to France and Prussia simultaneously on 22nd July, three days after the French declaration of war.

It was a historic moment. From the one source above all others from which the advocates of Peace of all camps had clamoured for sanctification—from the Churches—no gesture

---

[1] *H. of P.* (1870), p. 94.

had come, or could be reasonably expected. The National Churches were correct Erastians; they obeyed the behests of their Governments. The Dissenting Churches in England and America, articulate first during the Crimean War, could be heard again now, though dimly. At last Rome herself, transcending class and frontier, a unity standing four-square across earthly distinctions of nation and even race, resumed for a moment her medieval function of arbiter. But to no purpose. Prussia replied that she was fighting for "the honour and independence of her country," and would lay down her arms only if the Pope could assure her of "pacific dispositions and guarantees" from France.

In after years the Pope was often described, in virtue of his office, as the one possible arbiter for all international disputes. A movement had indeed already been set on foot within the Catholic Church itself to induce the Holy See to pronounce on the question of just and unjust war—partly as a moral gesture to the world, partly to enlighten Catholics as to their own duty. The London *Tablet* printed a petition to this effect in April 1869.[1] In the following month the *Weekly Register* prophesied a discussion of war and its justification at the next Œcumenical Council at the end of the year, and of a proposal that the Pope should approach the Powers on the problems of arbitration and disarmament. But the dual power of the Papacy, as a temporal as well as a spiritual sovereign, even after the seizure of Rome by the Italian Government in 1870, would effectually prevent any return to the medieval theory of the Pope as Arbiter of Christendom. Temporal power must be jealously guarded by the Vatican. But temporal power connoted a place in European politics; wherefore no Government would allow the Pope a pure spiritual aloofness and impartiality.

Layman and priest were ignored, then, and the war took its course. The result for the Peace Movement was twofold: rapid expansion, and a concerted onslaught on the Governments of Europe in the name of Arbitration.

[1] Cited in *H. of P.* (1869), pp. 199, 204.

In England efforts to avert the war gave place to lecture campaigns, designed to explain rationally its origin and its significance. Some dealt with the Franco-Prussian crisis, some with the scare which had suddenly risen late in 1870 when Russia abrogated the Black Sea clauses of the Treaty of Paris (1856). Prince Gorchakov's declaration that the neutralisation of the Black Sea would be no longer recognised by Russia nearly precipitated a repetition of the Crimean War. Peace was only maintained by the rest of the Powers accepting a *fait accompli*. The abrogation was condoned at a Conference in Paris in 1871. The scare, while it lasted, sent up the total of the British Peace Society's messages to the Press to 18,000. Sixty newspapers in London accepted these, and 290 in the provinces; while John Stuart Mill and Froude, in urging that the Concert of Europe must not be sundered a second time, imbued them with a respectability they would otherwise have lacked. In Parliament the cause of Peace in both crises was preached, at the opening of the new session in 1871, by Vernon Harcourt, G. O. Trevelyan, and Peter Rylands. The Society of Friends spent the winter in raising £162,000 for the relief of the destitute in France.[1]

The French pacifists themselves were driven underground. On 18th April 1871 Potonié-Pierre was arrested on a charge of sedition, and all the documents of the *Ligue du Bien Public* were seized by the police. The League ceased to exist until 1876, when he revived it in Berlin.[2] Passy and the League of Peace moved warily. Outside France, however, in neutral countries, the effect of the war was to create Peace organisations where none had existed before, and to multiply the demands of Continental statesmen for a saner internationalism. In Italy Signor Morelli asked the Chambers (without avail) to propose to the world the institution of an "Amphictyonic Tribunal" on the model of Ancient Greece. In Belgium Peace Societies were founded at Brussels and Verviens. More

[1] M. E. Hirst, *Quakers in Peace and War*, chap. x.
[2] It has been asserted that Potonié was betrayed by a woman clerk whom he had dismissed for theft.

important still for the future, a private meeting of fifteen men at The Hague, led by Jonckbloet Van Eck, established on 2nd September 1870 a Netherlands Peace Society (*Algemeen Neder-landsch Vredesbond*) which is to be regarded as the origin of a fourth Continental national Peace Movement. "Too long already," said the Society's declaration, "has the Netherlands failed to respond to the call." The time had come to oppose war "by means of persuasion, encouragement, and reasoning," and by co-operating "with some permanent international peace movement." At once, therefore, a periodical, *De Vredebond*, was begun, directed by the President, J. A. Tolles, and Van Eck. Within a year the Society had thrown out twenty-six branches, which were fused into the Netherlands Peace League (founded on 26th January 1871). While the war lasted progress was phenomenal; but after the Peace of Frankfort the League rapidly declined and became indifferent. By 1891 only two of the branches survived.[1] Political dissension, moreover, hastened the disintegration, when discussion became bitter on the question of revising the Netherlands Constitution in such a way that power to declare war should no longer reside exclusively with the Crown.[2]

In the United States Peace activity had been hesitant and circumscribed since the close of the Civil War. The American Peace Society had not resumed its lecture tours until after 1868, though fresh tracts had accompanied the regular circulat-ing of the *Advocate* to official bodies of all kinds. In 1869 enthusiasm was revived by Amasa Lord, of the American Bible Society, who recruited over fifty lecturers and agents in seven States, appealing for co-operation to all Christian ministers of religion. Lord took over the Secretaryship of the Society in Boston when Beckwith died in May 1870.[3] Beckwith's loss can hardly be exaggerated. He had laboured for the Society for thirty-five years at a meagre salary which he often

---

[1] J. van Beek en Donk, *Peace Movement in the Netherlands*, pp. 6–8; *H. of P.* (1870), pp. 119 *seq.*
[2] Information supplied by M. van der Mandere.
[3] E. L. Whitney, *American Peace Society*, pp. 118–9. Women members were admitted for the first time in May 1871.

sacrificed completely; and he had held the Peace Movement together during the Civil War, even in spite of itself. During the three years following his death, while the Peace advocates in Europe were proselytising, the American Society underwent extensive changes, emerging by 1873 with new officials and restored vigour to begin a more widespread propaganda than at any time hitherto. The signal was a series of Peace Jubilees organised in 1871 to celebrate the conclusion of the Franco-Prussian War. From now on the American Peace crusade centred on its President, Edward S. Tobey, and on Lord's successors after 1872. Burritt continued active until his death in 1879.

By far the most potent foundation of the year 1871 occurred in England, where, on 24th May, Cremer enlarged his Workmen's Peace Committee into the Workmen's Peace Association, signalising the event by drawing up an "Outline of a Plan for the Establishment of a High Court of Nations." The plan, which is of extreme historical interest in virtue of its relation to the League of Nations Covenant, was passed at a meeting held on 8th July. Its provisions for the equality of States before the International Court, for the codification of international law, and for limiting the jurisdiction of the Court to the "external relations" of the member States, contained no novelty. The distinctive features of the plan were two: that in the event of an award being ignored, sanctions were to be peaceful only—"the other Governments shall thereupon suspend Diplomatic intercourse with such Government and prohibit Commerical intercourse with the Nation it represents until it shall conform to the decision of the Court"; and that disputes not covered by the International Code (that is, non-justiciable disputes) were to be arbitrated by the Court, whose award was to be binding in advance and enforceable by the same pacific sanctions.[1] Thus there remained no fundamental difference of principle which could hinder full co-operation between the Workmen's Peace Association and the Peace

[1] Text in Howard Evans, *Sir Randal Cremer*, pp. 84–5 ; *H. of P.* (1871), p. 231 ; and reprinted in *Arbitrator* (March 1928).

Society.   That co-operation hitherto had been directed towards the negative end of checking in England a desire to intervene in the war on behalf of France.   It was now to take the positive direction of a European campaign for Arbitration Treaties.

(b) *The Campaign for Arbitration*: 1871–75

At no time had the fact been lost sight of that, logically, the development of arbitration in international disputes and the recognition of its value by means of stipulated provisions in treaties was the readiest way to Peace.   Codification and disarmament would follow rather than precede the realisation by Governments of a truly international outlook.   On a rough generalisation the first twenty years of the organised Peace Movements, from 1815 to 1835, can be regarded as the period of insistence upon dogmatic principle—the unchristian character of war; the next ten years, as dominated by the theory of a Congress of Nations; the next twenty years, to 1865, as devoted primarily to "stipulated arbitration"; and the years leading to the Franco-Prussian War, as the campaign for disarmament. After 1870 two concentrated efforts stand out from the general routine of pacifist and internationalist propaganda: one a revived campaign for arbitration, originating in England; the other an entirely new movement, largely academic, for the codification of international law, emanating from the continent of Europe.   At the same time the theory of Peace was to be elaborated in several epoch-making studies, and the *Alabama* question, outstanding from the American Civil War, was to provide an age-long triumph for arbitration.

Richard's campaign for arbitration began in the summer of 1871.   Though its success was achieved in England first, it was from the start a universal campaign throughout the Peace Movements of both continents.   Early in 1871 a paper on "International Arbitration" had been read before the Social Science Association in London (then recently formed) by Professor Leone Levi.   As a result a Committee of the Association was set up to examine "whether some General Scheme of

International Arbitration or Conciliation cannot be usefully recommended for adoption." The Committee's report, issued in the following July, explored the whole field of international obligations, and wound up by declaring that the world's needs could best be satisfied by a Congress of Nations—a permanent federation on the model of the United States of America—meeting whenever two or more States should desire. No barbarous States were to be accorded membership, but the federation was to be as wide as possible. The Committee hesitated, however, to recommend the adherence of North and South America. The Congress was to have no power to determine the domestic problems of Governments, but its jurisdiction should cover all international disputes, which would be heard before a Court of Reference (set up by the Congress), whose awards should be binding. On the question of sanctions the Committee was not unanimous. It tabulated the arguments for and against the use of military force—the deterrent value of a knowledge of certain punishment—as against the view that a system based on arbitration and the renunciation of force could not logically rely on force for its maintenance. There was thus a unity among the Peace projects that had sprung from Ladd and Jay—the four of Noble, Lorimer, Cremer, and Leone Levi. Each centred on a Congress and a Court, functioning through channels prescribed by a Code of International Law, and resolving political and legal disputes respectively. But sanctions presented an insoluble problem. Lorimer had bowed to realities and postulated an international army ; the others stopped short at the moral sanctions of Ladd himself.

The Committee's report was published in July. On 11th August Henry Richard, in the House of Commons, gave notice of a motion to the following effect, for discussion early in the next session: "That an humble address be presented to Her Majesty, praying that she will be graciously pleased to direct her principal Secretary of State for Foreign Affairs to enter into communication with Foreign Powers with a view to the further improvement of International Law, and to the establishment of a permanent system of International Arbitration." [1] He had planned the motion some months previously, and lectures and meetings in support of it were already in full swing throughout the British Isles. The three regular agents—Stokes, O'Neill, and Conder—were reinforced by nine others specially commissioned to canvass the country for the coming motion. The twelve addressed over 420 audiences during 1871, and were kept working at full pressure into the next year, as the debate on the motion was twice postponed on account of difficulties which arose over the settlement of the *Alabama* claims between Great Britain and the United States.

On 8th May 1871 the two Governments had concluded the Treaty of Washington, by which nine disputes, some of them precipitated by the predatory voyagings of the *Alabama*, were to be submitted to arbitration. The Treaty in itself was a triumph of diplomacy, for it had taken seven years to negotiate, from the moment when Mr. Shaw-Lefevre first urged the arbitration of the questions from his seat in the House of Commons. Of two Conventions arrived at thereafter, one (1868) had proved abortive, while the other (1869), negotiated by Clarendon and Reverdy Johnson, had been rejected by the United States Senate. At last, by the Washington agreement, the nine disputes were to be separated into four groups, of which the *Alabama* claims were to be arbitrated at Geneva. In the following December, after sundry hesitations which served to retard Richard's motion in the Commons, the Geneva Tribunal opened. There were five arbitrators: Sir Alexander Cockburn, nominated by Great Britain; Charles Adams, nominated by the United States; and three others, chosen respectively by the King of Italy, the Swiss Federal Government, and the Emperor of Brazil. After thorough investigation their award was issued on 14th September 1872. The *Alabama* depredations were laid at the door of Great Britain on the score of negligence as a neutral. The United States were awarded £3,237,000 as satisfaction. Before the year was out

[1] Text in L. Appleton, *Henry Richard*, p. 128.

two of the other arbitrations had been satisfactorily resolved—one by the German Emperor, the other by a Mixed Commission. The fourth was ultimately settled in 1877.[1]

The Geneva Arbitration is still regarded as a landmark in the history of international relations. It was indeed the first occasion on which a front-rank question between two Great Powers had been settled without war. Whether or not this agglomeration of disputes would have precipitated war if left unheeded is now a matter of futile speculation. The view was widely held at the time that no rupture would have occurred. "I am afraid," said Lord Salisbury, "that, like competitive examinations and sewage irrigation, arbitration is one of the famous nostrums of the age. Like them it will have its day and will pass away, and future ages will look with pity and contempt on those who could have believed in such an expedient for bridling the ferocity of human passions."[2] What is of more practical importance is that the whole transaction cast into stronger relief the need for a Code of International Law and a Permanent Court to dispense it. The arbitrations settled purely legal questions as to the rights and duties of neutrals in time of war, and could not be cited as a precedent by those who looked to arbitration as a panacea for all types of international dispute. Wherefore, in order that a maximum of possible causes of friction might be reduced to plain legal and justiciable terms, it was imperative that the rules governing international relations should be crystallised into a body of laws, universally recognised and entrusted to the keeping of a permanent body of jurists. The first proposal for such a Tribunal of Jurists

[1] The claims were (1) fisheries; (2) navigation of the St. Lawrence; (3) transit of goods through Maine; (4) Manitoba boundary; (5) *Alabama*; (6) San Juan water boundary; (7) British Civil War claims; (8) Canadian Fenian claims; (9) revision of rules of maritime neutrality. They were settled by four arbitrations: (1) Geneva, 1872—*Alabama*; (2) San Juan, by German Emperor, 1872; (3) mutual claims, by a Mixed Commission; and (4) fisheries, by a Mixed Commission, 1877. *See* R. L. Jones, *International Arbitration* (1907), pp. 182–9; L. S. Woolf, *International Government* (1917), p. 46; J. B. Moore, *International Arbitrations* (1899), vol. i, chap. xiv, pp. 495–678.

[2] 3rd March 1873: cited in W. I. Hull, *Hague Conferences* (1908), p. 46. Lord Salisbury completely changed his view later.

was made during this very dispute by an American, T. B. Balch.[1]

Meanwhile the campaign begun in England had extended its front. For the American Peace Movement the year 1872 was as momentous as 1842, culminating in David Dudley Field's *International Tribunal* as the earlier year had culminated in Jay's *War and Peace*. On 2nd January Senator H. B. Anthony of Rhode Island introduced into Congress a memorial urging the United States Government to initiate measures for "a permanent system of international arbitration by the adoption of a High Court of Arbitration." His plea was referred to the Senate's Foreign Relations Committee.[2] Four months later Sumner, now in the last year of his life, tabled a motion in favour of "arbitration as a substitute for war in determining differences between nations "[3] four days after the annual meeting of the American Peace Society, at which both motions were enlarged into a series of resolutions seeking "early steps" in the forma- tion of an International Code and an International Court.[4] All three demands were reinforced from an expert source when Field, "the most commanding figure at the American Bar," published his monumental project for an International Tribunal. Field had already inspired a movement among American jurists for the reform of both criminal and civil law, directed to drafting codes that would be "of the people, and by the people, and for the people." He was by no means a pacifist. "I do not say that war is the greatest of all calamities, for I think that national degradation and slavery, or general corruption and the reign of fraud, are evils still greater. . . . A nation attacked may and must defend itself. He who would not fight to the death in defence of his family or country is not fit for this world."[5] But he endeavoured, as a jurist, to find legal means of averting wars

---

[1] In a letter to W. H. Huntingdon at Paris, quoted in Balch's *International Courts of Arbitration* (1896), pp. 9–13 ; see also his *Arbitrage International* (1908), p. 108.

[2] E. L. Whitney, *American Peace Society*, p. 121.

[3] 31st May 1872 : it was repeated on 9th and 17th June 1874.

[4] 27th May 1872 : Whitney, p. 129.

[5] In H. M. Field, *Life of D. D. Field*, p. 239.

by removing their causes (so far as those causes could be reduced to legal rules) and of mitigating them, when inevitable, by a definite body of the Laws of War. His scheme hinged on Arbitration, an International Code, and a Tribunal. Nations concerned in disputes which could not be settled by ordinary diplomatic means were each to appoint five members to a Joint High Commission, which should issue a report within six months. If the Commission failed to agree, or if either party failed to ratify the report, the dispute was to be taken, within a further six months, to a High Tribunal of seven judges, chosen from a list of names contributed by the other States adhering to the International Code. The awards of this Tribunal were to be binding in advance. The merits of the plan were that it was the work of an eminent jurist and that it provided a safety-valve of twelve months' delay to allow passions to cool. But it contained no definitive articles for sanctions of any kind, and its detailed provisions for the selection of the seven judges did not meet all objections. Field remedied both these defects later.[1]

In Europe also, where Peace activity had revived after the Franco-Prussian War, arbitration was adopted as the watch-word of the moment. Frederic Passy reorganised his French League of Peace early in 1872 under the new title *Société Française des Amis de la Paix*, of which Adolf Franck became President. In a manifesto labelled *Revanche ou Relèvement* the principle of interdependence among nations was argued anew, and arbitration was hailed as the most rational and the simplest substitute for war, for it would prevent nations from being any longer judges in their own suits and would cost practically nothing to organise.[2] Visschers and Roussel—veterans of 1848—were at the same moment busy in Belgium radiating arbitration manifestos from the two centres of Brussels and Verviens. In Spain, where as yet there was no organised Peace Movement, the pioneer Arturo de Marcoartu opened a Prize

---

[1] Text in W. E. Darby, *International Tribunals* (ed. 1904), pp. 214–5.
[2] Text in F. Passy, *Pour la Paix*, pp. 63–6.

Essay competition on *The Best Means of Establishing a Representative European Arbitral Assembly*.[1]

Richard continued to flash the watchword over England. Two special International Arbitration Societies were founded in Yorkshire and Lancashire as a result of lecture tours by O'Neill and Lewis Appleton, Richard's future biographer. Their platform was not Peace at any price, but Peace through Law and Arbitration. Three religious Unions—the Baptist, the Congregational, and the Society of Friends—discussed and recommended arbitration in every central and local meeting during 1872. The Peace Society, besides securing this co-operation, sent out two more apostles to echo the twelve of 1871, canvassed every reputable newspaper in the Kingdom, secured the insertion of articles in over 200 of them (to the total of 11,000 articles), held on an average 75 meetings per month, and sent to Westminster a record of 1163 local petitions by the time Richard's motion was finally taken.[2] The Workmen's Peace Association also proved a tower of strength. Cremer himself toured Scotland, leaving in England no fewer than 140 lecturing agents, who amassed altogether 1,000,000 signatures in favour of Richard's motion. Propaganda had never before been so widespread or so intensive.[3]

In the midst of the campaign there arrived in Europe J. B. Miles of the American Peace Society, armed with a draft plan for a permanent system of arbitration drawn up by Burritt and himself in collaboration with other jurists (January 1873). He came to summon the leaders of the Peace Movement in all countries to attend a Congress and discuss the draft. His journey embraced England, France, Italy, Germany, Austria, and Belguim—all within five months. By 15th May he was back in Boston in time to present his report at the American Peace Society's annual meeting. It produced two important results: an International Congress of the Peace leaders at Brussels in the following October, and the formation of an

[1] December 1872 ; the prize was £300 : *H. of P.* (1872), p. 131.
[2] Annual Reports for 1872–73, *passim*.
[3] Details in Cremer's Annual Reports, cited in *H. of P.*

International Code Committee of America to draft a Code of International Law, under the direction of Miles himself and Field.[1] Both these results will be noticed later.

Richard's motion at last came before the House of Commons on the night of 8th July 1873. The *Herald of Peace*, elated at the phenomenal statistics of the campaign, was none the less apprehensive that apathy in the House might prove more damning to the motion than spirited opposition—the latter would at least be an advertisement. "What we have most to apprehend . . . is not so much hostility as indifference. . . . The only way to remedy this is to galvanise members by a stream of electricity from without, and to awaken their sympathies by proving that the subject is one which is near to the heart of a large body of their constituents." [2] But the fears were not realised. Richard rose to address a packed House When the debate ended he had scored the most resounding triumph of his career. War, he began, was still being provoked by trivial disputes which could readily be set right if an international tribunal of some sort were in existence to deal with them. It was the lack of such a tribunal that had produced during the century a rivalry in armaments so keen that Europe was devoting to it, during the current year, £550,000,000, while the Continent was everywhere pauperised by conscription and heavy taxation. This situation, he urged, was becoming daily more absurd in view of the growing economic interdependence among the European nations: the more so, indeed, since there was at hand an expedient by which statesmen could fashion a policy far less suicidal than the existing game of "beggar my neighbour." Arbitration had already vindicated its practicability in international disputes. Lord Russell himself had admitted that not one of the wars of the eighteenth century could not have been avoided by recourse to arbitration. The world must take its stand firmly on the Paris protocol of 1856, and advance towards a permanent system of international jurisdiction to *prevent* disputes from reaching a point at which

[1] *See* E. L. Whitney, *American Peace Society*, pp. 129–33.
[2] *H. of P.* (June 1873), p. 253.

national passion should overcome reason. He prescribed a
tribunal on the model of the United States Supreme Court.

Gladstone, the Prime Minister, was magnanimous in his
reply. He described the speech as that of "a great Peace
Minister." He echoed its sentiments with an eloquence finer
than Richard's. But he feared that the motion transcended
Cobden's motion of 1849 so far that it was altogether too
ambitious. Richard's dream, if ever it were realised, would
be realised in times of tranquillity and by a gradual widening
of the scope and practice of arbitration. For the moment
Europe was too unsettled. Germany was too elated, France
too humiliated for anything but harm to result to Richard's
cause if his motion were pressed to a division and acted on by
the Government. Nevertheless, when Sir Wilfrid Lawson had
followed Gladstone with a studied appeal to action, Richard
rose and claimed a vote. Amid general astonishment the
motion was carried by a majority of ten.[1] Its effect outside
Parliament was equally astonishing, despite the feverish zeal
with which it had been canvassed during the past two years.
The Press of England was almost unanimous in praise of it.
Most of the London papers, from the *Daily News* downwards,
accentuated Richard's arguments. Only the *Times* and the
Spectator condemned the motion as premature: the former
because "we must bide a better time . . . progress is very
slow "; the latter because arbitration would never be organised
into a stable system unless buttressed by sanctions of force.[2]
From the Continent also extravagant congratulations filled the
editorial columns of leading journals in France and Germany.
The American Press, though cordial, was on the whole restrained.[3] The debate had aroused an interest far exceeding
that of Cobden's motion in 1849.

Richard seized his opportunity. With his wife he left
England on 1st September for a second Continental tour,
designed to promote analogous motions abroad. The series

---

[1] 98 to 88 ; see debate in Hansard, 8th July 1873.
[2] *Daily News*, 10th July ; *Times*, 9th July ; *Spectator*, 12th July.
[3] Particulars in *H. of P.* (1873), pp. 287 *seq.* ; and Miall, p. 199.

of resolutions introduced during the final months of the year mark the stages of his journey: to Brussels, The Hague, Berlin, Dresden, Vienna, Budapest, Venice, Verona, Milan, Rome, Florence, Turin, and Paris.   On his return, just before Christmas, he left the arbitration crusade active in seven countries.[1] The motions which his visit inspired punctuated the whole of the next five years, down to 1878.   In the history of international arbitration they form a chapter of themselves.

Van Eck in Holland, supported by M. Bredius, exhorted the Second Chamber to take the lead in acting on Richard's victory (19th November), but was rebuffed by the Foreign Minister's admonition that nothing could be done unless and until Great Britain issued invitations.   In Italy Mancini was more fortunate.   As Minister of Justice he was in a favourable position for commanding a hearing.   As an eminently practical and cautious statesman he marshalled his points to the utmost effect.   Admitting that arbitration could never supersede war entirely and that in defensive war there lay an everlasting glory, he asked the Italian Deputies to realise that the vital questions which would defy arbitration were extremely rare. The adoption of arbitration clauses in all future treaties concluded by Italy would therefore be of inestimable value in promoting security at home and goodwill abroad.   His motion was carried unanimously (24th November).[2]

Early in the new year the excitement roused by the campaign led to the foundation of an organised Peace Movement in a most unlooked-for spot—in Berlin.   Germany had long distressed the Continental Peace workers by reason of the flamboyant theories of State elaborated by Neitzsche and Moltke from the writings of Kant and Hegel, to the effect that war was a law of nature, that "a good war makes everything holy," and that "without war the world would sink into materialism."   There had risen two German prophets of Peace, but their auguries had passed unheeded, to be discovered much later when the German Peace Movement had weathered its first storms.

[1] Details of the tour are in Miall, chaps. xv–xvi.
[2] E. Langlade, *La Clause Compromissoire* (1899), pp. 67–9.

Sartorius, looking to the future, had foreseen an era of peace in the light of which he forbore to condemn the unpractical schemes of the previous century. Kaufmann of Bonn (about 1850), on the other hand, had urged that the future be hastened by means of resolute Peace propaganda — Peace Societies, Peace Days, Peace Prizes—concentrated into a *Science of Peace*.[1] The first step in this direction (apart from the short-lived Königsberg Society of 1850) was taken in January 1874, when Edward Lowenthal formed a Peace Committee in Berlin, where a year later he began the publication of a pacifist journal, *Deutsche Laterne*. The importance of this foundation lies not so much in the practical assistance Lowenthal was able to lend to the propagation of Peace as in the momentous suggestion which he published in his journal for a universal Parliamentary Peace Union, recruited from the members of every legislature in the world. This was the first proposal of its kind: at the time utterly fantastic. Within fourteen years it was to be virtually a reality.

Meanwhile Richard's visits had borne fruit elsewhere. Couvreur tabled, in the Belgian Lower House, a motion for arbitration clauses which just failed to pass (19th January). The Belgian Senate later adopted it without a single dissentient. Two months later the Swedish Second Chamber adopted a resolution for an International Court of Arbitration introduced by Jonas Jonassen (21st March). The Upper House, however, rejected it.[2] In Holland Van Eck and Bredius returned to the attack in October, a year after their first effort. They moved (27th November) that the Netherlands Government should negotiate with foreign States in order "that arbitration might become the regular means of adjusting international differences." To this end an arbitration clause should be inserted in treaties thenceforth wherever possible. The motion was carried this time by 35 votes to 30. In both the national and the local Press it received prominent notice and charitable

[1] Valentin, *Völkerbundegedanken in Deutschland* (1920), pp. 104 *seq.*
[2] K. P. Arnoldson, *Pax Mundi*, p. 15. The voting was 71 to 64.

comment.[1] Lemonnier at Geneva went further than any proposal had yet gone when during the same summer he projected in his journal a system of Permanent Treaties of Arbitration.[2] But the most zealous of the European movements took place in Denmark, where, although there was as yet no Peace campaign as such, petitions totalling over 11,000 signatures were sent in to the legislature by the farmers of Jutland on their own initiative, calling for the establishment of an International Tribunal. The plea was sponsored by three members of the Folkthing, led by Dr. Winther of Copenhagen, who secured a date for its discussion (13th May 1875). The Committee of Reference set up to report on it declared, however, that small countries like Denmark would find it difficult to lead the world in matters of international organisation: and the petitions were therefore futile. Winther afterwards became for some years the leading Danish pacifist.[3]

Across the Atlantic also much had been done. Sumner had contrived to repeat his arbitration motion in the Senate of 1st December 1873 and get it printed. In the following June the Senate and the House of Representatives actually passed analogous resolutions moved by S. L. Woodford and G. S. Orth. Sumner carried all three motions to their logical conclusion later in 1875, when he asked the Senate to propose before the world a system of arbitration founded on the conviction that "arbitration is a substitute for war in reality as in name, and is therefore co-extensive with war in its jurisdiction." It is to be noticed that this position fell short of that adopted thirty years earlier in his *True Grandeur of Nations*. Nevertheless it was too advanced for the Senate of the United States, though a motion similar to it was carried in the Canadian Upper House by Senator Cameron on 27th March 1875.[4]

[1] *H. of P.* (1874), p. 153; and information supplied by M. van der Mandere.
[2] R. L. Jones, *International Arbitration*, p. 169.
[3] A. Gennadius, *Arbitrage*, p. 77 ; *H. of P.* (1878), p. 130.
[4] E. L. Whitney, *American Peace Society*, p. 159 ; E. Rouard de Card, *Destinées de l'Arbitrage International* (1892), pp. 80 *seq.*; C. C. Morrison, *Outlawry of War* (1927), p. 267; *H. of P.* (1875), p. 229.

Three years later, finally, when the campaign had abated, two echoes were heard: one in Italy, where Mancini repeated his motion of 1873 with special reference to arbitration clauses in future Italian commercial treaties; the other in France, where one Sigaud of Nîmes got up a petition to the Senate for identical provisions in French treaties. Mancini was successful; Sigaud, however, did not get beyond a committee of investigation.

By 1878, then, Richard's debate in the House of Commons had found counterparts in Italy, Belgium, Sweden, Denmark, Holland, the United States, and Canada. Eight Parliaments altogether had given approval (albeit it counted for little) to the principle which, among all the principles of Peace, must be admitted first.

(c) *International Law and Disarmament*: 1873–78

By that year also the second avenue of progress—that of International Law — had been explored to some considerable distance. The need for a Code had not only been revealed in the *Alabama* dispute; it was inherent likewise in Richard's scheme of arbitration and in the plans for a Court of Nations propounded since 1870. Nor was the realisation of this confined to Miles and his American Code Committee. Statesmen were finding it impossible to conceive the international future in terms of the past. "The greatest triumph of our epoch," said Gladstone in 1870, "will be the consecration of the idea of a public law as the fundamental principle of European politics." [1]

Though the consummation of this hope was a long way off, an academic beginning had been made before the end of 1873. The American Code Committee itself produced a series of *Proposals for an International Code*, the work of David Dudley Field, which served as the basis of discussion at a Peace Congress held in Brussels in October 1873 at the instigation of Miles himself. The 702 sections of the proposed Code covered nearly the whole field of international relations. But on the thorny question of sanctions Field still

[1] Cited in C. L. Lange, *Doctrine Pacifique* (1926), p. 415.

forbore to offer an uncompromising opinion. The nations were "to bind themselves to see to it that each nation thus a party [to the Code] shall not resort to war against any other party accepting the Code." But the means were not specified.[1] The problem of sanctions, however, was not yet to take the front rank in the discussions of Peace advocates. Arbitration itself still provided sufficient latitude for disagreement and even wrangling. At the Brussels Congress, which took place during Richard's Continental tour, the foremost German jurist present, Bluntschli, urged, against the most vehement protests of Richard and Passy, that the path of arbitration would be both easier and safer if disputes arising out of "vital interests" were excluded from it. The resolution finally adopted was a compromise, admitting that there might be exceptions to the universal application of an arbitral system, but declaring that such exceptions would be extremely rare.[2]

Their rarity, of course, would depend on the scope of the Code of International Law by which the future was to be moulded; and it was to fashion such a code that two academic juridical societies were founded in Europe at the end of 1873. The first, inaugurated at Ghent on 18th September, was the *Institut de Droit International*, a society of jurists and publicists drawn from several countries, with no official character and devoted to the study of arbitration and private international law. Among its founders were Miles and Lieber from the United States, Westlake from England, Bluntschli from Germany, and Rollins-Jacquemyns from Belgium. By means of a periodical, the *Revue de Droit International*, the Institute proposed to foster the development of international law, to codify its rules into an "organisation of the world's conscience," and thus to facilitate the settlement of disputes without resort to war.[3]

---

[1] Reviewed in *H. of P.* (1874), p. 69. The American Code Committee comprised J. B. Miles, D. D. Field, T. W. Woolsey, E. Washburn, and W. B. Lawrence.

[2] Brussels Congress *Report* (1873), *passim* ; Howard Evans, *Sir Randal Cremer*, pp. 90–1.

[3] *See* Rouard de Card, *Destinées de l'Arbitrage International* (1892), pp. 16–9.

The wider the code the greater the proportion of disputes that would be legal in character and therefore arbitrable.

The other society was founded, as a result of the Brussels Congress, on 13th October. Known at first as the Association for the Reform and Codification of the Law of Nations, it changed its name in 1895 to International Law Society. Here again the initiative came from America, in that the Society, like the Brussels Congress itself, resulted from Miles's mission to Europe earlier in the year. But the coincidence of the two bodies, Institute and Society, did not extend beyond their theoretical object. This is the reason for the double foundation. The Institute at Ghent was not founded *expressly* in order to frame a code for universal adoption; its purview, indeed, was limited to private international law. The Society, on the other hand, was to explore the whole field of public international law and promulgate a code.[1]

During their first seven years, punctuated by annual meetings in different cities, the two organisations transformed international law from a set of precepts into a science. The International Law Association adopted from the outset the standpoint of the Brussels resolution, that arbitration should be made obligatory for all nations and that the disputes which could not be settled by it were few. At the first annual meeting, in 1874, Field was elected President. Invitations were issued to all Governments to initiate at once an era of arbitration. In the following year an identical appeal was made to every ruler in the world. At the fourth meeting, in 1876, special attention was devoted to the legal relations that might be fixed between Christian and non-Christian peoples. Next year, at Zurich, Mancini and Bluntschli carried a resolution to the effect that all future treaties should contain a clause making arbitration in certain classes of disputes *obligatory*. But thereafter the universality of the Association ceased for twenty years, as no members of the American Peace Society attended from 1878 to 1898. In Europe it recruited Sir Robert Phillimore from England, and leading Continental jurists.

[1] See *H. of P.* (1874), p. 129; E. Rouard de Card, pp. 21–5; Miall, *Henry Richard*, p. 215.

The Institute of International Law meanwhile built on a more solid foundation. It set up, in 1873, a committee instructed to study the question of *procedure* in cases of arbitration. M. Goldschmidt, the chairman, presented his report two years later at the annual meeting at The Hague in 1875. It became the basis of a body of "Rules of Procedure for Arbitration" issued by the Institute in twenty-seven articles (28th August). This, together with the Mancini-Bluntschli resolution of 1877 (which was passed by both associations, meeting in the same city of Zurich), amounted to a declaration of both scope and method.[1]

The two bodies were wise in excluding disarmament from their agenda. Not only was the time not ripe for a reduction of armaments in Europe, but the folly of the growing Armed Peace was being adequately laid bare in pamphlets and petitions by the Peace Societies and their parliamentary adherents; and the remarkable change that was coming over the Press can be gauged from a leading article in the London *Times* of 1874, which Richard naïvely reprinted as a Peace Society tract. The article warrants quotation, despite its length.

"We hear everywhere of profound peace. . . . But the process of turning citizens into soldiers goes on all over Europe without any apparent limit. . . . That such conduct has a direct tendency to provoke war is, perhaps, the least important point that could be urged against it. . . . The excuse which each nation urges for increasing its own army is, of course, everywhere the same. The wishes and intentions of each are most peaceful, but each is in perpetual dread of very opposite intentions on its neighbour's part. . . . The spectacle we now witness is one of needless preparation on all sides, where no danger threatens, or rather where the only danger is such as necessarily arises from mistaken efforts for security. . . . Our present peace is such literally as the world has never known before. It is a peace not only full of mutual suspicion and

---

[1] *See* Rouard de Card, *Destinées de l'Arbitrage International* (1892), pp. 17–9; text of Draft of Procedure is in *Revue de Droit International* (1875), pp. 227 *seq.*

mistrust, but one which entails as great a burden as Europe collectively has ever borne as the cost of war. . . . The worst feature of the case is that the process which is now going on may go on apparently without end. . . . The evil is so great already that it is scarcely possible to exaggerate it. . . . If such a state of things is permitted to continue, it will be a disgrace to European statesmen. It is on their shoulders that the real blame is to be laid." [1]

This prophetic warning was echoed several times in the British Parliament during the next two years, while Cremer's association kept the burden of armaments fresh in the minds of the working classes. Even when abject failure resulted, as when a motion of Sir Wilfred Lawson to reduce the British Army was rejected in the House of Commons by 224 votes to 61 (March 1875), the occasion was at least valuable as having allowed the Peace body in Parliament to air its views. Richard himself was responsible for two heated debates on the national armaments expenditure, both of which very properly gave him no material satisfaction. [2]

Outside England there was little concerted effort in the same direction. The Austrian and German Reichstags, however, were the scene of disarmament proposals by leading pacifists between 1875 and 1878 whose efforts were undoubtedly connected. Ritter von Schmerling declared before the Austrian Chambers in October 1875 that the labour of a conscript people was of far higher importance than an army, and that the Dual Monarchy should "take the initiative in a general disarmament." Early in 1876 three cities canvassed petitions in this strain at the instance of their municipalities; while Adolf Fischhoff, the foremost pacifist in Austria, kept Richard and Passy regularly posted with information on the birth of a Peace party in Vienna. Herr Fux, a co-founder, moved the reduction of the Austrian army in February 1876 with unexpected results; for though discussion on the motion was

---

[1] *Times*, 27th May 1874; similarly on 18th January 1875.
[2] *See* Howard Evans, *Sir Randal Cremer*, p. 328; *H. of P.* (1875), p. 214.

precluded by the lateness of the session, thirty-six members of both Chambers met in April to discuss disarmament and arbitration.　Don Arturo de Marcoartu, who was touring Central Europe from his headquarters in Spain, and who had already published the winning essays in his Prize Competition, attended these discussions and bore the news northwards into Germany, where already negotiations had been opened between certain German deputies, led by Baron Ducker, and the Austrians under Fux and Fischhoff, for an International Conference on the Reduction of Armaments.　These tentative beginnings were to lead to stable results in 1879.　The only German effort before that date was an abortive resolution by Jean Dollfus and Von Bühler for a fifty per cent. reduction of all European armaments for the next ten or fifteen years.

Most noteworthy of all, Fischhoff propounded in the autumn of 1875 the idea which had been first conceived by Lowenthal in Berlin a year earlier—the idea of an Inter-Parliamentary Union of members pledged to future Peace.　He elaborated a scheme for an annual conference at which the various Parliamentary groups might discuss the best means of popularising arbitration and disarmament.　A first meeting was actually planned to be held in 1877 by Austrian, German, French, and Italian deputies, to draft a memorandum to their Parliaments calling for a reduction of armaments; but the Bulgarian atrocities and the Balkan wars of 1877 interrupted the fourfold negotiations.[1]　Nevertheless the idea of an Inter-Parliamentary Union gained favour from that date onwards, until its triumphant realisation in 1889.

The campaign for disarmament and an International Code, then, was not organised on the entire Peace front.　But there was a concerted activity in 1878, which came to a head after the Berlin Congress though not organically connected with the crisis in the Balkans.　This was a second offensive on the part of the working-class Peace Movement directed from London.　It produced a Congress in Paris in 1878 comparable to that

[1] Text of Memorandum is in Howard Evans, *Sir Randal Cremer*, p. 135.

of 1849.   While the British Peace Society was pursuing quietly
its career of domestic propaganda—signalised in the formation
of a Women's Peace Society in April 1874 and a Midlands
Arbitration Union at Birmingham and Liverpool in the following month—the Workmen's Peace Association in London,
with its 350 agents, was more concerned to preserve the
international character of the Peace crusade.   Cremer proposed in 1875 that the Association should form a new International, by means of a Conference in Paris.   The memories
of the war of 1870 were still acute in France, but Paris
was the only possible centre for a Continental crusade.   In
the autumn of 1875 he took fifty British delegates across to
inaugurate plans by conferring with twice their number of
French working-men's leaders under Auguste Desmoulins.
The result, apart from resolutions in favour of arbitration and
against bloated armaments, was the establishment of a Workmen's Peace Committee in Paris for the purpose of preparing
a Congress.

Hopes ran high, as revival was everywhere apparent.
Santallier had re-emerged in the autumn of 1874 with an
evening edition of his paper, *Le Havre*, devoted entirely to
pacifist propaganda.   He disseminated it throughout France.
Passy's *Société des Amis de la Paix* steadily recruited fresh
members, until by the beginning of 1877 it numbered 475 active
agents and opened a series of lectures to make known the work
of the two international law societies.   Franck and Bellaire,
its President and Secretary, sought the co-operation of kindred
spirits outside the society—Garnier, Desmoulins, and Limousin;
while at Potonié's house in Paris the meetings of the *Ligue du
Bien Public* began to be held more regularly than at any time
since 1870.   Progress in other countries was hindered by
stringent Press laws to a degree unknown even in France.
Nevertheless the Mennonite sects in Russia began an articulate
propaganda for Peace at Christmas 1875, led by one Ellen
Jansen, and in Germany there appeared next year a curious
echo of Burritt's voice—a pacifist journal issued from Berlin
by Jean Dollfus under the title of *The Olive Branch*.   Potonié

revived his *Ligue* in the same city with not one but three periodicals.[1]

When the Paris Congress assembled on 26th September 1878 it was found to contain spokesmen from thirteen countries. In all there were about 150 delegates, of whom 95 came from France. The business to be discussed fell into three categories. Foremost was the question of the best practical means for fostering Peace—by agitating for freedom of commerce, by utilising the Press, by encouraging International Congresses on literary and scientific subjects, by promoting Peace Congresses and universal Exhibitions, and by securing the election of pacifist candidates to Parliament in all countries. Secondly, in the matter of arbitration, means had to be discovered for obtaining from Governments something more than mere unctuous praise. And thirdly, the codification of International Law was to be examined, with special emphasis on the prohibition of crippling war indemnities. All this was thrashed out by Richard, Van Eck, Joseph Garnier, Dr. Sturm (Austria), Couvreur, Baron Holtzendorff (Germany), and the Marquis Popoli (Italy).[2]

Many of the resolutions passed are especially noteworthy for the light which they throw on the movement which inspired them. The usual denunciations of war as international brigandage were there, together with repetitions of the plea for arbitration advanced in former years. There reappeared also the easy theory that public relations should be determined by the same principles of justice and humanity that regulated private relations; and the Press and the Pulpit were at once hailed and chastised as of old. But there were innovations as well—of two types, administrative and political. On the one hand, the resolutions reflect a firmer grasp of the problems involved than the earlier Conferences could boast. Emphasis was laid on the value of the mediation protocol of 1856; an Arbitral Court was recommended, composed of two representa-

---

[1] *H. of P.* (1875), p. 333. Potonié's three organs were the *Journal de Berlin*, the *Feuille d'Ollivier*, and the *Cosmopolite*.

[2] Conference *Report*, *passim* : text of resolutions, pp. 153-5. See also L. Kamarovsky, *Le Tribunal International*, p. 273.

tives from each State, with annual re-elections; an International
Commission was demanded to estimate the armaments of each
nation.[1]   On the other hand, the strong political bias of the
delegates was manifest in the provision for a plebiscite to be
held before the annexation of any territory, and in the demand
for liberty of conscience in all countries.   The tenor of many
speeches during the six days had been that of John Bright in
the previous May at a meeting in Leeds: "If the Trade
Unions would speak out for peace, there would be no war.
There are men and classes to whom war is sometimes gain;
to the working-men it is only loss." [2]

From the standpoint of the Peace Movement itself, however,
the most vital question touched on was that of organisation.
Franck, who presided over the Congress, proposed that all
the Peace organisations should be united into a federation and
represented by a Permanent Committee, so that in times of
crisis a world-wide concentration of effort along lines laid down
by the central Committee could be brought to bear on public
opinion.   The advantages of such a federation were obvious;
but the suggestion tended to ignore the heterogeneous nature
of the Peace Movement as it then stood, and the radical differences which would have to be composed before a constitution
could be drafted that could incorporate every Peace body and
offend none.   Nevertheless Franck carried his resolution, and
a Commission of nine members, including Richard, Passy, Van
Eck, Lemonnier, and Couvreur, was set up to draft statutes for
the projected federation.[3]   This was begun in the weeks immediately following the Congress.   At the same time the
national delegates, back once more on their own fronts, prepared
a fresh attack on the three problems already attempted—arbitration, disarmament, international law.

The Paris Conference of 1878 represents the high-water
mark of the second Peace crusade during its first twelve years.
The same optimism was apparent as during the earlier period

[1] Resolutions 5, 13, 10.
[2] Cited in M. E. Hirst, *Quakers in Peace and War*, p. 296.
[3] Resolution 17 : Paris Congress (1878) *Report*, p. 31.

of Congresses; but if the old difficulties remained as insuperable as ever, there was at least a wiser understanding of them. Roussel, of disarmament fame since 1848, certainly had his counterpart still, in the person of one Alexander Laya of Switzerland, who called on the Paris delegates to demand forthwith the establishment of a European Parliament. But all the national Peace leaders, from Richard and Passy downwards, realised how very far off lay the consummation of their ideals, how little could be done to achieve them without profounder study and reflection, and how vitally necessary it was to avoid outbursts of optimism or fanaticism that could serve only to heap ridicule on the whole enterprise once more. The supreme need of the Peace Movement was still one of organisation.[1]

(d) *The Concert of Europe in* 1878

It is important also to pause at the year 1878 and examine the condition of the world which the Peace advocates were endeavouring to modify, for the expression "Concert of Europe" contained by now larger elements of truth than at the time of its invention in 1813–15. How far its approximation to reality had developed is shown by the diplomatic history of the Balkan insurrections of 1877–78.

Outside politics the Governments of the world had established the first universal international union ever formed—the Postal Union of 1874—to this day an institution more completely international than any other in existence. Since 1897 it has included every civilised nation in the world, each of which is represented at its Congresses held every five or six years. From the outset the Union was a startling achievement, not merely because it began with twenty-two adherent States pledged individually to submit to arbitration all disputes arising from its working, but also because it demonstrated how far international co-operation could be extended outside the field of political relations, slender though the hope might be as yet, of similar organisation within that field. The Peace Parties naturally derived from it a maximum of encouragement

[1] *Cf.* F. Passy, *Pour la Paix* (1909), pp. 76–7.

"The concert which is to end war," declared Benjamin True-blood,[1] "which is even now working itself out on a grand scale in the movements of the world society, is to be one of unarmed, trustful co-operation—a force more powerful to hold in check the demon of violence than all the combined steel-clad ships that ever furrowed the ocean."

And within the political field, cut up by national economic interests and national traditional prejudices, the Balkan crisis of 1878 illustrates that the conception of community among the Powers of Europe had already given rise to something like an international legislature.

The Berlin Congress is noteworthy here partly for this reason, partly for the opportunity which it afforded the Peace Parties to repeat the mission of 1856, and partly for the obstacles to international organisation which it threw into relief.

When the Balkan insurrections began in 1876 the five Great Powers came forward as mediators between the Ottoman Porte and its rebel subjects. Conferences were held by the five to decide what terms the Porte should be recommended to offer. It was even resolved to send an international police force to the Balkans to restore order; and when the Porte rejected the suggested terms, the Russian Government first turned to its fellow-mediators with plans to force an acceptance, and then, in default of support, opened war alone on behalf of the insurgents. These exchanges in themselves are striking evidence of a determination among the Powers that matters of paramount importance to all should be discussed and resolved by all. So much so, indeed, that when Russia carried her war to a successful issue and dictated, in the early summer of 1878, a Treaty of San Stefano which enhanced her own position in the Balkans, the rest of the Concert intervened—led by Great Britain—to substitute within three months an *international* settlement at Berlin in which Russian predominance was far less apparent.[2]

[1] B. F. Trueblood, *Federation of the World* (1899), p. 97 ; also an article on the Union in London *Times*, 10th May 1929.
[2] *See* the study by L. S. Woolf in *International Government* (1917), pp. 34 *seq.*

During the two years of the insurrections the British Peace Parties strove to avert a crisis among the Powers. The Peace Society, torn between its traditional defence of Turkish integrity and a recent disgust at the oppression of the Slavs under Ottoman rule, sent memorials to Lord Derby at the Foreign Office in favour of Non-Intervention, and printed fresh editions of Richard's old Crimean pamphlets. There emerged from the Foreign Office deputation a body known as the Eastern Question Association, founded in December 1876 with the express object of preventing a war with Russia or an alliance with the Porte. The Workmen's Peace Association took the more positive line of urging the Government to use its influence to secure the independence of the revolted districts.[1] Over 10,000 articles from the two bodies appeared in the Press during 1877: and when the danger of war became really acute in the early days of 1878 the Peace Society sent to Parliament over 1300 local petitions within a month. Richard hotly contested the order to send the fleet through the Dardanelles (11th February), and sent a memorial to every signatory of the Treaty of Paris of 1856, invoking recourse to the mediation protocol to curtail the Russo-Turkish war. When the reserves were called out in April he carried with him sixty-three members into the Opposition lobby. On 10th April he joined Cremer and Appleton in a monster meeting in London, at which Gladstone appeared and spoke for Peace, and from which resulted similar meetings in most of the large towns during May. Finally, when the Berlin Congress opened in June, the supreme gesture was made of sending a deputation bearing a memorial from the Peace organisations of all Europe.

Three delegates—Richard, Leone Levi, and Frederic Passy—arrived in Berlin on 1st July with a specific commission to bring the question of arbitration before the assembled plenipotentiaries of the Powers. The memorial they carried contained the signatures also of Mancini, Couvreur, Van Eck, Adolf Franck, and others. They were able to present it in person to three of the Congress delegates—Lord Odo Russell

[1] Howard Evans, *Sir Randal Cremer* (1909), pp. 98–100.

(Great Britain), Von Bülow (the German Foreign Minister), and Count Corti (Italy)—all of whom praised the motives which had prompted the mission, though all feared, to quote Corti's words, that "the plenipotentiaries would not be brought to accept the proposal of a clause binding the Congress to arbitration, as that might be thought inconsistent with the independence of Governments." Written replies to like effect were received from Lord Salisbury and Lord Beaconsfield (Great Britain), Baron Shuvalov (Russia), Count Haymerle (Austria), and the Comte de Saint-Vallier (France). The deputation was finally dismissed with the technical objection that the Congress could discuss no matters that had not been treated in the Treaty of San Stefano. Thus it failed. The one consolation was that the mediatory clause of 1856 was indirectly re-enacted by Article 63 of the Treaty of Berlin, which maintained the Balkan treaties of 1856 and 1871 "in all such of their provisions as are not [herein] abrogated."[1]

The London *Times* hailed the Berlin Congress as "the first instance of a real Parliament of the Great Powers." The criticism contains a modicum of truth in so far as the Congress marked a climax in the development of "Government by Concert and Conference" which had begun at Vienna in 1815. But the essentials of a true international legislature were lacking. Settlement by Conference could be little more than a matter of mere convenience while the question of submitting disputes to a Conference remained itself a point for diplomatic discussion. The need was "to *define* the cases in which a Conference must or could be called," and, further, to co-ordinate the means by which (through mediation and arbitration) diplomacy could hope to avert war. These tasks were not attempted by Government until the very end of the century.[2]

[1] Text in K. Strupp, *Diplomatische Aktenstücke zur Orientalischen Frage* (1918), p. 160.
[2] *Cf.* L. S. Woolf, *International Government* (1917), pp. 43, 65.

CHAPTER VIII

IF achievements are to be judged by their motives and direction as well as by their quantity, it is true to say that the decade following the Congress of Berlin is the most fruitful period in the whole history of the Peace Movement. Not only was there during those years an expansion of the various movements within the countries in which they had originated, nor only a persistence in the endless series of disarmament and arbitration motions laid before Senates and Parliaments, but in addition, while the body of academic theory behind the pacifist efforts increased, and while the Churches now awoke to the part they might play in the eradication of war, three new and vital threads emerged.

One, created partly by the expansion of Peace Societies throughout Europe, was the problem of organisation. The second was an attempt on both sides of the Atlantic to secure for the first time a permanent treaty of arbitration between two Great Powers. The third was an attempt, purely American, to forge a Pan-Continental Union which would render war no longer possible among the States of the Western Hemisphere. By the end of 1889 one of these problems—that of organisation —had been solved. The second, though much headway was made during the ten years, remained insurmountable until 1897, when Great Britain and the United States gave a lead to the Powers by concluding an arbitration treaty. The third effort— towards a Pan-American Union—bore its first fruit in 1890. At the same time there was a marked development of the Peace Movement in its several national centres, both old and new. This must be noticed first.

(a) *Great Britain:* 1878–89

In England it seemed for the moment that a schism was about to sunder the Peace Movement as the American bodies had been disrupted in 1839, for in the summer of 1880, when the two British Peace organisations were emerging from a year's campaign of lectures and petitions against the Afghan and Zulu wars, a third body was suddenly formed which, while professing the same ends as the Peace Society and the International Arbitration League (Cremer's organisation), was hotly denounced by Henry Richard.

The new society was the creation of Hodgson Pratt, a private gentleman of means and a great traveller, who had for some years shown an interest in the work of the Peace advocates. He was a man so energetic that when, a few years later, his new society had taken root in a dozen places on the Continent, Richard could not but declare in frank amazement that "Mr. Hodgson Pratt is a Peace Society in himself." Pratt's inaugural meeting was held on 16th August 1880 in London. He called his society the International Arbitration and Peace Association of Great Britain and Ireland. Its declared objects certainly do not explain the wrath with which Richard heard of its inception. They were threefold: to form a public opinion in Europe favourable to the substitution of arbitration for war; to promote friendly feelings between the citizens of different countries; and to correct erroneous statements in the Press or in European Parliaments on international questions. All this Pratt proposed to do by means partly of Continental tours and partly of a monthly journal entitled *Concord*.

But the reasons for the cleavage are not far to seek. In the first place, Pratt chose as his secretary Lewis Appleton, who actually resigned from the Peace Society to take up the post—to Richard's intense chagrin. In the second place, Pratt maintained that the Peace Society would remain severely handicapped so long as its standpoint was primarily spiritual and Christian, and that there was needed a purely *secular* organisation wider in scope than Cremer's International Arbitration League.

Richard denied the force of both assertions. "No one completely acquainted with the subject can believe that there is any necessity, or that there is any room, for a second organisation to carry on precisely the same work . . . as is already done by the institution which has been in existence for upwards of sixty years." [1]   A third and deeper point of difference was seen a few years later when, on 9th January 1885, Pratt published in the *Echo* a letter which showed that his society was not strictly a pacifist body at all.   Taking as his title the question, "Can England secure for herself immunity from war?" he declared that the hope of future peace lay in the spread of democracy, in close international ties between the democracies, in the recognition of the just claims of foreign nations, in fairer Press comments on the interests of foreign nations, and in maintaining adequate armaments for *insisting* on justice from foreign Governments.   The Peace Society refused to endorse this last point, as being thoroughly Palmerstonian and the greatest menace to peace.   But though the letter was not retracted, relations between the two societies afterwards improved until, by the summer of 1887, when the campaign began for an Anglo-American Arbitration Treaty, they were in full co-operation.

Cremer and Richard meanwhile pursued their own separate courses.   The appeal of the former lay to the masses, both in England and abroad.   While he changed the name of his society from International Working-Men's Peace Association to International Arbitration League, Cremer continued to head delegations from England to Continental meetings: notably in 1879, when there was held in Paris a Workmen's Conference of representatives from England, France, and Italy.   On his return Cremer carried a disarmament motion through the annual meeting of the British Trade Union Congress. [2]

Richard, on the other hand, utilised the opportunities furnished by his seat in Parliament.   In 1880 he projected a motion for disarmament to be raised in the Commons.   As in

[1] *H. of P.* (1880), p. 134.
[2] Howard Evans, *Cremer*, p. 95.

1873, he prepared for it by a six months' lightning campaign of lecture tours, beginning with a Peace Society demonstration at Liverpool on 23rd January.   It was obvious that the passage of this motion would be incomparably more difficult than that of his motion for arbitration in 1873; for, besides the "practical" men who would condemn disarmament in Europe as an interference with the *status quo*, there was also a strong military element in the Commons to be reckoned with.   The motion, however, was debated on 15th June, by which time 1100 petitions in its favour, totalling 85,000 signatures, had poured into Downing Street.   Richard moved "that an humble address be presented to Her Majesty, praying that she will be graciously pleased to instruct Her Principal Secretary of State for Foreign Affairs to enter into communications with other Powers with a view to bring about a mutual and simultaneous reduction of European armaments." He received strong support, especially from L. Courtney, who, less sanguine, secured the addition of the words "on all occasions when the circumstances admit of it."   But the motion was not pressed to a division.   Nevertheless it was of greater value than that of mere publicity; for Gladstone, in a cordial reply on behalf of the Government, reasserted his faith in a future conditioned, if not by immediate universal disarmament, at least by a rapid spread of the practice of arbitration.[1]   The Press also, adding to its comments the fact that Europe's armaments bill for 1880 stood at £161,000,000 out of a total budget of £586,000,000, was unstinted in its praise—from the *Daily News*, which believed that an earnest effort by the British Government in response to the motion might have had some effect, to the *Broad Arrow* (a military paper), which warned the Peace Society that in the last resort the country must be "able to defend her own shores successfully when these are threatened."

Almost a year later, during the Transvaal crisis of 1881, Richard introduced his third great motion in Parliament. Cremer had been carrying petitions to Gladstone from working-men protesting against any annexation in the Transvaal.

[1] Debate in Hansard, 15th June 1880.

Similar protests had arrived also from Van Eck in Holland and from meetings of the Belgian Flemings. Richard, taking a longer view, sought to prevent all annexations for the future by legislative means. On 29th April 1881 he moved in the Commons that the power vested in British representatives abroad of making contracts and annexations and of going to war without the prior authority of Parliament should be withdrawn, as being inimical to international law and dangerous to the peace of the world. The debate on it was spirited, Peter Rylands, the Manchester philanthropist, staunchly endorsing the arguments raised by Richard. But Gladstone countered that the Home Government had almost invariably ratified the actions of colonial governors, and the motion was lost by 72 votes to 64. In the Press of the following morning two constructive points stood out from the general body of qualified praise. One, in the *Times*, was to the effect that moral restraints on colonial governors were more potent than mechanical restraints, and that the effectual corrective would be to "teach people to distinguish between showy annexations, which are burdensome and useless, and wise acts, which strengthen and enrich the Empire." The other, in the *Daily Chronicle*, suggested that the telegraph and the speeding-up of communications were already achieving the end which Richard desired.[1]

This was almost Richard's last Parliamentary gesture; but he remained active as Secretary of the Peace Society for four years longer. During 1882 he was among the founders of still a fourth body—academic rather than propagandist—set up under the title of the Anti-Aggression League (22nd February). The event is important chiefly for the personnel of the society, for its founders were all men of letters—men of science or publicists—whose words would command respect. Among them were Sir A. Hobhouse, Herbert Spencer, Frederic Harrison, and John Morley (editor of the *Pall Mall Gazette* and the *Fortnightly Review*). Their objects were to amass reliable information on British foreign policy, to call attention to

[1] Debate in Hansard, 29th April 1881.

"forward" proceedings, to increase the control of Parliament over the executive in international and colonial transactions, and to explode the doctrine that the British Government was "bound to use force in defence of every British subject wherever he may choose to wander."

It can be seen from this that the new league appeared as a result of the Transvaal annexation; and there was immediate work for it to perform when the Egyptian insurrection broke out four months later (June 1882). The columns of the *Pall Mall Gazette* thenceforth spoke for rationality and moderation in foreign policy.

The Egyptian War, which began with the revolt of Arabi Pasha and dragged on until after the death of Gordon in 1885, kept all the Peace bodies active for nearly four years. Both Richard and Cremer protested against the bombardment of Alexandria in July 1882. The one petitioned Parliament, the other tabled question after question in the Commons, until he was afforded a day for debate on the war which gave him the melancholy satisfaction of bearing with him into the Opposition lobby only nineteen members (eleven of them Irish). Early in 1883 again, during the debate on the Address, the Peace Party in Parliament, headed by Richard, Thomas Burt, Sir Alfred Illingworth, and Sir Wilfrid Lawson, called the Government to account—again without avail. Every opportunity was seized for airing their detestation of aggression, even the day on which the Commons discussed the grant of peerages to Admiral Seymour and Sir Garnet Wolseley; while the *Pall Mall Gazette*, in which Morley had bitterly satirised the Day of Thanksgiving for the victory of Tel-el-Kebir, joined with the *Spectator* in demanding a withdrawal from the Sudan. Conferences were held, moreover, throughout the North of England, at which Sir Joseph Pease and his family (who provided the Peace Society with three Presidents between 1872 and 1911) were always active, in company with the Quaker, Theodore Fry. But no tangible effect was produced. And when Richard delivered his two final Parliamentary speeches on the war early in 1885, denouncing the sending of reinforcements to Gordon, the *Herald of Peace* could claim no more than that it had done its best.

In that same summer, after a fresh scare over the Penjdeh incident with Russia in March, in which he invoked the Paris Protocol of 1856, Richard resigned his Secretaryship of the Peace Society and retired. He was seventy-three years old, and had striven continuously in the *Herald*, in Continental tours, and later in Parliament, for thirty-seven years—from the day when he succeeded Jefferson in 1848. No Englishman has ever devoted more of himself to the cause of better understanding among nations. When Richard died in 1888 his friends called him the Apostle of Peace, and the title was used by each of his biographers in turn. He shares it with William Ladd, with whom also he shares to-day an almost complete oblivion. Each of them was born a century before his time. They both devoted their whole lives to the cause of Peace, preaching watchwords which, from being empty phrases, they transformed within fifty years into household expressions, and which have since become the axioms of world politics. There is room for a feeling stronger than regret that, of two such men, to whose plans for the future no subsequent Peace efforts have added a single new idea, only a tiny fraction of the English-speaking public has ever heard mention.

Richard was succeeded by William Jones, one of the Peace Society's travelling agents, who, however, was soon ordered off to Australia for reasons of health and had to relinquish his post in 1889. The Peace Society was still fairly prosperous, to judge from its balance-sheet and from the reports of its agents.

The local work of the branches had its own peculiar value; but Parliamentary action was more hopeful. It was therefore a great moment for the Peace Party when Cremer was elected to Parliament for Haggerston in 1885 along with seven other members of his own association. For several years the International Arbitration League had had over a thousand agents active, under the Presidency of Thomas Burt, M.P. (Beales had died in 1881), but not until now was the body given the tactical advantage held by the Peace Society since 1868. From

1885 onwards Cremer held his seat until his death in 1908, with only one interruption (1895–1900). He and his fellow-members took an active part in the debate which Richard inaugurated in the Commons on 19th March 1886—the last motion of Richard's life. It sought to deprive the Crown of its right to make war, annexations, and treaties, and to vest that right in Parliament as representative of the people: the very question, in fact, which was disrupting the Peace Party in Holland. Rylands, Pease, and Illingworth spoke in favour of the motion, but it was finally lost by 115 votes to 79. The speeches suggest that those who opposed it were misled in believing that Richard's object was a House of Commons entrusted with executive duties. The Press on the whole was sympathetic.[1] Cremer revived the topic two years later (7th March 1888) in a motion for setting up a Parliamentary Committee, on the lines of the Foreign Relations Committee of the United States Senate, "for the consideration of all questions of a foreign or colonial nature, and the ratification of treaties with foreign Powers." But still to no purpose.[2]

In the Lords a resolution introduced in July 1889 by the Marquis of Lansdowne for the establishment of an International Court of Justice is of importance for the opening it afforded the *Pall Mall Gazette*. For Lord Salisbury's cautious reply, which took refuge behind the argument that a High Court would presuppose in all States a new condition of mind, and that even with a Court in existence the world would still be at the mercy of any strong Power which might choose to flout an award, was torn to pieces in the *Pall Mall* as a "dyspeptic survey." The *Pall Mall* at this time had changed its editorship. The new editor, W. T. Stead, carried out a Continental tour in 1888 from which he returned to produce a series of impassioned leading articles, based on his observations, on the "folly and dangers of the European armed camp."

[1] *H. of P.* (1881), p. 260 ; Miall, *Henry Richard*, p. 353.
[2] *H. of P.* (1888), pp. 43–4 ; K. P. Arnoldson, *Pax Mundi*, p. 90 ; the voting was 219 to 44.

On 20th August 1888 Henry Richard died. William Jones, his temporary successor since 1885, was on the point of leaving for Australia. In January 1889 the Secretaryship of the Peace Society was entrusted to Dr. W. Evans Darby, a Nonconformist minister of Watford. No better choice could have been made. Darby continued Richard's work, with all Richard's energy and more than Richard's learning, until the close of 1915. His monumental book, *International Tribunals*, written in time for the Hague Conference of 1899, still remains the one authoritative record of every scheme for world organisation from the Greek Amphictyonic Council down to 1900; and when, after 1889, the Peace Movement throughout the world took on a real unity, he contrived to keep in touch with, and link up, all its activities in both hemispheres.

One other achievement belongs to this period of the British Peace Movement—Leone Levi's *Draft Project of a Council and High Court of Arbitration*, propounded in May 1886. Leone Levi, Professor of International Law in King's College, London, was a Vice-President of the Peace Society. His scheme appeared at a time when Great Britain could point to three successful arbitrations of delicate disputes since the *Alabama* award of 1872,[1] and when a treaty was being negotiated with Greece in which figured a clause providing for the establishment of a committee of arbitration, nominated by the two Governments, to settle certain classes of disputes.[2]

The project had the merit of leaving no difficulty unresolved, to Levi's own satisfaction. No problem was shelved. The scheme was, in brief, that the Peace Society and the International Arbitration League should invite the Governments of the civilised world to join in appointing a Permanent Council of International Arbitration, composed of men appointed by the various States, sitting as international judges and not in any national capacity. The Council was to sit in some neutral city such as Berne or Brussels, and its expenses were to be shared by

---

[1] They were the Delagowa Bay dispute (1875), a dispute with Nicaragua (1879), and the Halifax Fisheries dispute (1880).

[2] K. P. Arnoldson, *Pax Mundi*, p. 10.

the member States. On the outbreak of any dispute, involving members or non-members, a meeting of the Council was to be summoned by the Secretaries to offer mediation or arbitration, and if the dispute were arbitrated the award was to be binding. All was plain sailing so far. The crux of the scheme lay in its twelfth section—on sanctions. "It is not contemplated to provide for the exercise of physical force in order to secure reference to the Council or to compel compliance with the award of the Council or Court when made. The authority of the Council and Court is moral, not physical." For the rest, Council and Court would function as in Ladd's scheme, dispensing a Code of International Law as soon as such Code should have been drafted.[1]

In virtue of his declaration in favour of pacific sanctions Levi was able to submit his *Draft Project* to both the International Arbitration League and the Peace Society. Both bodies heartily endorsed it. The Peace Society took the line that there was now sufficient organised theory in existence for Governments to attempt a beginning; for to Levi's plan could be added the *Rules of Procedure for a Court of Arbitration* drawn up by the International Law Association in 1875. But there was needed something more than an explorer to bring the promised land nearer. "In Professor Levi's scheme," said the *Times*, "we recognise an old friend in a slightly altered dress. . . . The only novelty of the project . . . is that it provides a definite sphere for the international lawyer, that amphibious being who works midway between law and morality. . . . The most that can be said is that it is free from the airy grandiloquence which has distinguished previous schemes of international arbitration. . . . No scheme is likely to be successful, because no amount of recitals that war is disastrous will make people more disposed to arbitrate. . . . When a nation considers that its honour or its vital interests are at stake, nothing will persuade it, if strong enough, to allow the

---

[1] Text in L. Appleton, *Tribunal for Europe*, pp. 26–8 ; E. Rouard de Card, *Arbitrage International*, pp. 215–8 ; W. E. Darby, *International Tribunals* (ed. 1904), pp. 216–23.

question to be settled by third parties." And national honour, the bogey in international relations, is even to-day far from being killed.

(b) *The United States*: 1878-89

Across the Atlantic there was the same steady emphasis, in Congress and in the States, on arbitration and disarmament; and the same realisation also, that the spiritual cries of the older Peace Societies were becoming less and less potent as the Peace Movement became more practical. The thought which prompted Hodgson Pratt to found his International Arbitration and Peace Association in 1880 is well paralleled in a leading article in the Rochester, New York, *Morning Herald* during the summer of 1884. "The English Peace Society believe nothing but that the claims of Christ and of universal humanity are paramount to any other consideration. While no one would wish to damp the ardour of the Society in that direction, there may be a question whether the object cannot be sooner gained by bringing home to individuals the cost to them, in money, of wars and warlike armaments, and the cruelty of battlefields."[1] The criticism is not altogether just, whether applied to the British or to the American Peace Society. The truth is rather that, having broadened and secularised their outlook since 1848, these two original foundations survived to leaven the economic and internationalist movement of the second half of the century. The work for Peace, in America as in England, was twofold: in part missionary, "charged with the duty of urging on Christians, as such, an almost forgotten article of faith"; and in part political, "seeking to proclaim a more humane and reasonable international policy" for Governments and peoples.[2]

This work was pursued in America after 1878 with little direct co-operation with the simultaneous efforts in Europe until 1887, when the inter-continental crusade for a permanent

[1] Cited in *H. of P.* (1884), p. 102.
[2] *Cf.* a letter from William Pollard to the *Pall Mall Gazette* in September 1882 (reprinted in *H. of P.* (1882), pp. 124-5).

arbitration treaty was inaugurated. A link with the past was
severed when Elihu Burritt died in Connecticut in March
1879, after thirty-eight years of devotion to the cause of Peace.
From 1848 to 1861, and again during his tenure of office as
American Consul at Liverpool, Burritt had been the strongest
personal link uniting the American and European Peace men.
With Ladd and Richard he forms the triumvirate of the nine-
teenth-century Peace crusade. Others also had died: Miles,
Amasa Walker, and Reverdy Johnson (in 1875) among the most
prominent. The greatest international thinker left in America
was David Dudley Field, who took an active part after 1880
in promoting branches of Hodgson Pratt's International Arbitration and Peace Association.[1]

Two lines of progress are visible during the decade: one,
a fresh onslaught on President and Congress by the Peace
Societies in the name of arbitration and disarmament; the
other, an effort, shared by both the Peace Societies and the
Government, to weld the American Continent into an international unity. These two aims were pursued concurrently.

At the beginning of 1879 a memorial was delivered to
President Hayes by Jacob M. Troth (of the Universal Peace
Union) and C. Gillingham (a Quaker of Baltimore) to secure
the putting into operation of the Joint Resolution passed in
Congress on 17th June 1874 to promote arbitration. The
President did no more than recommend the Peace Party to
persevere with its propaganda and attain a maximum of publicity.
His successor, however (President Garfield), was blessed with a
true international outlook. At the instigation of the Secretary
of State (J. G. Blaine) he issued in 1881 an invitation to every
Government in the American Continent to attend a Conference in the following year for the purpose of uniting the whole
Continent on a basis of arbitration. This was the theme that
had been the keynote of the abortive Pan-American Conference in 1847. Garfield's death in the September following
his invitation delayed the negotiations by bringing into prominence the arguments of his opponents, who feared that the

[1] *See* E. L. Whitney, *American Peace Society*, p. 125.

establishment of a United America would inflame Europe. A large part, moreover, of South America was at the moment engaged in war. It is due to the efforts of the United States National Arbitration League, founded expressly in 1881, that the project did not fail altogether. The League held a Conference at Washington in May 1882, presided over by Edward S. Tobey (President of the American Peace Society) and attended by representatives of fifteen States. Means were discussed of giving publicity to Garfield's gesture, and resolutions were passed to hasten the formation of a Congress of Nations—a fully empowered arbitral body meeting annually. The latter question was raised again in the Senate at the end of the year by Senator Hoar of Massachusetts, whose resolution (20th December) was sent to die in the Senate's Foreign Relations Committee.[1]

Encouragement appeared meanwhile in two series of diplomatic negotiations in the middle of 1882. The first was an Arbitration Treaty concluded between Honduras and Colombia (10th April), which prompted the foundation of a vigorous Central and South American Arbitration League.[2] The other was a remarkable offer, made to the United States by the Federal Government of Switzerland in July, of a treaty embodying the arbitration of *all* future disputes between the two Governments. Each dispute as it arose was to be resolved by a tribunal of three judges—one appointed by each contracting party, and these two to choose a third. The treaty was to remain in force for thirty years. But the negotiations were interrupted by the death of the Swiss Secretary of State, and not resumed, though Switzerland concluded three such treaties elsewhere by the end of the century, all of which rank high in the history of "all-in" arbitration.[3]

---

[1] E. L. Whitney, *American Peace Society*, pp. 154–8 ; *H. of P.* (1882), p. 107 ; (1883), p. 239.

[2] Text in *H. of P.* (July 1883) ; see also K. P. Arnoldson, *Pax Mundi*, p. 20.

[3] With Salvador (30th October 1883), Ecuador (22nd June 1888), and the Congo (16th November 1899); see W.P.F. pamphlet on *Arbitration* (1926), p. 497.

In the light of these two events the agitation went on. While the United States National Arbitration League held a second Conference in November 1883, at which, among other things, severe strictures were passed on the prevailing methods of teaching history with strong national bias, the chain of resolutions in Congress grew steadily longer. Early in 1884 a Bill was introduced by I. Newton Evans, empowering the President to invite all the States of the world to a Conference at Washington to establish an International Tribunal. This secured a second reading before passing to the Foreign Relations Committee (3rd March). Senator Wilson of Iowa reintroduced it in December 1885 with like result, and again in December 1887. During the year 1886 Congress discussed no fewer than twelve Bills on international arbitration, all of which perished. Outside Congress the American Peace Society had hired a new corresponding secretary in 1884, having reduced its outstanding debts to 1200 dollars. The recruit, the Rev. R. B. Howard, reformed and enlarged the *Advocate of Peace*, whose circulation had recently fallen; and at the annual meeting in May 1885 a suggestion made by the Spaniard, Don Arturo de Marcoartu, was adopted, whereby a correspondence was at last opened with the other Peace bodies throughout the world for "mutual fellowship and co-operation."

A year later the fruits of Garfield's Pan-American scheme began to be gathered. Congress passed a Bill on 17th June 1886 authorising the President to invite Mexico and all the States of Central and South America to attend an International Arbitration Congress in Washington. A further resolution to the same effect two years later (11th May 1888) led finally to the opening of the First Pan-American Congress on 1st October 1889. This, rather than the earlier Congresses of 1826 and 1847, was the origin of the present-day Pan-American Union. It met "with a view to establishing a Tribunal of Arbitration for settling the differences that may arise between them [the American nations] and for establishing commercial treaties." Secretary Blaine, who presided, sounded the keynote of the proceedings in his opening address. "We believe that standing armies larger than are necessary for public order and the security of internal administration should become unknown in the two American Continents." How far this object was attained by the Conference must be left till later.

(c) *Europe and Elsewhere*: 1879–89

In Europe the expansion of the Peace Movement during the same decade was phenomenal; and the credit lies with two indefatigable Englishmen no less than with the Peace leaders in the various countries concerned. Hodgson Pratt toured the whole of Europe and America after 1880, setting up branches of his International Arbitration and Peace Association in nine European countries. His association became the model for every arbitration society afterwards founded. William Jones meanwhile, who succeeded Henry Richard, carried out a Continental tour in 1883 while still a local agent of the British Peace Society, directed towards the extension of organised Peace efforts and the preparation of a new International Peace Congress. He travelled through six countries, interviewing the leading pacifists in each and acting as a clearing-house for information as fresh societies sprang up. Then in 1888, when he sailed for Australia to recuperate his health, Jones sowed the first seeds of an internationalist movement in Japan and China. Importance also attaches, though to a far less degree, to the European tour of W. T. Stead (in 1888, after he became editor of the *Pall Mall Gazette*) and to Marcoartu's American visit in 1885, which resulted in regular communications being opened up between American and European Peace men. The work of these four—Pratt, Jones, Stead, and Marcoartu—has to be borne in mind in tracing the development of the European Peace Movement after 1880. Their influence as missionaries and as advisers was invaluable.

In Belgium there began, during 1881, an anti-conscription campaign led by two pacifists, Bats and Van den Bernde. For several years the two existing Peace centres at Brussels and Verviens lived on alone; but in 1889 a branch of Pratt's International Arbitration and Peace Association was founded at

Brussels by Emile de Lavelaye, with Couvreur as one of its Vice-Presidents.[1]   Across the Netherlands frontier Van Eck persisted in his series of motions every year (notably in 1878 and 1879) urging the States General to incorporate the principle of arbitration in all its future treaties.   In 1886, at the time of Richard's last motion in England on the right of the Crown to make war, the Netherlands Peace Society sent a memorial to the Second Chamber of the States General framed in similar terms, insisting that Parliamentary consent should be sought by the King *before* issuing a declaration of war.   This memorial failed.[2]   In Switzerland there was no such continuous effort. The League of Peace and Liberty, founded by Lemonnier at Geneva in 1867, continued to flourish, but its orbit remained circumscribed until 1889, when it threw off a branch at Lucerne — the *Schweitzer Friedensgesellschaft* — which was later to become extremely active.[3]

In Central Europe less was to be hoped for, by reason of militarist traditions and Press censorships.   The burden of armaments tended rather to strengthen the cry for offensive and defensive alliances than to stimulate retrenchment along lines of economy.   The growing strength of this conviction was well illustrated in a declaration by the Financial Committee of the Hungarian Parliament in 1879.[4]   Nevertheless remarkable progress was made.   The members of the Austrian Parliament who had met in April 1876 to discuss the future of international relations met again in March 1879 after the Paris Congress, under the chairmanship of Dr. Sturm.   They resolved to do all in their power to form a Peace Society for Austria - Hungary. Actually they got no further than setting up a Committee under one Beer.   And even though two young proselytes joined them in 1882 in the persons of Ferdinand Gilles and Friedrich Neumann, who developed a regular correspondence with Richard

---

[1] *H. of P.* (1881), *passim* ; (1889), p. 201 ; A. H. Fried, *Handbuch der Friedensbewegung* (1911), p. 292.
[2] *H. of P.* (1880), p. 36 ; (1886), p. 147 ; A. Gennadius, *Arbitrage International*, p. 77.
[3] A. H. Fried, *Handbuch* (1911), p. 292.
[4] See *H. of P.* (1879), p. 216.

in England, Austria remained without a Peace Society until the advent of Baroness von Suttner.[1]

Similarly in Germany. Sturm's motion for disarmament in the Austrian Reichsrath early in 1880 was anticipated in the German Reichstag in March 1879 by Dr. Bühler of Swabia. Both motions arose from Richard's initiative in planning the offensive which culminated in the Commons debate of 1880. Both naturally failed, and in Germany no further attempt was made inside Parliament for some years. An unofficial petition, got up in Berlin in 1882 for the promotion of disarmament and an International Court of Arbitration, came to nothing. Lowenthal's organisation, famous for its original scheme for an Inter-Parliamentary Peace Union, slowly atrophied. Until Bertha von Suttner startled the world in 1889 with her *Lay Down Your Arms* and her propagandist tour, the only other attempt to organise a Peace Party in Germany, apart from Pratt's local branches, was that of Paul Bendix in 1883. This also expired.[2]

Across the Alps, however, a vigorous Peace Movement spread throughout Italy after 1879. Already a Cosmopolitan League had been founded in Florence in 1877 by a Miss Pieromaldi, but the first Italian Peace Society proper—the League of Peace and Brotherhood—was created by E. T. Moneta in the following year. Its first great demonstration was made in 1879, when an Italian Peace Congress assembled at Milan (11th May), organised largely by four thousand delegates from Workmen's Associations. Resolutions were passed in favour of arbitration and disarmament, and the right of declaring war was claimed exclusively for "representative bodies elected by popular suffrage." A later meeting at Naples issued invitations to the Peace Societies of all other countries. Richard crossed from England to attend, and Holtzendorff came from Germany. But when Hodgson Pratt arrived in 1880 during his tour of Europe, the latent energy was concentrated into one central body, the *Associazione per l'Arbitrato e la Pace*

[1] *H. of P.* (1879), pp. 260–2 ; (1883), p. 185.
[2] L. Appleton, *Henry Richard*, p. 176 ; *H. of P.* (1879), p. 225 ; (1882), p. 71.

SIR W. R. CREMER

BARONESS BERTHA VON SUTTNER

tra le Nazioni, led by the deputy Ruggiero Bonghi. Within ten years it had evolved seventy-nine branches. Italy's record for arbitration clauses in her treaties meanwhile was becoming an object-lesson for the rest of Europe. Between 1856 and 1871 five treaties were negotiated embodying provisions for the arbitration of commercial disputes; and when in 1878 an Italian commercial treaty with France was ratified without such a clause, Mancini (the Father of the Italian Peace Movement) repaired the omission as soon as he became Foreign Minister. In 1883 alone nineteen arbitral clauses (including one with Great Britain) appeared in Italian treaties. There was justification, therefore, for the series of four congresses held by the numerous Italian Peace bodies in 1889. At all of these disapproval of the Triple Alliance with Germany and Austria-Hungary was strongly marked; and it was with this as his text that Moneta, the founder of the first society of 1879, toured the whole peninsula at the close of the year.[1]

In France the ten years represented a revival and reorganisation of existing bodies rather than a creation of new ones, though the first signs of new life after the Balkan crisis of 1878 came from two fresh organisations. One of these was a Workmen's Peace Association launched in Paris by Desmoulins and others in March 1879 on Cremer's model. This became extremist as time went on, until in 1885 one of its meetings was broken up by anarchist uproar. Georges Clemenceau was among its members.[2] The other body, the creation of Hodgson Pratt, was founded in 1883 under the grandiloquent title of *Comité de Paris de la Fédération Internationale de l'Arbitrage et de la Paix*. It soon absorbed Passy's Society of the Friends of Peace, which, though Passy himself had reconstituted it in 1872 on the framework of his 1867 *Ligue de la Paix*, had not been thriving of late. The union became known as the *Société Française de l'Arbitrage entre Nations*.[3] Passy broached the

---

[1] *H. of P.* (1877), p. 340 ; (1879), pp. 267, 329–30 ; (1884) p. 51 ; (1883), p. 265 ; A. H. Fried, *Handbuch* (1911), p. 298 ; K. P. Arnoldson, *Pax Mundi*, pp. 123, 127 ; *H. of P.* (1889), p. 291.

[2] Howard Evans, *Cremer*, p. 110.

[3] K. P. Arnoldson, *Pax Mundi*, p. 118.

various topics of Peace machinery from his seat in the Chamber of Deputies whenever an occasion offered. In November 1883, during a debate on a French dispute with China, he invoked (unavailingly) the mediation protocol of the Treaty of Paris. In the following January he joined with Santallier in an arbitration petition to both Chambers, which met with so favourable a treatment in committee that the editor of a social service journal, *Le Devoir*, was encouraged to agitate in his paper for the neutralisation and disarmament of Alsace-Lorraine (July). When a fresh Balkan crisis occurred in 1886 between Turkey and Greece, Passy besought Freycinet, the Foreign Minister, to offer arbitration by the French Government. But Freycinet, as a student of diplomatic history, knew that the only possible arbiter of Balkan problems was the Concert of Europe—whether from a lofty conception of duty or from mutual distrust among the Powers. The Concert, moreover, had already taken action. Three other motions, all for the creation of an Arbitral Tribunal and all abortive, were introduced into the French Chambers before 1890. Outside the Chambers the Peace Movement recruited Jules Simon and Ferdinand de Lesseps—the latter of whom carried the message of international goodwill on a tour through Germany in 1886. But by far the most fruitful advance was the creation, in April 1887, of the Nîmes Association of Young Friends of Peace, a society founded in the south of France for people of less than twenty-five years of age. This was the work of L. A. Barnier of Geneva. It spread rapidly throughout France, changing its name in 1895 to *La Paix par le Droit*, and functioning by means of fortnightly meetings in all its branches. It exists to-day as the most active Peace organisation in France, still under the guidance of its original Secretary, M. J. Prudhommeaux. One other body raised its cry in France in the summer of 1889—the Second Workmen's International, modelled on Marx's foundation of 1864. Among schemes for organised socialist congresses and demands for an eight-hour day (May Day thereafter became Labour Day) the assembled artisans planned a propagandist campaign against armaments and the dangers of war as "an expression of the bourgeois capitalist régime." [1]

It was in Scandinavia, however, that the most astonishing progress was made. None of the three Scandinavian countries had a Peace organisation in 1880; by 1885 all three were honeycombed by local branches of three separate national societies, all of which had co-operated in a gigantic Scandinavian Peace Congress at Gothenburg. The distinctive features of the Movement north of the Baltic are two. The societies recruited from the start a valuable contingent of newspaper editors, and they concentrated on the potent argument that Norway, Sweden, and Denmark, being self-contained nations, geographically remote and politically harmless, might well be made the first testing-ground for practical disarmament and arbitration.

The first Scandinavian Peace Society was founded in Denmark on 1st December 1882 under the title of *Dansk Fredsforeningen*. Among its founders were sixteen members of the legislature and two newspaper editors, the latter of whom secured for the venture a maximum of publicity in the Press. The President of the Society was A. Holck; but its life-force was the Vice-President, Frederick Bajer, the greatest Scandinavian Peace advocate of all time. Adler, the Secretary, edited the Society's journal, *Freden*, which was directed during its early months to dispelling the cloud of ignorance and fear that surrounded the dispute with Germany over Schleswig. Very soon twenty-five branches were in existence. [2]

In Sweden it was chiefly the influence of Hodgson Pratt that secured the foundation of the Swedish Peace and Arbitration Association in April 1883, under the leadership of B. A. Hedlund and J. Jonassen. For the rest, the initiative lay with K. P. Arnoldson, the first chronicler of the Scandinavian Peace

[1] *H. of P.* (1883), p. 319 ; (1884), p. 17 ; (1889), p. 218 ; F. Passy, *Pour la Paix* (1909), pp. 82–6 ; A. Gennadius, *Arbitrage International*, p. 77 ; E. Rouard de Card, *Arbitrage International*, pp. 61–2 ; C. L. Lange, *Doctrine Pacifique* (1926), p. 402.

[2] *H. of P.* (1883), pp. 177, 198 ; (1884), p. 21 ; K. P. Arnoldson, *Pax Mundi*, p. 123.

Movement, who in 1884 became editor of the *Stockholm Times*, which he used to further the Society's objects. From the outset the Society maintained regular relations with its counterparts in Denmark and England. Of the Parliamentarians who were among its original members Carl Lindhagen periodically canvassed the project of arbitration treaties in the Chambers, with at first few encouraging results.[1]

Simultaneously a similar society—the Norsk Union against War—was founded in Norway to co-operate with Stockholm and Copenhagen. Its organ (*Daun*) flourished for several years, and it received useful publicity from Anna Bugge, the President of the Norwegian Association for the Cause of Women; but, with its branches, it waned by 1889, and the Norwegian Peace Movement proper is of later date.[2]

At Stockholm a motion was introduced in the Rigsdag during the summer of 1883 for the permanent neutralisation and disarmament of Sweden as an example to the world. It failed by a surprisingly large minority of 70 to 112. Two years later three men came forward to found a fresh branch of the 1883 Society in the capital. All of these—Branting, Sandstedt, and Strindberg — were afterwards famous for literary and social services to the whole world. With Hedlund and Arnoldson they found themselves, by the end of 1886, at the head of an energetic movement which boasted 250 travelling agents, and which was steadily making itself more widely known in a new journal started by Arnoldson called *Freds Vannen*.[3] In Denmark Bajer concentrated on Parliamentary action, while his daughter built up a women's branch of the Peace Society by the spring of 1886. Three times before 1890 Bajer bearded the Chambers. On the first occasion, in 1884, his proposal for an arbitration clause in a commercial

---

[1] Arnoldson, p. 123 ; *H. of P.* (1883), p. 214 ; and information supplied by Miss A. Jacobson of the Swedish League of Nations Society.

[2] *H. of P.* (1883), p. 215, and (article by Axel Lunenberg) October 1889, p. 287.

[3] *H. of P.* (1883), p. 256, and information from Swedish Peace Society.

treaty pending with Spain was lost through the eloquence of the Foreign Minister, Estrup, who carried the House with him in doubting the efficacy of peaceful methods of settlement when applied to grave issues. In the January following, on his return from a tour in Germany, Bajer raised the question of permanent neutralisation, already discussed in the Swedish Parliament—and with like results. His third effort, in March 1888, was successful. He secured the passage of a motion advocating that all differences, of whatever kind, arising among the three Scandinavian countries should in future be settled by arbitration. This noteworthy resolution was carried in the Folkthing by 50 votes to 16.[1] It was only a step, of course. Grave dangers would attend the negotiating of a treaty providing adequate arbitral machinery. The difficulties were realised in the discussion of the question which had taken place in August 1885, when a three-day Peace Congress was held at Gothenburg by the combined Peace Societies of Scandinavia under the Presidency of S. A. Hedlund. Herein lay the supreme gesture of the Baltic Peace Movement during its first decade.[2]

Such, in brief, was the expansion of the idea of Peace in Europe by 1889. Elsewhere, though there is much evidence of dissatisfaction with the existing order of international relations, no organised *propagandist* bodies appeared. Russian jurists founded an International Law Association at St. Petersburg in 1880; the Spanish Royal Academy of Moral and Political Science appointed a committee to study the theory of arbitration (1884), in the light of whose report the Prime Minister later urged drastic reductions in the Spanish army (1889). Marcoartu, in the year of his visit to America (1885), elaborated a scheme of International Arbitration noteworthy for the manner in which it provided for gradual *evolution* as against direct creation. Its code of international law was to be built

---

[1] *H. of P.* (1886), p. 71; (1884), p. 117; (1885), p. 165; A. Gennadius, *Arbitrage International*, p. 77.

[2] E. Rouard de Card, *Arbitrage International*, p. 28; *H. of P.* (1885), pp. 278–9.

on the double basis of existing rules and future experience, while, pending the appointment of an International Assembly and Court, a system of inter-parliamentary conferences should be resorted to for the settlement of international problems. This was a new and temporary use for the institution originally conceived by Lowenthal in Germany.[1]

But the only other attempt at expansion—William Jones's journey to the Far East at the end of 1888—was unproductive. Jones found a cordial reception among the Quakers of Australia, who had already formed a Peace Society at Adelaide. He even sailed to China to interview the Viceroy at Tientsin on the blessings of arbitration, and to Japan, where he approached the Foreign Minister and the Minister of Education to the same purpose. At this time Miss Priscilla Peckover of the Wisbech Peace Auxiliary was personally financing the export to Japan of British Peace tracts, which were being translated into Japanese by the Rev. George Braithwaite of Tokio. Two men, however, were insufficient to evangelise a continent. Jones passed on to the United States, where he attended the Pan-American Conference of 1889.

(d) *The Churches and Peace:* 1879–89

"The Committee," said the annual report of the British Peace Society for 1885, "venture to say a word on a somewhat delicate topic, not in a censorious spirit, but in profound sorrowfulness of heart. They refer to the little help they receive in prosecuting what they claim to be their eminently Christian work from the Christian Churches of this land. The Church of Christ . . . stands aloof and holds its peace in the presence of this, the most stupendous of all the evils that afflict humanity. . . ." [2] This was in large measure true, with the one notable exception of Canon W. H. Fremantle, of whose sermons, *Pleading against War*, the Peace Society had just circulated 3000 copies. And the continued lack of support from the Churches was a matter for genuine distress throughout the

---

[1] *H. of P.* (1880), p. 115 ; (1884), p. 94 ; (1885), p. 153.
[2] *H. of P.* (1885), p. 241.

Peace Movement generally. It was part of a deeper dissatisfaction, very widespread, which found expression in the bitter indictments uttered by Tolstoy in *What I Believe*. For though the economist and democratic sections of the Peace Movement did not demand, with Tolstoy and the older Peace Societies, a literal acceptance of the Sermon on the Mount, and though they did not delude themselves that a condemnation of war by every Christian Church would be of much practical value in eradicating the war system, they did maintain that such categorical denunciation ought at least to be delivered.

Nor did the Peace advocates ignore the difficulty which State Churches would certainly experience in promulgating a denunciation. There was no gainsaying these; they were implicit in the very theory of an Establishment. What was condemned was rather the Erastian system itself for forcing the national Churches of Christ into a political servitude which entailed religious apostasy. What the *Herald of Peace* said of the Church of England was applicable to every other State Church as well. "The whole aim and method of the Christian Church, in all its directions, seems to be to adapt itself, its teaching and its conduct, to its *temporal* conditions. And the result is a hybrid, emasculated form of Christianity, in which the fundamental assumptions and seeming necessities of the temporal State are accepted as axioms and truisms of the Christian faith. In regard to a Church as by law established, this does not surprise us. . . . The marvel is that the Nonconformist—the so-called 'Free'—Churches should be held captive by the same principles and assumptions. Surely this arises from the necessity placed upon the leaders and teachers of these Churches to stand well with their flocks, and as a matter of practical expediency and necessity to consider and even court the conventional ideas and the practices that follow from them. . . . The principles and ideals of Christianity do not get a fair trial; the episcopal blessing is still given to the soldier and his standard, and the Christ is made . . . the ally and the aide-de-camp of Cæsar."[1]

[1] *H. of P.* (1907), p. 7.

To this it was sometimes objected that State morality was not identical with individual morality, and that the Peace Societies were guilty of the same confusion of thought that had led them, during the years of Congresses in 1848–53, to regard the State as a mere aggregation of individuals. But this objection pre-supposed the existence of Established Churches, the abolition of which was the whole crux of the Peace Societies' position. For Richard and Darby in England, therefore, and Tobey in the United States, it had no validity. The religious pacifists were more concerned with pointing out the way in which at least the Dissenting Churches in all countries might help the work of Peace by moral encouragement. Many of these Dissenting bodies were internationally organised; they held international conclaves, which could be made to proclaim a denunciation of war and convey it downwards to every member through a channel of national, provincial, county, and local gatherings. Steps might be taken, moreover, to include the principles of Peace in the curricula of theological and seminary colleges, as the Wesley Guild began to do in England before 1900, and as Cremer was to do during his Anglo-German Church campaign. "We cannot fight the militarists with money, nor imitate their tactics; but we may emulate their zeal." [1]

The shining example throughout the world was the Society of Friends, which had been the core of the early Peace Societies, and to whose credit stood the mission to the Tsar before the Crimean War. The part played by the British and American Friends in the agitation for an Anglo-American Arbitration Treaty in 1887 has to be noticed later. Apart from this activity there was no organised Peace effort as yet within any Church, though two tentative beginnings appeared in England. The first was a discussion on "Scripture and the Attitude of the Church towards War " at the Annual Conference of the Church of England in October 1885 at Portsmouth—the first occasion on which the Church of England had formally debated the question. The second, a signal advance, occurred during the Canterbury Diocesan Conference at Lambeth Palace in July

[1] *Cf.* Rev. M. J. Elliott in *H. of P.* (1910), pp. 7–10.

1889, when, sponsored by Canon Westcott and the Archbishop of Canterbury (Dr. Edward White Benson), a resolution was passed "to decide whether to appoint a special day for a Peace Prayer." By 1892 Canon Westcott, afterwards Bishop of Durham, was presiding at the annual meeting of the International Arbitration League.

The Papacy also made repeated efforts both to preserve peace in actual moments of crisis and to substitute for war a universal recourse to papal mediation. Offers of mediation had been made by the Pope to the States of the American Union in 1861, and to France and Prussia in 1870. Leo XIII actually carried out two successful mediations of delicate disputes—the Caroline Islands quarrel between Germany and Spain in 1885 (at the invitation of Bismarck), and a dispute between Belgium and Portugal in 1891. But Leo XIII's zeal in endeavouring to revive the Pope's function as Arbiter of Christendom met nowhere a stronger criticism than that of the internationalist bodies founded after 1867.

It was in 1881, in the Encyclical Letter *Diuturnum Illud*, that the Pope, declaring that all modern wars had arisen from the lack of a central mediatory, suggested that such a mediatory could be found in the Holy See. A Catholic Congress at Madrid in 1889 went further, advocating that the Pope should definitely assume the function of Universal Arbiter.[1] And Leo XIII's concern for the peace of the world was shown also in an Allocation issued in February 1889 condemning aggressive war. The Catholic Church had never condemned all war; Monteith's *Discourse on the Shedding of Blood and the Laws of War*, which appeared in 1886 with the *imprimatur* of the Pope, urged no more than that the Church should "henceforth uphold a qualified and discriminating, instead of a blind, obedience to military commands." The Pope's Allocation was more precise. "Arms alone," it declared, "cannot suffice to avert the perils of the time. Moreover, even though it be permitted to employ arms in self-defence, Nature does not tolerate might being held sufficient surety for right. Peace must be preserved by

[1] See *H. of P.* (1881), pp. 266–7 ; (1889), pp. 225, 231.

rendering to each what belongs to him, and by strictly adhering to the dictates of justice." [1]

But while manifestos of this sort were above criticism, the idea of universal papal arbitrament in international disputes provoked objections at once political and personal.   Not only was the Pope a temporal sovereign, but he was domiciled sufficiently near the capital of a Great Power for his impartiality not to be everywhere trusted.   Moreover, his training would hardly fit him to be an international judge in equity.   These were strong objections: never perhaps entirely surmountable so long as the Papal State remained a temporal domain with diplomatic relations of its own.   Cremer saw fit to add that Popes in general, and Leo XIII in particular, were aged men, too feeble for the task of arbiter. [2]

(e) *The Climax of* 1887–89

By the close of 1889 three momentous developments had occurred in the history of Peace.   The Peace bodies of Europe and America at last secured Governmental action along the lines that had been advocated since 1830; the whole of the Peace Movement throughout the world was at last linked up both within and outside Parliaments; and an experiment in Pan-Continental organisation was inaugurated at Washington.

The first of these developments was the agitation which began in 1887 for an Anglo-American Treaty of Arbitration. The first campaign for "stipulated arbitration" had begun with the publication of Jay's *War and Peace* in 1842, and had been concentrated in the Congresses of 1848–53.   This second campaign of 1887 is remarkable, not only for its intensity and its ultimate success, but for the fact that it enjoyed the concerted strength of *all* the British and American Peace organisations, despite their differences of principle.   The Peace Society in London, for instance, though it still disavowed the renegade Appleton in a minimum of words, called Hodgson Pratt "a

[1] Text in *H. of P.* (1889), p. 187.
[2] See *Arbitrator* (August 1890), and *H. of P.* (September 1890), p. 136.

Peace Society in himself," and was content to be led by Cremer.[1]

It is interesting that the first active steps taken to promote an Anglo-American Arbitration Treaty were taken by the Society of Friends. The British Friends resolved, in May 1887, to join with their American brethren in bringing pressure to bear on the United States Government,[2] but the real beginning of the movement was a meeting held in London on 16th June between Cremer and Andrew Carnegie, with Thomas Burt presiding. The express purpose of the meeting was to decide on the best means of obtaining an arbitration treaty between the two Governments. Carnegie was convinced that all political opinion in America was favourable to arbitration, and that a similar manifestation in England might produce striking results. Cremer undertook, therefore, to prepare, and Carnegie to introduce to the United States Government, a petition signed by British Members of Parliament calling for such a treaty. Signatures were canvassed, and in its final form the memorial bore the names of 232 members : 175 Liberals, 44 Liberal Unionists, and 13 Conservatives, among the number being Asquith, Bright, Bryce, Joseph Chamberlain, Grey, Haldane, Lubbock, and Morley. Approval was added by 37 members of the House of Lords.[3] Thus armed, Cremer and Carnegie sailed for the United States, where on 31st October the memorial was presented to President Cleveland at the White House by a deputation of 14 (10 from the House of Commons, 1 peer, and 3 delegates from the Trade Union Congress).

The only immediate result was a sympathetic reply from the President. In the meantime William Jones of the British Peace Society landed at New York on 18th September to co-operate with the American Quakers to the same end. A memorial similar to that from the House of Commons was presented, in January 1888, by the Quakers of the United

[1] *H. of P.* (1889), pp. 167, 211.
[2] *H. of P.* (1887), p. 229.
[3] Text of memorial in Howard Evans, *Cremer*, p. 126, and E. L. Whitney, *American Peace Society*, p. 162.

States, England, Ireland, and Canada.[1] Jones returned to England by Christmas to tour the whole country and collect further petitions before his departure for Australia. The Press in England was cordial throughout, insisting that, whatever the future of arbitration, it was fitting that the English-speaking peoples should take the initiative. The *Times* admitted frankly, however, that, Europe being so much an armed camp, "our wishes in this matter are very far in advance of our hopes"; while the *Saturday Review*—least charitable among the critics—foresaw nothing more than a second amiable protocol like that of 1856.[2]

Passy meanwhile had followed the Anglo-American initiative by organising among French deputies a memorial to the Foreign Minister (Goblet) in favour of a simultaneous Arbitration Treaty between the United States and France. His memorial, signed by 112 deputies, was presented in December 1887. In the following April, after four months of deliberation and propaganda, he led 50 deputies in presenting the *text* of such a treaty, on which the Chamber reported favourably in June. But for the moment nothing came of the effort, and it was not repeated till July 1895,[3] though Goblet was shortly to serve the cause of Peace in another direction.

Three days after the French Chamber reported on Passy's treaty welcome encouragement came from the United States, where the Peace men, inside and outside Congress, had been spurred on by the conviction that the next move lay with their own Government. In April 1888 Senator Allinson proposed a credit of 80,000 dollars for negotiating a permanent treaty of arbitration between the United States, Great Britain, and France. In the House of Representatives the same suggestion was advanced by Kerr of Iowa and Belmont of New York. The American Peace Society, all through the spring, canvassed

---

[1] *H. of P.* (1887), pp. 266, 285–6 ; London *Times*, 27th January 1888.

[2] Quoted in *H. of P.* (1887), pp. 296, 306–8.

[3] F. Passy, *Pour la Paix* (1909), pp. 88–90. Text in E. Rouard de Card, *Arbitrage International*, pp. 73 *seq.*

literally masses of petitions to Congress; while Carnegie and
David Dudley Field sent in memorials (10th January) on the
wider issue of arbitration generally.[1] Reward for these labours
came on 14th June, when both Houses of Congress passed
resolutions, introduced by John Sherman, the Chairman of the
Senate's Foreign Relations Committee, inviting the President
to initiate negotiations with foreign states for treaties of arbitration.[2] The seed planted by Cremer and Carnegie had borne
fruit.

Although nine years were to elapse before the first of the
treaties foreshadowed in these resolutions was concluded, the
success here achieved by the twelve months' campaign would
alone be sufficient to make 1887–88 a memorable year. But
a far greater triumph followed immediately. This was the
birth, in 1888–89, of the Inter-Parliamentary Union and the
Universal Peace Congresses, by means of which the Peace
forces of the world have been concentrated once a year ever
since (save during the World War).

The idea of an Inter-Parliamentary Conference of members
working for Peace had been germinating since 1874, when
Lowenthal first conceived it in Berlin. Three other men—
Marcoartu, Virchow, and Richard—had elaborated it during
the following ten years. Marcoartu had examined it in his
Internationalism published in 1876,[3] had broached it to the
Italian deputies in Rome and the Austrian deputies in Vienna
later in the same year,[4] and had finally incorporated it in his
arbitration proposals of 1885. Virchow had advocated it in
August 1878, at the time of the Paris Peace Congress. Richard
had urged it in a letter to Passy in January 1882. The practical
initiative, however, lay again with Cremer. It was on 31st
October 1888 that Cremer and a number of Members of Parliament went to Paris for a meeting with Goblet and French

[1] E. Langlade, *La Clause Compromissoire*, p. 61 ; Whitney, *American
Peace Society*, pp. 164–6, 197 ; *H. of P.* (1888), pp. 31–3.
[2] Text of the resolutions in Carnegie Endowment for International
Peace, *Year Book* (1927), p. 2 ; also Howard Evans, *Cremer*, p. 129.
[3] Pp. 19–21.
[4] *H. of P.* (1892), p. 295.

deputies, out of which grew the Inter-Parliamentary Union. The thirty-three men assembled (nine British and twenty-four French) resolved to call a Conference for the following year, to which Peace advocates in other Parliaments should be invited, for a special discussion of the most practical means of organising World Peace by simultaneous concerted agitation, along pre-arranged lines, in every legislature in which a Peace group could be formed.

The invitations were issued in the spring of 1889, and the first Inter-Parliamentary Conference opened in Paris on 29th June following. At the same time a Peace Demonstration in St. James's Hall, London, on 19th May issued invitations to the Peace organisations of the world to inaugurate a series of annual World Peace Congresses, which should be held in the same city as the Inter-Parliamentary Conference, either immediately before or immediately after it, whereby the whole of the Peace Movement might be represented every year in some capital town.[1] The distinctions between the two groups of conferences will be noticed later.

In the inaugural year (1889) the Universal Peace Congress preceded the Inter-Parliamentary Conference. It sat for five days (23rd to 27th June). It was in effect a revival of the series of 1848–51, which had been curtailed at the outbreak of the Crimean crisis and never resumed, despite the insistence of Lemonnier and Hodgson Pratt, with whom lay the initiative for this ultimate revival. Passy presided, the gathering consisting of delegates from both Europe and America. The emphasis throughout the proceedings was on arbitration. It was resolved that arbitration should not only form a fundamental part of the constitution of every State, but should be embodied in principle in every future treaty as an obligatory and not an optional undertaking. Darby, the newly appointed Secretary of the British Peace Society, urged further that the two campaigns (in England and France) for permanent arbitration treaties with the United States should be intensified, and that every Government throughout the civilised world

[1] *H. of P.* (1889), pp. 221, 226–7.

should be petitioned to take diplomatic steps towards the same end.[1]

When the Inter-Parliamentary Conference assembled on the two following days (29th and 30th June) only those delegates of the Congress could attend who were Parliamentarians. It became the custom in later years for the rest of the Congress to hold banquets and receptions during these days in order that the universality of the Movement and its impressiveness should be preserved to the end.

The Inter-Parliamentary Conference proved so large a gathering that it had to adjourn to the Continental Hotel. Fifty-five French senators and deputies were present (including Passy, Simon, Trarieux, and Jaurés); thirty British Members of Parliament (among them Thomas Burt, Cremer, and the Hon. Philip Stanhope, later famous as Lord Weardale); and representatives from seven other Parliaments—the United States, Italy, Spain, Denmark, Belgium, Hungary, and Liberia. Passy and Jules Simon presided. Here again the emphasis was on arbitration. The Conference formally invited Governments to conclude permanent arbitration treaties (without prejudice to their national independence)—especially the United States, France, Great Britain, and Italy; and an arbitral clause was advocated for all future commercial treaties, to provide for their interpretation without risk of war.[2]

Both assemblies still meet every summer, in a different capital each year. Their work has always been in large measure complementary. While engaged on the same problems and canvassing the same expedients for solution, their orbit and methods have been different. The Inter-Parliamentary Union, when finally organised in 1892, could assail Governments from within; its declarations had an official standing higher than that of any Peace Society or Arbitration League petition. The Universal Peace Congresses, on the other hand, represented

[1] U.P. Cong. *Report*, Paris, 1889; E. Rouard de Card, *Arbitrage International*, p. 32.
[2] I.P. Conf. *Report*, Paris, 1889; also E. Rouard de Card, *Arbitrage International*, p. 39.

the combined strength of these societies and leagues, which, while they could continue to address Parliaments from without, as had been done since the early days of the Anglo-American Christian Peace Movement, still found their greatest field of action and their own particular mission in propaganda among their several national publics. The principle, however, that a country's policy should be guided by its citizens through their elected representatives (the principle already voiced in the Parliaments of Great Britain and Holland) was common to both groups.

To put the distinction in another way, it has been said that the Universal Peace Congresses were idealistic and popular, while the Inter-Parliamentary Conferences were positive and practical;[1] that the former elaborated the abstract idea of international justice and recommended it to the world at large, while the latter, avoiding exaggerations and speculations, aimed at a gradual progress from theory to fact. This generalisation is certainly true of the early years, though the idealism of the unofficial Peace bodies became gradually tempered as the practice of arbitration advanced after 1900.

The beginnings, indeed, of the Inter-Parliamentary Movement were modest. There was at first little discussion except on the theme that "the differences between States shall be submitted to an arbitral tribunal to be definitively settled"; and the words "for International Arbitration" were not deleted from the title of the annual conference until 1899, when by force of logic and force of events it was found necessary to explore "other questions of public international law."[2] But the deliberations ultimately spread to the furthest limits, embracing not only the pacific settlement of disputes, but also the organisation of a Society of Nations and an International Tribunal, neutrality, armaments, the laws of war, prizes, the treatment of foreigners, private international law, and current international questions as they arose. In this way it was

[1] E. Langlade, *La Clause Compromissoire* (1899), p. 59.
[2] Inter-Parliamentary Union pamphlet on the Conferences (1921), p. 11 (quoting from the Berne Conference of 1892).

will surely be resented as an interference with the prerogative of government, and expose us to the charge of arrogant meddlesomeness." [1]   And the aim of the Movement finally, even on the part of its extreme pacifist adherents, was not merely negative, not a static condition of freedom from war, but "a condition where the adequate power of the community maintains the common law and common justice, and public order reigns." [2]

[1] W. E. Darby at U.P. Cong., Chicago, 1893; cited in *H. of P.* (1893), pp. 335–8.

[2] *Cf.* P. B. Potter, *International Organisation* (1928), p. 268.

PART FOUR

THE TWO SYSTEMS—WAR AND PEACE
1889–1918

We do not desire to be confounded with revolutionary cosmopolitanism ; we therefore exclude from our program everything that might cause the Governments to look on us with suspicion. We do not talk of changes in the map of Europe, nor of the rectification of boundaries, nor of any attack on the principle of nationality. . . . We take up only the study of those proposals which aim directly at doing away with war and substituting for it the solution of difficulties through a regularly constituted jurisdiction—that is a ground on which the broad-minded patriots of all countries may meet.—L. TRARIEUX in 1893 to BERTHA VON SUTTNER

CHAPTER IX

THE CLOSE OF THE CENTURY: 1889–99

SIMULTANEOUSLY with the first real unification of the Peace Movements there appeared the greatest Peace novel of all time, Bertha von Suttner's *Lay Down Your Arms* (*Die Waffen Nieder*), a book that shares with Bunyan's *Pilgrim's Progress* and Defoe's *Gulliver's Travels* the distinction of having been translated into almost every known tongue. When the Baroness von Suttner wrote it she was not yet an active Peace Crusader, though she had developed an interest in the work of Hodgson Pratt since 1887 and had long wished to give literary expression to the lofty ethical philosophy and the horror of war which were part of her being. But after its publication she devoted her whole life to the cause of Peace, attending every Universal Peace Congress until her death, striving might and main to organise Peace Movements in Germany and Austria, and forming, with A. H. Fried and Alfred Nobel, a link between Continental pacifist groups and a constant inspiration. Fried, Nobel, W. T. Stead, and the Baroness von Suttner are the giants of these vital ten years.

It was only with difficulty that the book was published, for the Press censorship in Prussia was severe. But from the day of publication it took the world by storm, and was soon available in twelve languages and hundreds of editions. Stead reprinted it in England in 1896 at a penny. The author's own summary of the story described it as "the history of a young woman whose fate was closely involved with the wars fought in our own day." Its literary value consists in the vivid battle scenes, all of which were built up on patient and accurate historical research. Psychologically the book was the most trenchant propaganda that Peace had ever had, for its appeal was at once ethical, rational, emotional, and universal. Though its critics scoffed at the author as "Peace Bertha," and at the book itself as "emotional silliness," "obtrusive inartistic didacticism," and "feminist sentimental pacifism," there remains its circulation to testify to its world-wide popularity and its overwhelming success. Few books have a more enduring record as both propaganda and literature.[1]

Bertha von Suttner's subsequent devotion to Peace and the vigour which she infused into the organised pacifism of Central Europe constitute one thread in the history of the closing years of the century. For the rest, besides the steady expansion of all the national movements (particularly in Scandinavia) and the elaboration of schemes and programmes by the Inter-Parliamentary and Universal Peace gatherings, the decade brought to a triumphant issue the campaign of Cremer and Carnegie for an Anglo-American Arbitration Treaty, produced a grandiloquent call to Peace on the part of the Churches of at least one country, and closed with what seemed a fitting headstone for the tombs of the early pioneers, in the shape of the first Hague Conference.

(1) *The National Movements*

(i) *Great Britain*

The year 1890 was heralded in England by an acute but now forgotten dispute with Portugal in Africa, which called forth memorials to the Government from Darby and lamentations from Cremer for the studied neglect of arbitration as a ready solution, however overwhelming the British position might appear. But Lords Salisbury and Lansdowne were not yet the vigorous converts to the principle of arbitration that they afterwards became.[2] Nor were the Peace Societies more successful in the following summer, when, on the strength of an undenied rumour that the German Emperor had proposed

---

[1] Suttner, *Memoirs*, i, 295–7; H. Wehberg, *Die Fuhrer der Deutschen Friedensbewegung* (1923).

[2] Details in *Arbitrator* (January 1890); *H. of P.* (January 1890); Evans, *Cremer*, p. 143.

to the Powers a disarmament conference, they memorialised Wilhelm II himself during his visit to London in July. The British and Foreign Arbitration Association earnestly reminded him that the cure for international competition in armaments was nothing more nor less than a gradual renunciation: for which the Chancellor Hatzfeld thanked them.[1]

Propaganda did not slacken. In the same year Darby sent one Manuel Vasseur to open a Peace Society agency in Paris in order to link more closely the British and the growing Continental Movement. Two years later, when the Berne Peace Congress explored the question of an Anglo-American Arbitration Treaty, a petition to Parliament in support of the project was carried to a total of 80,000 signatures, in addition to which, as the *Pall Mall Gazette* conceded hopefully, "if you go on every year holding 400 meetings, preaching 500 sermons, and issuing 400,000 circulars, perchance you will make some impression even on the untameable elements." But there were mortifications to come. Lord Meath founded the Empire Day Movement in 1893, to the annual disgust of the *Herald of Peace* ; and in the General Election of 1895 Cremer lost the seat which he had held continuously for eleven years; [2] while friction with the United States grew ominous.

The most signal advance in England, however, was the sudden prominence into which the *Pall Mall Gazette* was thrown by W. T. Stead, who had succeeded John Morley as its editor in 1883. Stead was far from being a pacifist, but he devoted his energies to keeping the public correctly and sanely informed on questions of foreign policy, and on fostering by his "new journalism" an international outlook conditioned by "sober defence, no jingo, and more arbitration." He was already a public figure since his flamboyant editorials during the Gordon crisis and the Navy scare of 1885; and as a power in the land he had it to his credit that his "Modern Babylon"

---

[1] L. Appleton, *Fifty Years of Disarmament* (1899), p. 4 ; *H. of P.* (1890), p. 49.

[2] *H. of P.* (1890), *passim* ; (1891), pp. 314 *seq.* ; (1893), pp. 184, 239, 253 ; London *Times*, 12th October 1929.

revelations of the same year had secured the passage of the Criminal Law Amendment Act. Since 1890 he had concentrated his demand for a saner internationalism in a creation of his own—the *Review of Reviews*.[1] And this enterprise bore him into the current of Peace activity on the Continent, where he became the friend of Suttner and Fried.

By the end of the century the British Peace crusade was enjoying the moral support of the Prime Minister (Lord Salisbury), who foreshadowed the Hague Conference as early as 1897, when he used the occasion of the Guildhall Banquet (9th November) to deprecate the growing race for armaments, and even to visualise the future of civilisation in terms of an inevitable "Federation of Europe." [2] But the outbreak of the Boer War opened a new chapter.

(ii) *The United States*

Progress across the Atlantic was still more chequered. Expansion was quickened and tempered at once by the Behring Sea and Venezuelan disputes with Great Britain, while renewed onslaughts were made on Congress in the name of a general Arbitration Tribunal and a particular Arbitration Treaty.

The two disputes with Great Britain, involving straightforward legal rights that could be arbitrated and intangible political issues like the Monroe Doctrine that could not, produced several threatening situations.   In the matter of the fur seal fisheries in the Behring Sea, the United States Government, which had purchased all Russian rights in Alaska in 1867, had legislated against the killing of seals in the neighbourhood of certain islands and "the adjacent waters," and had captured sundry British sealers between 1881 and 1887 for alleged infractions of the law. The British Government repudiated the American interpretation of "adjacent waters," but offered to negotiate on a second claim advanced by President Harrison that the protection of the seals was an international

---

[1] See F. Whyte, *Life of W. T. Stead* (1925), i, 100, 155, 315.
[2] Cited in *H. of P.* (1897), p. 325.

duty and should be regulated by treaty.   In August 1890 Lord Salisbury suggested that the dispute should be arbitrated. Throughout the subsequent negotiations the Peace organisations in both countries canvassed people and Government without ceasing.   The arbitral tribunal set up in 1892, consisting of seven persons (appointed two each by the disputants and one each by three European sovereigns), eventually declared for Great Britain on 15th August 1893.   But it was not until a tense situation had been created by the United States House of Representatives refusing to vote the $425,000 awarded that a Joint Commission was able to settle the dispute in 1896.[1]

The Venezuela dispute, nearly a century old, was much more acute, especially as its resurgence occurred during the revived negotiations for a permanent Arbitration Treaty in 1895. President Cleveland himself was in favour of arbitration from the start.   But the British Government was thrown for a time into a panic.   Cremer set his agents hastily to work before Christmas 1895, while the American Peace Society circulated throughout the Press of America a manifesto against allowing the two nations to be stampeded into war, and against any extension of the Monroe Doctrine to cover boundary disputes such as this.   On 22nd February 1896 monster demonstrations were held simultaneously in Philadelphia (warmly acknowledged by Cleveland) and in London.   Felix Moscheles, Secretary of Pratt's Arbitration and Peace Association and later a friend of Bertha von Suttner, repeated this meeting annually for several years.   The double cry for arbitration was amplified into a national demand by Stead (in the *Review of Reviews*) and by the London *Daily Chronicle*.   Support was lent by Asquith, Balfour, Bryce, Rosebery, Gladstone, and countless other public men in both countries, including the heads of the Church of England.   Finally—and undoubtedly as a result of the publicity secured by the Peace advocates—an arbitral tribunal was appointed in the following November,

[1] Full account in *Fur Seal Arbitration Proceedings*, Washington, 1895. *See also* A. Wishart, *Behring Sea Arbitration*, and E. L. Whitney, *American Peace Society*, p. 153.

made up of two judges from the Supreme Court of each country and a fifth chosen by the four. By the end of 1899 the Venezuelan frontier was satisfactorily delimited. So that the dispute provided a triumph for the Peace organisations and for the principle of arbitration, though on political grounds this success was offset by the argument that, in submitting to the arbitration, Great Britain had in effect sanctioned the Monroe Doctrine and its extensions.[1]

During these disputes the wider application of American pacifist efforts was not lost sight of. Encouraged by the Senate's reiteration in February 1890 of the resolutions passed two years earlier in favour of arbitration treaties with foreign Governments, and at the same time chagrined that no initiative had been taken in Europe in response to the draft treaty signed by the Pan-American Conference at Washington, Senator Sherman introduced into the Senate on 23rd June 1892 a Bill authorising the President to appoint a committee to visit foreign Governments in person to negotiate for the creation of an International Tribunal; and when it seemed that the Bill had expired in the Senate's Foreign Relations Committee, to which it was automatically referred, he reintroduced it in the following spring, and a third time in January 1895—but with no result. Nevertheless there were strong grounds for hope. President M'Kinley was cordially disposed towards the principle of arbitration, and was bitterly disappointed in 1897 when the Anglo-American Treaty proved so sorry a travesty of what had been anticipated (see later). Both M'Kinley and Sherman followed with interest the agitation which was rapidly gaining publicity through the zeal of Albert K. Smiley of Lake Mohonk, who had inaugurated in June 1895 a series of annual Lake Mohonk Peace Conferences destined to last for twenty-one years (until curtailed by the Great War in 1915). Smiley's object was to awaken in America a wider sympathy for

[1] See E. L. Whitney, *American Peace Society*, pp. 190, 191; Suttner, *Memoirs*, ii, 104; F. Whyte, *W. T. Stead*, ii, 78; *H. of P.* (1896), p. 168 ; T. W. Balch, *Arbitrage International* (1908), pp. 90 *seq.*

arbitration treaties and an international arbitration tribunal. His gatherings grew from 56 in the first year to 300 in 1904 —all influential citizens whose expressions of opinion carried weight in their local districts.   The Mohonk forces joined with the American Peace Society and the various arbitration associations in a National Conference on Arbitration held in Washington in April 1896 under the Presidency of Senator G. F. Edmunds.   This Conference collectively, and its constituent bodies individually, memorialised the Senate in favour of arbitration treaties "providing for the widest practicable application." [1]

But early in 1898 the crisis which culminated in the Spanish-American War, despite M'Kinley's efforts to avert hostilities, produced a fresh series of protests—completely ineffectual— in the columns of the *Advocate of Peace*; protests which did not cease with the end of the war after a few months, but dragged on in a vain endeavour to discredit the Government's policy of subjugating the Philippines.   One principle emerged among these denunciations which had lain dormant since the Congresses of 1848-53—the principle that the consent of a people be obtained, by plebiscite and in advance, to any extension of sovereignty over them by an outside Power.   But the diplomatic history of the rights of minorities, except in the Balkans, was yet to begin.   And the domestic history of the Peace Movement, in both England and the United States, entered a new century in the throes of a war fever that the pacifists had been unable to stem.

(iii) *The Rest of the World*

In Europe, on the contrary, there was everywhere apparent a double movement of revival and expansion, stimulated partly by the travels of Suttner and Fried and partly by the steady evolution of programmes and theories in the annual Peace gatherings.   Each Inter-Parliamentary Conference welcomed

[1] E. L. Whitney, *American Peace Society*, pp. 199, 200, 202, 229 ; *H. of P.* (1892), p. 148 ; (1895), p. 161 ; Lake Mohonk Conference *Reports*, 1895 onwards.

a new national group hitherto non-existent; while by 1895 the Peace Movement had taken firm root in Central Europe.

In France, while Frederic Passy remained pre-eminently the mainstay of the Movement on its domestic side, new leaders emerged to intensify the campaign within the Chambers and to maintain full co-operation with pacifists across the frontiers. M. Barodet revived in 1895 Passy's motion of 1888 for a Franco-American Treaty of Arbitration, and carried it unanimously in the Chamber of Deputies. A year later Gaston Moch, famous as a military strategist, founded a French Peace Bureau destined to link up all the French Peace organisations and serve as their channel of communication with the rest of the world (by this time there was already an International Peace Bureau at Berne). After the Hague Conference, again, an Association for International Conciliation was created in Paris by the Baron d'Estournelles de Constant, who devoted his life to keeping public opinion healthy on matters of foreign policy, as Stead was doing in England. Among his triumphs was the founding of a branch of the Association in Japan, where a Peace Society at Tokio had been struggling to keep alive since 1891.[1] For the rest, the most flourishing of the French organisations was the Nîmes foundation of 1887, which concentrated on domestic propaganda through its organ *La Paix par le Droit*.

In Belgium, too, leaders emerged at this point who were to pilot their organisations through the storms of the Great War and beyond. Chief among them was Henri La Fontaine, who resurrected the Brussels Peace Society in 1892 by starting a periodical, *Annales de la Paix*, and seized every opportunity to canvass the burning question of arbitration in the Chambers. In July 1897, when the Deputies had been induced to pass a general resolution in favour of the principle of peaceful settlement, La Fontaine repeated the attempt in the Senate, where the strong convictions of the Foreign Minister (Favreau) augured a stormy passage. In the end, after being diluted by Emile Descamps, whose reputation as Secretary of the Inter-

[1] Toulouse Peace Congress (1902), *Report*, p. 47 ; *H. of P.* (1891), p. 283 ; and see p. 215 below.

Parliamentary Bureau commanded him a respectful hearing, the motion was passed on the following day.[1]

In Holland the emphasis was less Parliamentary and more educational. The Parliamentary strength of the Netherlands Peace Movement declined on the death of Van Eck in 1895, at a critical moment, when the funds of the central society stood at only £21. But the new President began a campaign of propaganda in the schools, to no small effect. The foundation in 1897, however, of a rival organisation calling itself the Women's League for International Disarmament for a time distracted the older Movement, until the double stream of activity was united four years later. Both organisations were comparatively inarticulate during the Hague Conference, when more than ever their vigorous co-operation would have been valuable; for funds were low, and the general attitude of the members was that "popularisation" properly belonged to the Bureau at Berne. The Dutch Peace Movement, though shorn of its atrophied branches, had not yet reached its second harvest.[2]

Death also robbed the Italian Movement of a founder when Ruggiero Bonghi ended a brilliant Parliamentary career in 1895. But there was left a strong Italian Parliamentary Peace group which he himself had created in 1890. By the end of 1891 Italy had forty-eight local Peace Societies in operation. In Sicily a federation of local Peace bodies was established in 1890 (on the model of the earlier Lombard Union) with a combined organ, *La Pace Internazionale*. In the north a memorable meeting between the Baroness von Suttner and Felix Moscheles of London resulted in the foundation of yet another Arbitration and Peace Association—in Venice, under the patronage of the Marquis Pandolfi, who thereafter strove to recruit a larger Parliamentary Committee.[3]

---

[1] *H. of P.* (1892), p. 69 ; E. Langlade, *La Clause Compromissoire* (1899), pp. 73–4.

[2] *H. of P.* (1891), p. 298 ; (1896), p. 39 ; J. van Beek en Donk, *Peace Movement in the Netherlands* (1915), p. 11 ; and information supplied by M. van der Mandere.

[3] *H. of P.* (1890), p. 100; (1892), pp. 19, 163 ; Suttner, *Memoirs*, i, 317–9.

14

Bertha von Suttner pushed on into Austria for the same purpose; and here, in remarkable contrast to the trend of development elsewhere, the creation of a Parliamentary group preceded, and indeed prompted, the foundation of the first Austrian Peace Society, though officially the two organisations began simultaneously. The Baroness inspired both. She had started a periodical of her own, named after her book (*Die Waffen Nieder*). In this, and in the Vienna *Neue Frie Presse*, she appealed in September 1891 for recruits for an Austrian Inter-Parliamentary group which she proposed to found. Simultaneously she planned a society to popularise the cause of Peace in an appeal primarily æsthetic. Both projects bore fruit in the following October, when the *Oesterreichische Friedensgesellschaft* came into being with a membership of 2000. Its periodical, the Baroness's own *Die Waffen Nieder*, was published by Alfred Fried, her warmest friend in the Movement and the first chronicler of Pacifism. Fried became sole editor in 1901, when the name was changed to its present form of *Friedenswarte*. From the start the enterprise flourished. In 1892 it was sponsored and largely financed by Alfred Nobel, whose astounding antitheses—dynamite and pacifism, Socialistic beliefs and a vast fortune—have made him one of the most fascinating studies of the century. Within another year a sister organisation, again the work of Suttner, had taken root in Hungary, at Budapest, with the novelist Maurus Jokai among its 1100 members. Both bodies at once canvassed throughout the country the various motions that were tabled in the Chambers; as, for instance, when Herr Peez demanded to know in March 1893 why a recent treaty with Serbia had contained no arbitration clause, and when the occasion of a Hungarian frontier dispute in 1896 enabled the Peace Party in the Austrian Lower House to carry a motion for such a clause in all future commercial treaties entered into by the Dual Monarchy.[1]

In Germany, where also there was no organised Movement in

[1] Suttner, *Memoirs*, i, 335–47; *H. of P.* (1896), p. 19; A. H. Fried, *Handbuch der Friedensbewegung* (1911 edition), p. 301; E. Langlade, *La Clause Compromissoire*, pp. 80–1.

1890, Fried rather than Bertha von Suttner was the "Apostle of Peace." Here again the first step was the formation of a small Inter-Parliamentary group, which won the influential support of Virchow, who, together with Fried and others, formed the *Deutsche Friedensgesellschaft* in November 1892. Within two years they had added 14 branches and federated the whole into a German Peace Union, numbering 4000 active members, who further increased the number of societies to 70 by the middle of 1897. Legislative action, of course, was not forthcoming: the policy of Imperial Germany precluded it. But the decade shows patient attempts by the pacifist deputies to gain more than an amused indulgence in the Reichstag. All failed; but what is remarkable is the volume of support which they contrived to find. In both Germany and Austria-Hungary there is no doubt that the Peace Movement, however unproductive of tangible results, was a thriving plant.[1]

In Spain alone of the western countries was there no effective progress. Don Arturo de Marcoartu, despite his age, still bearded the Senate regularly with motions for a Permanent International Tribunal. In June 1890 he even prevailed on the Chamber to authorise definite negotiations by the Government to this end. But Suttner was lamenting two years later that Peace sentiment in Spain seemed to be confined to Marcoartu himself. Strictly the reflection was not true; for the orator Emilio Castelar had pledged the remainder of his life to a crusade in favour of disarmament, and Marcoartu's repeated motions ultimately converted not only the President of the Senate, but the Bishop of Salamanca as well. Nevertheless the Peninsula developed no organised Peace Movement until 1899, and then only in Portugal. Mme. Alice Pestana founded a small society which by 1903 became the Portuguese League of Peace.[2]

[1] Suttner, *Memoirs*, i, 389 seq., 445 seq.; ii, 26; K. P. Arnoldson, *Pax Mundi*, p. 86; E. Langlade, *La Clause Compromissoire*, p. 80; F. Stratmann, *The Church and War* (1929), p. 108; *H. of P.* (1897), p. 195.

[2] K. Arnoldson, *Pax Mundi*, p. 14; A. Gennadius, *Arbitrage International*, p. 78; Suttner, *Memoirs*, i, 428; E. Langlade, *La Clause Compromissoire*, p. 78; *H. of P.* (1892), p. 135; (1893), p. 290; (1899), p. 259.

Most militant of all, apart from the Anglo-American agitation for an Arbitration Treaty, was the crusade in Scandinavia, where societies had grown up during the eighties (though even the reverberations of the Pan-Scandinavian Peace Congress at Gothenburg had met with no response in Norway). Not until after a second Congress, held in Copenhagen in 1890, did the Norwegian Peace Movement begin; and when it did, it found at once a vitalising and an exhausting force in the question of Norwegian independence from Sweden. The *Norges Fredsforening*, founded by one Konow in February 1885 to agitate for arbitration and military retrenchment, was re-formed twice, by Ullman and Bjornsen in turn, before it finally expired in 1892. The Storthing was sympathetic whenever pacifist proposals came before it for debate; as, for instance, when the Norwegian group of the Inter-Parliamentary Union carried, the day after its formation, an arbitration resolution which utterly confounded Stang, the militarist foreign minister. But the creation of a national movement had to be achieved by first founding local societies. The consummation of this work lay with two men—K. P. Arnoldson of Sweden, who lectured up and down the country, and Paul Koht, who kept Peace questions alive in the Storthing from 1890 onwards. As Norway wished to proceed with arbitration treaties independently of Sweden, and the Swedish Storthing would not consent to separate action, the resolutions, though often unanimously concurred in, were usually shelved. And not even this precaution averted political crises between the two parts of the Union. But on its popular side the Movement scored its first triumph when a new and durable *Norges Fredsforening*, consisting at the outset of a hundred members, was formed on 31st July 1895. Its leaders were Koht and Bernhard Hansen. Two problems dogged its progress. In the first—the question of armaments— Koht stressed the need for retaining an adequate defence force, and so drove a wedge between the extreme pacifist members and others, comparable to that which had sundered the American Peace Society in 1838. The other problem—that of independence from Sweden—reappeared every time arbitration came up for discussion in the society, for the question of separate arbitration treaties for the two countries remained insoluble. As a result, the society came to eschew practical issues, and steadily degenerated into an abstract movement. Even co-operation with the Swedish Peace bodies in and after 1898 only revealed that the Norwegian people would never sacrifice their army while there was a likelihood that they would need recourse to force to secure their independence. The most unanimous action taken in Norway before 1900 was an address to the King delivered when the Tsar issued his Rescript summoning the first Hague Conference (1898).[1]

These difficulties similarly dissipated the energies of pacifists in Sweden, where, however, the Peace organisations were older and more vigorous. At the lower level of synchronised agitation on non-controversial measures opportunities were occasionally seized. Outside the Chambers the popular movement took a fresh turn in 1898 when a Swedish Women's Peace Association was founded in Stockholm by Emilia Broomé. This was destined to become one of the most widespread of the feminine pacifist bodies in Europe. By 1911 its many local groups were fused into the Swedish Peace Society under the Baron Carl Bonde.[2]

In Denmark only was there no distraction by Scandinavian domestic politics. Bajer's proselytism produced 89 local Peace committees by 1893, and 40 more within the next two years; until by the close of 1895 his lists totalled 10,000 members. Propaganda in Denmark was encouraged by the consideration that the country, being self-contained and politically isolated, might well be made the first testing-ground for schemes of Peace. And certainly Bajer's agitation was rewarded at times by magnanimous gestures on the part of the Government. The Lower House set up a committee in

---

[1] P. Koht, *Mouvement Pacifique en Norvège* (1900), *passim* ; K. P. Arnoldson, *Pax Mundi*, p. 144 ; A. H. Fried, *Handbuch der Friedensbewegung* (1911 edition), p. 299 ; *H. of P.* (1890), p. 37 ; (1895), p. 167 ; (1897), p. 265.

[2] K. P. Arnoldson, *Pax Mundi*, p. 144 ; and information from Miss Alida Jakobson of the Swedish League of Nations Society.

1890 to explore the possibilities of arbitration treaties between the three Scandinavian Powers and foreign countries. In November 1892 a more specific resolution was passed, inviting the Government to negotiate such a treaty with the United States. But in 1894 Bajer censured the Ministry for allowing a treaty with Spain to be ratified without inserting even an arbitration clause. Bjornsen, the Norwegian poet, meanwhile toured Denmark, addressing a Peace meeting of 15,000 in July 1892 and stressing the need for capturing the interest of clergy and women. More than one approach, again, was made by Bajer's society to King Christian IX himself; but the King, while cordial and sympathetic, could offer no more than that Denmark would loyally follow the lead of any larger Power that should take the initiative in organising the world. It was because there was so much interest taken in all three countries that the Third Pan-Scandinavian Peace Congress, held at Stockholm in August 1895, urged, as an example to the world, a threefold Scandinavian Treaty of Arbitration. Petitions for this had already secured a quarter of a million signatures in each country during the first two months of the year; and so great was the effect on public opinion that by the end of the century Sweden could boast thirty newspapers pledged to the principle of arbitration treaties, while the whole of the Danish Cabinet had endorsed a motion for Denmark's neutrality in any European war, and the left wing of the Norwegian Parliament had included in its political programme the neutralisation of the three Northern Kingdoms.[1]

Elsewhere in Europe prophets of Peace arose, but with little material result. The five societies existing in Switzerland were federated in 1894 to form one Swiss Peace Society, but this itself was merged into the Geneva League of Peace and Liberty, which had played its part in the second Peace Movement of 1867.[2] In Russia there was for some time a hope that

---

[1] E. Langlade, *La Clause Compromissoire*, p. 75 ; *H. of P.* (1890), p. 175 ; (1892), p. 103 ; (1893), pp. 222, 228 ; (1894), p. 49 ; (1895), pp. 179, 220, 226, 242 ; (1896), p. 126 ; (1897), *passim*.

[2] *H. of P.* (1894), pp. 59, 75 ; (1895), p. 271. The five were Neuchâtel, Berne, Geneva, St. Gall, and Zurich.

an organised campaign of pacifism might be worked up, for
Mennonite immigrants, despite persecution, were spreading
their evangelical doctrines among the peasantry, and the poet
Vasili Vereshchagin, famous for his picture "Apotheosis of
War," travelled widely demanding an international congress to
hasten the simultaneous disarmament of all Europe (1897).
Prince Peter of Oldenburg, moreover, a grandson of the Tsar
Paul, had slowly developed a plan, which he had outlined to
Bismarck as early as 1873, to abolish war by international
agreement and settle all subsequent disputes by means of
"international commissions of arbitration," whereby taxes
might be universally lowered and the standard of living appre-
ciably raised.   But it was not until 1899, after the close of the
Hague Conference, that a Russian Peace Society was founded
by Prince Dolgoruki under the patronage of the Imperial
Government.[1]

Three years earlier the first Balkan Peace Society had
emerged—the creation of Dr. Barvić—in Bohemia.   This,
aided after 1899 by the Moravian Women's Central Pacifist
Alliance, endured until 1914, when it was engulfed in a deluge
of war feeling.[2]   The only other action traceable in the Balkans
before 1900 is in Roumania, where an Inter-Parliamentary
group, formed in 1892 under M. Urechia, twice interpellated
the Foreign Minister; the first time demanding what the
Government proposed to say in reply to the Washington Treaty
of 1890, and the second time carrying a motion for arbitration
clauses in future Roumanian treaties "wherever possible."
The motion was at once carried into effect in a treaty with
Switzerland.[3]   Further east the only other Peace Societies
were in Australia (at Adelaide and Melbourne) and at Tokio.
In China there was no pacific influence at work outside the
columns of a single prominent newspaper, the *Shih Pao*, which

---

[1] *H. of P.* (1892), p. 30 ;   (1894), pp. 75, 116, 203 ;   (1897), p. 304;
(1899), p. 307 ; *Contemporary Review*, London, January 1892 ; Suttner,
Memoirs, ii, 9–14, 44.
[2] Information supplied by MM. Syrovy and Hyka.
[3] E. Langlade, *La Clause Compromissoire*, p. 79 ; *H. of P.* (1893),
pp. 215, 234–5.

produced in the summer of 1890 a comprehensive (albeit stereotyped) scheme for the peace of the world based on alliance, democracy, arbitration, non-intervention, and an international army.[1]

Such in brief were the main lines of domestic progress during the decade leading up to the Hague Conference.   But the most resounding moral success had been meanwhile achieved in definitely enlisting the organised co-operation of the Churches in a large part of Europe and America.   The initiative in this lay with W. Evans Darby, the Secretary of the London Peace Society, who clamoured for four years amid the opposition even of his own allies, until in the end he built up what came to be known as the Arbitration Alliance in the Anglo-American Churches.   Darby realised the practical futility of deputations to leading ecclesiastical dignatories, like the deputations which he headed to the Archbishop of Canterbury and to Cardinal Manning in 1891.   He had striven since 1889 to bring the question of propaganda in the Churches to the notice of the Universal Peace Congresses.   But in point of time he had achieved his end in other ways before the annual Congress finally condescended to listen to him.   At Paris, in 1889, religious issues had been excluded from the agenda.   At the London Congress of 1890 nothing more was done than to appoint the fourth Sunday in Advent as "Peace Sunday," on which the ministers of all Churches were invited to deliver special Peace sermons and prayers.   At Rome, in 1891, a specific resolution on the power of the Churches in promoting international fellowship was defeated by 65 votes to 30, as being beyond the scope of the Congress.   Darby deplored this rejection as a tactical mistake likely to rob the Peace Movement of its universality; nevertheless in the following year at Berne a similar resolution was simply reported without discussion, and it was only in 1893 at Chicago that the Congress for the first time recommended the world's Churches to forward the cause of arbitration.   But Darby had long since taken other action.   As early as 1890 he had formed a committee

[1] H. of P. (1890), p. 147 ; (1891), p. 283.

of the British Churches on Arbitration, directed towards agitating Peace questions within the various Churches. Encouraged by the response received in 1891 from two world congresses (the International Congregational Council in London and the Œcumenical Methodist Alliance in Washington) which discussed the future of arbitration as a means of supplanting war, Darby's committee united with a committee of the Society of Friends formed for the same purpose. The result was the Arbitration Alliance of Great Britain and Ireland (April 1893). It was a national body, entirely British; but within a year it had become truly international, for its petition in favour of disarmament, ultimately presented to Lord Salisbury in November 1897, bore 35,000 signatures, representative of 165,000 people, from 112 Churches in Great Britain, the United States, Holland, Belgium, Switzerland, and Australia. An appeal was made simultaneously to every ruler in Christendom. By 1896 the *Herald of Peace* was justified in its reference to "a perfect chorus for arbitration," supported in high places within the Churches. Cardinal Vaughan was among the speakers at Pratt's annual meeting in 1894, and devoted his Easter Sermon in 1896 to an appeal for a Permanent International Tribunal. So that, while it must be admitted that this Movement within the Churches was largely secular and that its energy later flagged, the chorus of 1894–97 transcended that of later years, when the World Alliance for Peace through the Churches was founded in 1914.[1]

Thus by 1899 the world's Peace Movement, internationally organised since 1889, was still primarily secular on a popular and parliamentary basis. Its case for arbitration had been tested in the two Anglo-American disputes and vindicated; the danger to it of domestic politics cutting across it had been revealed in Scandinavia; the power of resolute propaganda had similarly been proved in Scandinavia among the people and in Central Europe inside Parliaments. In the Anglo-Saxon countries, above all, though on its popular side the Movement

[1] U.P. Cong. *Reports*, 1889–93, *passim*; *H. of P.* (1894), pp. 83, 100, 102, 108–10; (1895), p. 228 and *passim*; (1896), pp. 60–1.

was more or less stationary, an ironical success ultimately crowned the efforts to put through the first Treaty of Permanent Arbitration.

(2) *The Anglo-American Arbitration Treaty of* 1897

The work done to achieve this object, by Cremer in England and by Carnegie, Sherman, and D. D. Field in America, has already been traced as far as 1890. No lull was allowed to weaken the force of the agitation. Cremer transferred his attack from Washington to London in June 1893, when, after two years' unavoidable delay, he managed to bring the question of the Arbitration Treaty into open debate in the House of Commons. Seconded by Sir John Lubbock, he drew the moral of his visit to Washington and of the Pan-American Conference, and tabled a resolution providing for *pourparlers* to be opened at once between the two Governments. Gladstone's reply was sympathetic, but suggested, as a less ambitious expedient, the erection of a "Council of the Great Powers" functioning in Europe only, and finally amended the resolution so that it invited the British Government merely to "co-operate" with that of the United States in any action the latter might take on a basis of the Congress resolutions of 1888.[1] This amendment was passed, with the result that the next move lay with the American Government. Cremer was not disappointed, for the debate not only produced a subsequent dinner at which he was able to approach the Prime Minister privately, but also indicated two lines of action which indeed ultimately led to the Treaty.

The first was the line taken in America. Sir Julian Pauncefote, the British Ambassador at Washington, transmitted a copy of the Commons resolution to W. Q. Gresham, the American Secretary of State. In this way it found mention in Cleveland's Presidential Address to Congress at the end of the year. But simultaneously with the motion, in the same June both Houses of Congress had been assailed with similar resolutions—the

[1] Texts in Howard Evans, *Cremer*, pp. 152–5 ; also *H. of P.* (1893), pp. 255 *seq.*

Senate by Allinson, and the House of Representatives by J. F. Lacey.[1] Both these were referred to committees which eventually shelved them. But with Sherman's two resolutions on arbitration discussed in 1893 and 1894 and with Cleveland's Address they contrived to keep the question alive until Cremer opened the second line of action.

This took the form of a second memorial to the President of the United States from members of the British Parliament, armed with which Cremer crossed the Atlantic in November 1894. There were 354 signatures this time: 232 Liberals, 71 Nationalists, 30 Unionists, and 21 Conservatives. On 18th January 1895 the memorial was presented to Cleveland at the White House. Thereafter nothing seems to have been done for almost a year, as the Peace men in both countries were occupied with the Venezuela arbitration crisis. But in 1896 the attack was reopened. In America resolutions were introduced into both Houses in January and again in April, though only to pass on to the Foreign Relations Committee; and Lord Russell of Killowen (the Lord Chief Justice of England) delivered an epoch-marking speech on International Law and Arbitration to the American Bar Association in August; while in England Cremer headed a deputation in June to Lord Salisbury at the Foreign Office, bearing a petition signed by 5359 Trade Union and Pacifist leaders.[2] The occasion for these renewed attacks lay in that diplomatic negotiations between the two Governments for the desired treaty had already been opened in March. Both Salisbury and Cleveland warmly encouraged the project—the latter from long conviction, the former from a chastened realisation that arbitration was no longer "one of the famous nostrums of the age" but the only sane alternative to international armed conflict.

The negotiations are particularly important, as they revealed the fundamental barriers against which all attempts at

---

[1] Evans, pp. 158–60; Whitney, *American Peace Society*, p. 200; *H. of P.* (1894), p. 81.

[2] *H. of P.* (1896), pp. 37, 119 *seq.*; Howard Evans, *Cremer*, pp. 182–3.

international organisation from 1897 onwards have tended to break.   The chief difficulty was to determine what kinds of dispute could be agreed on permanently for arbitration whenever they should arise, and what types must be reserved for decision individually as they arose.   Cleveland and Olney (his representative) urged that the treaty should provide for the arbitration of all questions without exception.   Lord Salisbury, through Pauncefote, who negotiated for Great Britain, insisted that no dispute could be arbitrated which involved "the national honour or integrity," and that Her Majesty's Government were "not prepared for this complete surrender of their liberty of action."   So that, for Great Britain, any treaty signed would be obliged, after providing for the arbitration of disputes, to reserve that the award should not be binding in advance where questions of territory or jurisdiction were involved, and that "questions of honour" fell outside the scope of the provisions altogether.   Thus emerged the two bogeys, national honour and national sovereignty.   Olney replied to this that it amounted to arbitrating first and then deciding whether or not to accept the verdict—which would convert the practice of arbitration into a farce.   But there was an obstacle on the American side also, which the British Government no less warmly contested.   The United States Constitution of 1787, drafted at a time when jealousy between President and Congress was acute, and based on the mutual limitation of the powers of government, had made the "advice and consent" of the Senate necessary, by a two-thirds majority, to all treaties and obligations entered into by the President as Executive.   This control of American foreign policy the Senate had always held very dear.   In the light of it, all awards given in disputes submitted to arbitration would have to come before the Senate for ratification—and could not, therefore, be made binding in advance.   Olney himself was of the opinion that the Senate should modify its attitude; that an award concurred in could hardly be regarded as appealable.   But the Senatorial veto was a constitutional matter, and would require a constitutional amendment (almost an impossibility) for its removal.   The obstacle therefore remained.

Likewise the British reservations. The Anglo-American Treaty of Arbitration, ultimately signed by Olney and Pauncefote on 11th January 1897, was at once a signal advance in governmental recourse to the machinery of Peace and a realisation of what the Peace advocates had expected. Both parties agreed, in the first article, "to submit to arbitration, in accordance with the provisions and subject to the limitations of the Treaty, all questions of difference between them which may fail to adjust themselves by diplomatic negotiations." None of the Great Powers had ever before gone so far in pledging itself to pacific settlement. But the reservations inserted by the United States Senate when the Treaty was presented for ratification robbed it of its greatest value, and rendered it a travesty before the final rejection of even the amended text. Not only were the President's hands tied at every point by the addition of the formula "by and with the advice and consent of the Senate," but the first article was extended as follows: "No difference shall be submitted under this treaty which, in the judgment of either Power, materially affects its honor, the integrity of its territory, or its foreign or domestic policy. . . ." In other words, either party could refuse, on any of these three undefined grounds, to arbitrate any dispute that might arise. But worse followed. The Treaty, even thus crippled, never came into force; for the Senate, moved partly by distrust of Great Britain, partly by lack of complete confidence in Cleveland, and partly by the fear that its own two-thirds majority veto would be lost in cases of dispute between the United States and foreign Powers, rejected the Treaty on 5th May by 26 votes to 43. "We will be purblind," said Senator J. T. Morgan, "if we put a paper guarantee of peace in place of the moral and military forces that are the supreme elements of strength in our splendid Republic."

Three important reflections follow from this defeat. First, it has been computed that the bulk of the United States was in favour of the Treaty and that a Senatorial vote *by population* would have secured ratification. Secondly, national honour and national sovereignty had been invoked to jettison the first

Permanent Arbitration Treaty concluded by two Great Powers —a disaster that was often to be repeated after 1900. And thirdly, the Senatorial treaty veto, so salutary in preventing secret diplomacy in the United States, had again shown itself capable of safeguarding the isolationist policy enshrined in the Monroe Doctrine—as it was to do still more tragically when the Senate rejected the League of Nations Covenant in 1920.[1]

The triumph that had been Cremer's lasted, therefore, just four months. The autumn of 1897 found him once more in Washington with the same end in view as before. But the new President (M'Kinley), though an advocate of arbitration, declared the moment inopportune to revive the Treaty. The American Peace Society met with a similar reply when it petitioned the Government to reopen negotiations (September 1898).[2] A treaty of permanent arbitration was concluded between Chile and Argentina in July 1898 on the exact model of the unratified Anglo-American treaty;[3] but the first experiment among the Great Powers had failed—and failed without even stirring the Anglo-Saxon Press to appreciate it.[4]

(3) The International Movement

On its international side, meanwhile, the Peace Movement had cleared away many obstacles from its path. The Inter-Parliamentary Conferences and the Universal Peace Congresses had both set up central secretariats to act as permanent clearing-houses; the programme of Peace had been developed and defined; the annual gatherings were attracting more and more official recognition by Governments every year; and by 1897 a concerted inter-parliamentary agitation was in full swing to achieve the calling of a Conference of the Powers—secured two years later. At the same time, however, the problem of

[1] E. L. Whitney, *American Peace Society*, p. 202; A. H. Montgomery in *H. of P.* (1897), pp. 184 *seq.*; R. M'Elroy, *Pathway of Peace* (1927), pp. 28–33, 175, and chap. vii, *passim*; D. F. Fleming, *The Treaty Veto of the American Senate* (1930), *passim*; text of Treaty and amendments in W.P.F. pamphlet on *Arbitration* (vol. ix, Nos. 6, 7), 1926, pp. 509–13.   [2] Whitney, p. 229.
[3] *H. of P.* (1899), p. 228.   [4] Suttner, *Memoirs*, ii, 152.

sanctions and the doubt as to how far arbitration could be universally applicable tended to cleave a fundamental difference of outlook between the two groups.

All this became manifest by the end of 1896. For the first few years the annual meetings were confined to preparatory work. Both gatherings met in London in July 1890. The Universal Peace Congress, despite faulty organisation and a lack of capable interpreters, spent five days in evolving, under Field's presidency, a series of resolutions which revived several projects long dormant. History teachers throughout the world were urged to emphasise the horror and futility of war; the Inter-Parliamentary Conference was recommended to issue an international newspaper; an attempt was made to secure popular control over declarations of war by the suggestion that National Juridical Courts, independent of the Executive, should be set up in all countries to examine the causes of disputes as they arose and notify the public accordingly; all minor Powers, further, should be permanently neutralised by treaty, in the manner of Belgium and Switzerland.[1] At the Inter-Parliamentary Conference, which occupied the following week, however, the agenda was more restricted. The two hundred representatives from twelve European Parliaments, including that of Greece, concentrated on the problems of organisation and tactics. Resolutions were indeed passed for the conclusion of arbitration treaties and, in the interim, of arbitration clauses; but the most important decision of the meeting was that "the Conference recommends the appointment of a Parliamentary Committee for each country, with a view to the interchange of ideas and the consideration of disputes as they may arise." At intervals during the proceedings the President (Lord Herschell) read letters of commendation from Gladstone, Clemenceau, Count Crispi, and Baron Andrassy.[2]

Organisation was the major issue at both conferences in the following year at Rome, though the Italian delegation, led by

[1] U.P. Cong. *Report*, London, 1890; *Revue de Droit International* (1890), p. 368; *H. of P.* (1890), *passim*.

[2] I.P. Conf. *Report*, London, 1890; Howard Evans, *Cremer*, p. 142.

Bonghi, would have had both meetings devoted almost entirely
to exploring arbitration, since Italy, the weakest member of the
Triple Alliance, was crippled by the burden of armaments.
The British and French Parliamentary delegations too were
disposed to have the problem of Alsace-Lorraine thrashed out;
but the Austrian group urged the danger of discussing current
international difficulties before the organisation had won a
sound reputation, especially as the German representatives
might be regarded at home as guilty of high treason if they
appeared to question their Government's right to the annexed
provinces. "The Peace Movement," commented Bertha von
Suttner, "was a very tender plant; it must be kept away from
any over-chilly draught." Accordingly the sixteen Parliamentary groups present forbore to become too concrete in their
discussions.[1] The Baroness, though absent from the Parliamentary Conference, took a leading part in the Universal Peace
Congress held immediately afterwards (11th to 16th November).
"It is not the first time that one of the sisterhood has quacked
on this spot," said one journal in recognition of her oratory,
"and this time it was not even a matter of saving the Capitol." [2]
But of all the proceedings the most significant was a proposal
adumbrated in the Inter-Parliamentary Conference by Bajer
and Hodgson Pratt, that a permanent Inter-Parliamentary
Bureau should be established at Berne, in which city both
Conferences were to assemble in the following year. The
Universal Peace Congress at the same time projected an International Peace Bureau. By the time the meetings fell due a
third gathering had been held in Rome (at the end of 1891)—an
International Working-Men's Congress. But here all resolutions for Peace were vitiated by other motions carried by
political demagogues, to the effect that Peace could only be
secured when their own proletarian programme had first been
carried into execution.[3]

The International Peace Bureau opened at Berne in January

---

[1] I.P. Conf. *Report*, Rome, 1891 ; Suttner, *Memoirs*, i, 360–1.
[2] E. Rouard de Card, *Arbitrage International*, pp. 34–5; Suttner,
Memoirs, i, 366.　　　　　　[3] *H. of P.* (1892), p. 8.

1892: the first (and only) international federation of Peace organisations. It was directed by Dr. Albert Gobat of the Swiss National Council, and had for Secretary Elie Ducommun, perhaps the most energetic figure of the International Movement. The purpose of the Bureau was to represent the Peace organisations when they were not in annual session, to knit them more closely together, to circulate information, and to build up a library. From the start the expenses of upkeep were small.

Thus the popular side of the Movement was centralised before the Parliamentary side. But simultaneously the popular Movement fought its first two engagements on matters of principle. At the Berne meeting in August 1892, while uncontested resolutions were passed in favour of arbitration treaties and in furtherance of the Pan-American Treaty of 1890, a sharp issue was encountered in a motion, tabled by E. T. Moneta, S. J. Capper, and the Baroness von Suttner, for a "Confederation of the European States" on the model of the plan put forward by the Geneva League of Peace and Liberty in 1867. This resolution eventually passed, though a section of the Congress feared it as postulating absorptions and annexations. The other critical discussion, on Sanctions, also produced a resolution, despite the strenuous expostulation of Darby, who denounced all element of material force in holding Governments to their pledges. As finally carried, the resolution declared that no international sanctions would be justified that amounted to acts of war. The older (religious) Peace Societies voted against it.[1]

An Inter-Parliamentary Bureau was set up in Berne at the end of the year, founded by the Conference held in the same August and directed by the Marquis Pandolfi. It began immediately to issue a journal, the *Courier Diplomatique*. Both bodies, the International Peace Bureau and the Inter-Parliamentary Bureau, are still in existence—the former at Geneva since 1925, the latter at Brussels since 1909. The two

---

[1] U.P. Cong. *Report*, Berne, 1892, *passim*; Suttner, *Memoirs*, i, 426 ; E. Langlade, *La Clause Compromissoire*, p. 45.

wings of the Peace Movement functioned, therefore, through the annual reunions every summer and through these permanent secretariats in the intervening months.[1]

From now on, with administrative matters resolved, the two Conferences could give themselves more particularly to questions bearing on the organisation of Peace : and the expedient most unceasingly pressed was that of an International Tribunal. The Universal Peace Congress, meeting on American soil for the first time in August 1893 (at Chicago), discussed a plan for an International Court of Arbitration which had been prepared, at the instigation of the American Peace Society, by three American jurists. A special Church convention at the same moment prepared a petition to the Governments of the world to be presented along with that of the Arbitration Alliance in Great Britain.[2] In the Inter-Parliamentary Conference there was no similar discussion, as the meeting of 1893 (held in Brussels) was an interim meeting of the Central Committee only. But in 1894, whereas the Universal Peace Congress (welcomed in Brussels by the King of the Belgians) marked time again, aspiring to nothing more than that "the most practical and just means of settling international disputes is that of permanent arbitration treaties with definite pacific sanctions,"[3] the fourteen Parliamentary groups in session at The Hague took a great step forward. Attempts by the Roumanian group to get a quarrel between their Government and Hungary discussed were quashed, and the Conference devoted its attention to a report on a Permanent International Court of Arbitration drawn up in England by the Hon. Philip Stanhope. It was objected that all discussion of a tribunal would be futile until the Powers had accepted the principle of general arbitration treaties. But the report was nevertheless adopted, and a

[1] *H. of P.* (1892), p. 55 ; E. L. Whitney, *American Peace Society*, pp. 173-5 ; *Annuaire* of the International Peace Bureau (Geneva), 1924, pp. 7 *seq.* and 19 *seq.*

[2] *A. of P.* (October 1893), pp. 237-8; Whitney, pp. 194-5 ; Suttner, *Memoirs*, ii, 8.

[3] E. Langlade, *La Clause Compromissoire*, p. 37 ; F. Passy, *Pour la Paix*, p. 140.

commission of six was appointed to work it out in detail by the time fixed for the next annual conference.[1]

Stanhope's project is important both for itself and for its results. It laid down four principles as fundamental to any tribunal established. National sovereignty was to remain inalienable and inviolable; the adhesion of Governments to the Court was to be optional; all States members of the Court were to be recognised as equal in status; and the judgments of the Court were to be binding in advance ("to have the force of an executive sentence"). On this basis the commission of six drafted the plan for a Permanent Court of International Arbitration which they presented to the Conference at Brussels in August 1895, with the Belgian Senator Honzeau de Lehaye as spokesman. In fourteen articles the plan provided complete machinery for a Court. Two members were to be appointed by each Government for five years, and to sit permanently in some neutral city unless the adherent Powers should transfer the Court elsewhere by a three-quarters majority. Expenses were to be paid by the Governments in proportion. Suits were to be submitted either to the full Court or to a tribunal of two of its members nominated for each occasion by the President of the Court (who would be elected annually). Notification of the dispute by either party would automatically invest the Court with full jurisdiction. And when the judgment had been given (within two months), an appeal lay within a further three months for judgment by the same procedure as in the first instance. The execution of the final award lay "with the honour of both parties"; there were no sanctions apart from the moral obligation. [2]

Passy declared in his elation that within five years the Powers would be actually in conference to erect such a tribunal (as indeed they were to be). And besides this moral encouragement created, the plan has historical value in that it formed the basis of the official British plan put forward at the Hague

[1] I.P. Conf. *Report*, Hague, 1894; Suttner, *Memoirs*, ii, chap. xlv, *passim*.

[2] Text in E. Descamps, *Organisation of Arbitration* (1895), pp. 29–32 ; *H. of P.* (1894–95), *passim*.

Conference in 1899.[1] Its immediate practical result was a
valuable analysis published by Emile Descamps in 1895, entitled *The Organisation of Arbitration*, which coincided in time
with the appearance of a further contribution of immense
importance from the International Law Association.

At the annual meeting of the International Law Association
in October 1893, held in London, Darby had secured the
nomination of a committee to draft a project for Arbitration
Treaties and an Arbitration Tribunal. This body had
completed its task in two parts by April 1895, and its Report
was passed at the annual meeting at Brussels in the following
October. It is the first part of this project, concerned with the
scope and structure of Permanent Arbitration Treaties, that
forms, with the Inter-Parliamentary project for a tribunal, an
outline of pacific machinery more complete than any yet
evolved. The thirteen articles of the Association's plan
recognised two classes of Arbitration Treaty—"all-in" treaties
with no reservations, and treaties in which certain specified
types of dispute were excluded from arbitration on grounds of
honour or national independence. Every treaty, of whichever
type, should lay down rules as to the formation of the arbitral
bodies it proposed. If these tribunals consisted of more than
two persons the awards should be given by a majority vote, and
the opinions of the minority should be appended to each award
as a report. Should there be doubt as to whether any dispute
was arbitrable under the treaty, this uncertainty should itself be
resolved by arbitration. Procedure should be always by case,
counter case, printed arguments presented simultaneously, and
a final oral discussion. Neither party was to use documents
which at the time the difference arose had been unknown to the
other party. The arbitrators' award, finally, was to be published within a fixed time.[2]

Much ground, then, had been cleared by the two series of
conferences and by the learned societies when the Hague

[1] *Cf.* Whitney, p. 210.
[2] International Law Association, *Annual Report*, Brussels, 1895;
H. of P. (1895), pp. 281 *seq.*

Conference ultimately met. The first direct step taken to promote an assembly of the Powers to execute the plans outlined in 1894-95 occurred at the next Inter-Parliamentary Conference, at Budapest, in September 1896. A resolution by Count Apponyi, passed on the second day, sought to strengthen the influence already being brought to bear on Governments, by providing that delegates appointed by constitutional Governments should be admitted to the Conference, and also representatives from the Russian Council of State and from any analogous institution in States which had no constitution. The Parliamentary groups were invited, further, to fix a time for demanding of their Governments *simultaneously* the conclusion of special and general arbitration treaties and the convening of an international conference to establish a Permanent Court of Arbitration on the lines planned by the Union. The Universal Peace Congress of the same year advanced a further step by adopting a draft project of an International Code, for which it invoked the blessing of Pope Leo XIII.[1]

In the interval, between these first overtures and the assembling of the Hague Conference, a difference in theory showed itself between the idealists of the Universal Peace Congress Movement and those who adopted the more practical and more prudent standpoint of the Inter-Parliamentary Conferences. "To see that there is something wrong in the world," said the *St. James's Gazette*, "and to propose a remedy which, on inquiry, turns out to be a radical change in human nature, is the same thing with them."[2] The Universal Peace Congress of 1897 gave point to the gibe. Hodgson Pratt, ever practical, had questioned how far a Government could specify beforehand in a treaty the types of dispute which it could undertake invariably to submit to arbitration. When a resolution came before the gathering asking Governments to amend their constitutions so as to admit of the arbitration of *all* disputes, he had pleaded for a less categorical wording, for the plan

[1] I.P. Conf. *Report*, Budapest, 1896; U.P. Cong. *Report*, Budapest, 1896, pp. 46 *seq*. Suttner, *Memoirs*, ii, 118-9.
[2] Cited in Suttner, *Memoirs*, ii, 134-5.

of the Inter-Parliamentary Union had recognised definite limits to the scope of arbitration after a careful juridical examination. But the committee set up to scrutinise his objection brushed it aside. The Universal Peace Congress declared composedly that arbitration was applicable to all disputes without exception. [1]

Neither conference met in 1898; for Lisbon, the city intended for their next assembly, was the scene of domestic upheaval and rioting. But in point of fact there was no need of further measures to secure their immediate object. The link which was to bridge the gap between unofficial and official Government action had already been forged.

M. Vasili, the Russian Consul in Budapest, had attended the Inter-Parliamentary Conference of 1896 in the private capacity of an interested spectator. He had forwarded to his Government a copy of the proceedings, with a report on them by himself. They were placed in the archives at St. Petersburg and forgotten. But when Count Muravev came into power, Vasili was recalled to take up a post in the Russian Foreign Office, where, now in an official capacity, he unearthed his documents and had them conveyed to the Tsar. Two considerations, according to W. T. Stead, influenced him in this course of action. One was the pressure of his Government's armaments bill, which an international conference might do something to alleviate. The other was Lord Salisbury's denunciation of armaments at the Guildhall Dinner on 9th November 1897. Vasili's first approach to the Emperor failed; but his second, buttressed by Count Lamsdorff, produced the famous Rescript which summoned the Hague Conference. [2]

(4) *The Hague Conference of* 1899

How far other agencies and other considerations helped to bring about the Tsar's Rescript on 24th August 1898 is not

[1] U.P. Cong. *Report*, Hamburg, 1897; E. Langlade, *La Clause Compromissoire*, pp. 48–9.

[2] See discussion of this episode, with sources, in Howard Evans, *Cremer*, pp 177–80.

Hoppé

W. T. STEAD

yet fully known.   It is certain that the burden of armaments was in part responsible.   There is evidence too that Nicholas II was profoundly impressed by the work of a Russian (Jean de Bloch), *La Guerre*, which appeared in July 1898 with the message, proved up to the last of its six voluminous parts, that war would ultimately become impossible through sheer expense and deadliness.   The Baroness von Suttner's *Die Waffen Nieder*, again, is known to have affected the Tsar deeply.[1] Vasili's report may be best interpreted as suggesting a means of investigating the whole vicious circle of international relations through a conference of the Powers.   At all events, the facts of the Vasili episode are well established; and thereby the causal connection between the Inter-Parliamentary Union and the Hague Conference.

The Rescript, a circular letter from Count Muravev to all the ambassadors accredited to St. Petersburg, astounded the world.   In the name of the greatest autocrat in Europe it denounced war on scientific grounds as a destroyer of civilisation, and on economic grounds as the cause of an intolerable armament burden, in the light of which the world was invited to herald the new century by attending a Conference of Governments to discuss the gradual supersession of war by pacific settlements of all disputes.   At the end of the year definite invitations were issued for a preliminary exchange of views on the subjects of disarmament and arbitration.

Throughout the world the Peace Movement seized its opportunity.   While the bulk of the European Press recovered from the first amazement and settled down to a commentary in part sceptical and in part amused, and while Governments showed no inclination to deny the dictum of the German Kaiser that the only guarantee of peace was a well-drilled army,[2] the Peace organisations, national and international,

---

[1] J. de Bloch, *Le Rôle de la Guerre*, St. Petersburg, 1898; trans. W. T. Stead, London, 1900. See obituary of Bloch in *H. of P.* (1902), p. 195; also Suttner, *Memoirs*, ii, 183, 193; C. L. Lange, *Doctrine Pacifique* (1926), p. 402; W.P.F. pamphlet on *Arbitration* (1926), p. 464.

[2] *Cf.* Suttner, *Memoirs*, ii, 199-201.

bombarded the Imperial Russian Government with congratulations and began nation-wide campaigns of propaganda. Petitions to Governments were opened all over Europe, while in England forces were joined between the Peace Society, the International Arbitration League, the Trade Union Congress, and the Arbitration Alliance of the Churches. Darby, Cremer, Hodgson Pratt, and Felix Moscheles divided the British Isles among themselves and flooded the land with 300,000 pamphlets within the next twelve months. In the United States the American Peace Society appears to have been less active; but in Europe a universal campaign was promoted by the Peace Bureau at Berne and by an extensive tour begun by Bertha von Suttner early in 1899, well supported in the *Neue-Wiener Tagblatt* and the *Neue Freie Presse*. It was an anxious moment. "Governments are not humble enough," said Jean de Bloch, "and public opinion is not as yet ripe enough, to be able to obtain results from the Conference." The man who did most to foster what opinion there was favourable to the enterprise was W. T. Stead. On his own responsibility, after interviewing Balfour in London in September 1898, Stead spent four months touring the capitals of Europe to demand audiences of their sovereigns. The King of the Belgians would not see him; Clemenceau in Paris was sceptical; in Berlin Lord Lonsdale, the British ambassador, was fearful of securing him an interview with the Kaiser; in Russia he contrived to see the Tsar; in Rome, after twice appealing to "the Pope of the Middle Ages and of the Truce of God" to "come to the help of a weary and war-worn world," he was favoured with a letter from Cardinal Rampolla. On his return to England he founded, in January 1899, the newspaper *War on War* expressly to canvass the coming Conference. And when the Conference ultimately assembled he went to the Hague and addressed the Tsar in a continuous series of private letters.[1]

Nicholas II himself, declaring wryly that all his critics

[1] Howard Evans, *Cremer*, chap. xxii; *H. of P.* (1899), p. 200; Suttner, *Memoirs*, ii, 226, 236; F. Whyte, *W. T. Stead*, ii, 122–166, 218, 225; E. L. Whitney, *American Peace Society*, p. 208.

seemed merely to be asking him what he proposed to do, as if the future of the world was his business and his alone, issued a further circular in January 1899 defining more precisely the scope of his proposals. The additional matter has been criticised as foreshadowing the inevitable failure of the Conference. For whereas the original Rescript had concerned itself exclusively with the reduction of armaments and the use of good offices and mediation, there were now introduced considerations relating to the laws of war, weapons of war, submarines, and the Red Cross—a grim indication of the pressure that had been brought to bear on the Tsar in the meantime. It was finally on a basis of the new Rescript that formal invitations to The Hague were issued on 6th April.[1]

The Conference lasted two months—from 18th May till 29th July. At the outset its two great merits were that it was the first conference of the kind to be convened at a time of profound peace, and that its method of attempting to supersede war by establishing "laws of war" was logically and practically sound.[2] The ninety-six delegates, representing twenty-six Powers, did their work in three committees: one on Armaments, under M. Beenaert of Belgium; one on the Laws of War, under the Russian jurist Martens; and one on Arbitration and Conciliation, under Léon Bourgeois (a member of the French Inter-Parliamentary Group). Court functions punctuated the proceedings; the delegates spent most of their free evenings interviewing pacifist deputations; Jean de Bloch gave lantern lectures on war; the World's Press, after striving without avail to gain admission to the sessions, gave up in disgust and neglected the Conference—so that its only advertisements were the Baroness von Suttner's telegrams to Vienna and Stead's daily bulletins to London. Two panics arose within the committees themselves: the first on 11th June, when rumour had it that the German delegation had wrecked all hopes of an agreement on arbitration; and the second on 20th July, when the Roumanian delegation threatened to wreck the agreement

---

[1] Cf. Suttner, Memoirs, ii, 226–8.
[2] Cf. N. Politis, La Justice International (1924), p. 16.

already reached on mediation. Stead and Emile Descamps strove heroically each evening, at receptions and by interviews with the delegates, to restore equanimity. At the end the results were embodied in a Final Act on 29th July. Stead went off immediately on a second tour of the Continent, and the Inter-Parliamentary and Universal Peace gatherings, meeting in August in Christiania, congratulated the Conference on its labours.[1]

Those labours are important here only for their relation to the efforts of the Peace Movements of the preceding eighty-four years. From this standpoint only two sections of the work call for analysis—the first Convention (on arbitration) and the one resolution (on armaments). The other two Conventions decided respectively the relation of the Red Cross to Maritime Warfare and the preliminary codification of the Laws of War. There were added three "declarations" forbidding the use of expanding bullets, gas projectiles, and projectiles from balloons, and six "wishes" on less vital points of detail.

The resolution on armaments was a bitter disappointment to the Peace bodies and to the world in general. At best it was nothing more than a resolution; and it did no more than state a truism—"that the restriction of military budgets is . . . extremely desirable for . . . the material and moral welfare of mankind." A resolution to *provide* for such restriction, introduced on 30th June, had been defeated—largely through the hostility of the German von Schwarzhoff.[2]

The Convention "for the peaceful settlement of international conflicts" offered more grounds for satisfaction. Its three cardinal provisions marked a real advance in international understanding. In the first place, it established for every Government the right to offer mediation without the offer being open to interpretation as an unfriendly act. This was a logical corollary to the mediation article of the Treaty of Paris

---

[1] Narrative of the Conference (from inside knowledge) in Suttner, *Memoirs*, ii, chaps. lv–lvii ; text of Final Act in A. P. Higgins, *Hague Conferences*, pp. 60–71.
[2] Suttner, *Memoirs*, ii, 309.

of 1856. The fact of its deliberate formulation reveals incidentally how far international tolerance still fell short of the goodwill necessary for any International Tribunal to function serenely. In the second place, provision was made for Commissions of Enquiry, composed partly of neutrals, to be set up in moments of acute difference between two Powers, for the peaceful settlement of the points at issue. Most important of all, in the third place, a Court of International Arbitration was established at The Hague, to meet each time a controversy arose in which the parties had recourse to its jurisdiction, and functioning according to rules of procedure laid down by the Convention. There had been a stormy passage for each of the three parts. The mediation clause (Article 27) had nearly been destroyed by the Roumanian delegation, which refused for a time to undertake any obligation likely to prejudice national sovereignty; the clauses on Commissions of Enquiry had been diluted by strenuous opposition (again from the Balkans) until they merely recommended such commissions as "useful"; and the provisions for the Hague Court were a compromise between three plans submitted by Great Britain, the United States, and Russia.

A phrase of Frederic Passy's, uttered years later in his memoirs, sums up all that can be said about the first Hague Conference: "We have to secure not disarmament, but the disarmament spirit." [1] The Conference had to some extent recognised this in attempting to bring about settled peace by creating a machinery that might in time produce a feeling of security among the nations sufficient to atrophy the "custom of war." Nobody imagined the Conference would result in an immediate reduction of armaments. Even Stead, who believed in the Tsar's sincerity more firmly than did anyone else outside Russia, realised that the practical purpose of the discussions was rather "to bring about a cessation of the ever-increasing preparations for war." [2] Few others among the ministers and delegates indeed had the moral courage of the

[1] F. Passy, *Pour la Paix* (1909), p. 168.
[2] F. Whyte, *W. T. Stead*, ii, 136, 218.

Tsar. Lord Salisbury frankly doubted that the honourable fulfilment of their obligations by the Powers could be relied on; Delcassé at heart was resolved that there should be no promises to disarm; A. D. White, the United States chief delegate, was instructed to leave the initiative in disarmament to the rest of the Governments; the dispatches from the German Foreign Office glorified "the protection of its own interests" as the supreme aim of every State; the Kaiser, in a famous phrase, undertook to save the Tsar's face by voting for "this nonsense," but thereafter to "trust and invoke only God and my sharp sword." The universal fear was that arbitration proceedings would only allow the other side time to prepare itself for war.[1]

Judgment of the Hague Convention has to consider, therefore, the psychology of the negotiators no less than the aspirations of the Peace advocates. On the whole the achievement was remarkable, though juridically the Court of Arbitration had its limitations. The maximum that was hoped for was a World Court, a permanent body in constant session. Lord Pauncefote, the chief British delegate, urged the establishment of such a tribunal, but had no concrete plan to produce. The American delegation had a plan, drawn up by the New York Bar Association in 1896 on the basis of Ladd's "Congress of Nations," but opposition from the Italian and Belgian delegations precluded its discussion; and the Court as finally established was founded on a British memorandum drawn from the Inter-Parliamentary plan of 1895.[2] There were precedents for a World Court in the United States Supreme Court and the Swiss Federal Court at Berne; but the will to peace was lacking, and a Permanent Court enjoining obligatory arbitration remained a dream until 1920.

Nevertheless the Hague Court, with its record of fourteen

---

[1] German documents—*Die Grosse Politik der Europäischen Kabinette*, 1871–1914 (Berlin), vol. xv, pp. 170, 186, 305–6; A. D. White, *Memoirs*, ii, 253, 268; cited in G. L. Dickinson, *The International Anarchy* (1926), chap. xiv.

[2] Texts in L. Appleton, *An International Tribunal for Europe*, pp. 30 *seq.*; see also E. L. Whitney, *American Peace Society*, p. 210.

cases settled by August 1914, was "the first and most significant European and World experiment." [1] It was in composition an *ad hoc* body, a tribunal chosen in moments of crisis from a list of names. No provision was made for rendering effective the agreement as to its establishment. The Convention "made a declaration as to the legal value of certain approved means" of settling disputes, and set up a Court with a certain procedure; but there was no compact to arbitrate differences. The Powers party to the Convention were not precluded from using other means of settlement, and the older method of reference to a special arbitrator or tribunal (as, for instance, in the *Alabama* and Venezuela cases) was not affected by the Hague decisions. Reference to the Hague Court was optional, and could only be made obligatory by separate bilateral agreements among the Powers—of which no fewer than 942 would be needed for the obligation to be universal. [2]

Thus of the two essentials of a League of Nations—the legislative and the judicial organs—the second had been secured by 1899. The second Hague Conference, in 1907, was to attempt the other. The Balance of Power had already begun to be superseded by a community of power; and the fruits of the first Hague Conference can be seen in the fourteen cases arbitrated down to 1914, and in the fact that the early wars of the twentieth century were waged according to fixed rules. Above all, since the Conventions were the work of diplomats standing outside the Peace Movement, peace was thenceforward to be "an integral part of the creed of statesmen"; wherefore, by reflection, the phrase "Universal Peace" had become thoroughly respectable. [3]

[1] L. Sturzo, *The International Community* (1929), p. 63.

[2] See legal discussion by W. E. Darby at annual meeting of International Law Association at Christiania, 1905, cited in *H. of P.* (1905), p. 117 ; also *H. of P.* (1906), pp. 312-3 ; J. L. Tryon, *Proposals for an International Court* (1913) ; R. L. Jones, *International Arbitration* (1907), chap. xiii.

[3] *Cf.* E. L. Whitney, *American Peace Society*, p. 298 ; A. P. Higgins, *Hague Conferences*, pp. 38-51 ; Suttner, *Memoirs*, ii, 252.

(5) *The Situation at the End of the Century*

It is convenient, then, to pause at the year 1900 and review the international progress of the century from the angle of the pacifist and internationalist bodies; and the record is by no means a failure.

The solidarity of the whole world had become a fact universally recognised in every international sphere except that of politics. Between the Panama Congress of 1826 and the Hague Conference of 1899 there had been held over a thousand international congresses (like the Red Cross and Postal Congresses)—all of a diplomatic character, and all convened to promote objects of a social or economic nature. All had tended to prove the doctrine enunciated by the Peace Societies since 1815, and (on different grounds) by the Free Traders after 1840 and the Labour Movements since 1867, of "interdependence as a moral and material fact, and an effort to abandon an irrational isolation." The cumulative result, moreover, was that the work of Peace was no longer a negative avoidance of war, but a positive search for some durable and equitable form of international organisation—an effort towards a federative union of nation States.[1]

On the political side the century's progress has to be measured in terms of arbitrations and arbitration treaties. Here the result is far more considerable than is generally appreciated. The practice of arbitration had at first been used with little conception of its value. Its growth can be traced along several definite lines. The records of the century show (first) an increase which always synchronised with the termination of large wars; they reveal (secondly) that the general acceptance of arbitration developed parallel with the growth of democracy; and (thirdly) the admission of arbitration into the field of international law was due (perhaps in consequence) to the example of the Anglo-Saxon race. As the practice became general it

---

[1] *See* L. Sturzo, *The International Community* (1929), p. 62 ; C. L. Lange, *Doctrine Pacifique* (1926), p. 409 ; S. E. Baldwin in *American Journal of International Law* (1907), pp. 565–78 and 808–29.

fell into three well-defined methods of procedure. Disputes were referred to a congress of European representatives, or to a neutral sovereign friendly to both parties, or to an international commission presided over by an umpire.[1] The total number settled by one or other of these means between 1794 (the year of the Jay Treaty) and 1900 has been computed at 177, with 90 cases in the last twenty years of that period. Of these, some 40 per cent. had arisen out of warlike or illegal operations, 30 per cent. arose over titles and boundaries, 20 per cent. concerned the pecuniary claims of private citizens, and 10 per cent. determined the interpretation of treaties. This classification reveals both the strength and the weakness of the practice, for all the issues were legal issues. Potent to solve questions of law, arbitration had not yet been used to compose a political issue of the kind so easily construed as involving national honour or national independence.[2]

The treaties of arbitration likewise fell into three categories: some contained a "specific" arbitration clause, providing for the arbitration of specific points of dispute; some contained a "general" compromissory clause covering all kinds of disputes except those specially reserved; and a third category—arbitration treaties proper—established procedure for the permanent regulation of disputes (specific or general) between the contracting parties.[3] Altogether there were 314 treaties signed containing provisions for arbitration within the century ending 1909. Of these, eliminating duplicates and those that lapsed, 194 were in force in 1914.[4] International arbitration, further, had found its way into one State Constitution by the end of the

---

[1] Examples: (1) France and Prussia, 1867, by London Congress; (2) Great Britain and United States (San Juan), 1872, by Kaiser Wilhelm I; (3) *Alabama*, 1872, by Geneva Tribunal.

[2] *See* J. Gennadius, *Arbitrage International* (1904), *passim*; L. Appleton, *Arbitration* (1899), p. 3; H. La Fontaine, *Pasicrisie International* . . . 1794–1900 (1902); L. S. Woolf, *International Government* (1917), p. 46.

[3] Examples: (1) Postal Union (Berne), 9th October 1874; (2) Peru and Bolivia, 5th November 1863; (3) Great Britain and United States (unratified), 11th January 1897. See discussion in E. Langlade, *La Clause Compromissoire* (1899), pp. 82 *seq.*

[4] G. Moch, *Hist. Sommaire de l'Arbitrage Permanent* (edition 1910).

century (Brazil, 4th February 1891); but as a political instrument among nations there were still very definite limits to its application. It still needed to be raised to the level of an international *obligation*; the clauses and treaties in which it was established were still dangerously vague and general; and there was as yet no International Tribunal dispensing a Code of International Law which would clarify the legal issues involved in disputes. Governmental psychology, again, was still kept apprehensive on the questions of sanctions and national sovereignty; while, even further, there was no provision for *obligatory* recourse to mediation in disputes which were manifestly non-justiciable.[1] The ideal formula for settlement was not destined to be seen in an international document until 22nd June 1921. When it appeared, in a treaty between Afghanistan and Persia, it was found to be the shortest and simplest formula of its kind: "The two contracting parties have decided, in conformity with international usage, to submit to arbitration all the difficulties arising between the two countries of which a solution cannot be arrived at by diplomatic negotiations. Further, the high contracting parties undertake loyally to carry out the decisions of the arbitrators." There were to be no exceptions.

How far from this goal the world actually found itself in 1900 is now being elucidated in the flood of documents and studies which are exploring the diplomatic history of the years leading to the World War, and endeavouring to find a means of cutting the vicious circle of fear, insurance, armaments, more fear, and "re-insurance."

The contribution of the Peace Movement down to 1900 had been one of logical foresight, warning, and suggestion. No new idea on the subject of World Peace had been formulated since Ladd's *Congress of Nations*. But the popular Peace Movement of the first half of the century, besides its propaganda in towns and villages (where the effect cannot be measured), had forced its pleas on Governments in 1856 and 1871; while the wider Movement of the second half of the

---

[1] See discussion in C. de Mougins de Roquefort, *De la Solution des Conflits Internationaux* (1889).

century, after organising itself on a double basis, inside and outside Parliaments, had contrived at least one glorious failure (the Anglo-American Treaty of 1897) and had given the world the means of at least understanding the issues of the Hague Conference.

Nearly all the Peace thinking of the nineteenth century had visualised the ultimate goal of a "Congress of Nations." By its variety and its constant discussion, that concept and the means to it had been completely worked out. Lieber had pointed an eventual way to it through "facultative (optional) international jurisdiction." Sir Travers Twiss, Bulmering, and Kamarovsky had sought it through "specialised international tribunals." Bentham, Ladd, Burritt, Miles, Marcoartu, Lavelaye, Field, and Leone Levi had endowed the Congress and its awards with a moral sanction only. Sir Edward Hornby, Kamarovsky, and their disciples had stressed the need for sanctions of material force. John Stuart Mill, Lemonnier, Larroque, Lorimer, and Bluntschli had elaborated Victor Hugo's dream of a United States of Europe. One theorist had even offered the world a return to the papal arbitration of the Middle Ages.[1] Permanent neutralisation of the smaller States also had been advanced in theory by the British Peace Society,[2] and in practice by the Scandinavian Peace organisations, as a panacea for the majority of territorial disputes; while complete schemes of arbitral procedure and a tribunal had been evolved— and brought to the notice of the world's Governments in conference—by the Inter-Parliamentary Union and the International Law Association. Of the logical roads to Peace, only Disarmament and a Code of International Law were behind in the race for amplification. The first of these was by now recognised among pacifists to be a sequel rather than a forerunner of Peace; but the neglect of the second was lamentable, despite the colossal nature of the task of codification. The Prize Essay

[1] Lacointa, 1855. See discussion of all these in R. L. Jones, *International Arbitration* (1907), pp. 218–27.

[2] See *H. of P.* (1891), p. 186 and *passim*. There were five permanent neutralities by 1890—Switzerland, Belgium, Luxemburg, the Ionian Islands, and Samoa.

Competitions, finally, so beloved of the older Peace Movement, were now elevated to heights of permanence and universal respect in the Nobel Peace Prize, founded in 1897 by Alfred Nobel at Christiania, in the form of a diploma, a gold medal, and 150,000 Norwegian kroner awarded every year to the man or woman who, during that year, had contributed most, by word or action, to the cause of Peace.[1]

For the rest, the century closed with 425 Peace organisations in existence throughout the world.   By numerical classification Denmark had 94, Sweden 79, Germany 72, Great Britain 46, Norway 38, Switzerland 26, France 16, the United States 15, Italy 13, Austria 9, Holland 9, Hungary 2, Belgium, Portugal, and Russia 1 each.   The odd three were in Tokio and Australia.   They showed among them a threefold trend: in the Germanic countries towards unity, by the fusion of groups; in the Latin countries towards the multiplication and independence of groups—particularly in Italy; and in the Anglo-Saxon countries towards individual and local multiplication, the societies preserving their antinomy but striving for alliance and perhaps federation.[2]

[1] First awarded in 1901.   Particulars in International Peace Bureau's *Annuaire des Organisations Internationales* (1924), pp. 120–1.

[2] *Cf.* analysis by E. Langlade at French National Peace Congress, Toulouse, 1902 ; see its *Report*, p. 63 and *passim* ; also *H. of P.* (1898), p. 72 ; (1899), p. 309.

CHAPTER X

TO THE WORLD WAR: 1899–1914

THE bitter tragedy of the years that followed the Hague Conference lies in that the idea of World Peace was becoming more practically futile as it grew more theoretically axiomatic. Though the ranks of the world's Peace crusaders had broadened out from the older critics of the War system (like Dymond), and had by now recruited Prime Ministers and statesmen (like Salisbury and Cleveland), the Movement was quite incompatible with the existing system of international relations. The way to Peace lay elsewhere than in mere reform. The advance in arbitration was certainly phenomenal after 1900—sixty-three cases settled within the first four years of the century. But, as the London Peace Society urged in 1903, "we must be on our guard against supposing that the mere increase or perfecting of machinery involves all we want. That will avail little without a soul." Among competent observers some imagined that the progress of Peace would be hindered by hidden defects in the Hague machinery; others looked rather to outside sources of danger—for no Government invoked defects in the Hague machinery as a pretext for refusing to carry a case before the Hague Tribunal. But the real hitch proved to be the easy doctrine, condemned by the Baroness von Suttner, that "endeavours against war should be discreetly limited to its alleviation." [1]

There might be matter for rejoicing in the fact that the "provincialism of the United States" had come to an end. The time might also have arrived, as a Japanese enthusiast averred in 1905, to discuss the elaboration of a *Universal* Peace Society.

[1] Suttner, *Memoirs*, ii, 373 ; *H. of P.* (1904), p. 200.

But the diplomatic world was not likely to follow the example set by the Pope when, in 1900, he melted down barrowloads of old swords and sold them as pig-iron. For the ten years that preceded the World War were a chronic period of "international anarchy," whose awful implications were only half-realised at the time. The security of the State, in a community of nations almost completely unorganised, still depended in the last resort on material strength. Thus insecurity bred armaments and alliances and a consequently greater insecurity. The Powers were "States armed, and therefore a menace to one another; policies ostensibly defensive, but really just as much offensive; these policies pursued in the dark by a very few men who, because they act secretly, cannot act honestly; and this whole complex playing upon primitive passions, arousable at every moment by appropriate appeals from a Press which has no object except to make money out of the weakness of men." Nevertheless, anarchy is a dynamic condition, containing elements of good in so far as it is "an awakening from stupor and a yearning after what is new and better." The prophets hoped to reform the world without a cataclysm.[1]

Most remarkable of all among the cross-currents that thread the fourteen years is the strength which Peace arguments drew from new and powerful sources. To the earlier lessons of humanitarianism, Free Trade, religion, and socialism, were now added morals drawn from sociology, economics, and finance. The *Great Illusion* of Norman Angell, published in 1901, revealed for all time the suicidal nature of modern war and the fact that it literally did not pay, since the nations were growing ever more interdependent. The same doctrine, already preached from the strategic standpoint by Gaston Moch and the Russian Novikov, was fortified still further by arguments drawn from sociology and biology by Prince Kropotkin in his *Mutual Aid* (1902). Both books had a world-wide circulation.[2] Wealthy pacifists, at the same time, began to leave vast

[1] G. Lowes Dickinson, *The International Anarchy* (1904–14), p. 46; *Quarterly Review* (London), vol. ccviii, p. 231 (1908); F. Stratmann, *The Church and War*, p. 10.

[2] *Cf.* also the works of Max Huber and Schücking in and after 1910.

endowments for propagating the gospel of Peace. Alfred
Nobel's bequest had been the first. It was to be followed in
1910 by the establishment in America of the World Peace
Foundation at Boston—the legacy of the publisher Edwin
Ginn, who had been stimulated by his annual visits to the Lake
Mohonk Conferences. His Foundation began to spread abroad
cheap editions of the more famous Peace classics. It never,
however, aspired to the position of authority and respect
secured later by Carnegie's Endowment for International
Peace; while a far more ambitious project, to form an international union of the leaders of the Press to foster Peace, conceived in Europe in 1907, failed altogether.[1]

For the rest, the years leading to the World War show a
vigorous increase of Peace propaganda in England and America,
concentrated on forging a new and better Arbitration Treaty—
ultimately achieved in 1914; comparative stagnation of the
Peace Movement on the continent of Europe; preoccupations
and fears at each moment of crisis among the Powers; and a
logical working out of the forces set in motion at the Hague.
The period is bisected by the second Hague Conference.

(1) *Great Britain*, 1900–1907

Within a few months of the first Hague Conference Great
Britain was in the throes of the Boer War, and national feeling
was at a pitch of excitement which not only drowned the cry of
the foreign Press that here was a case for submission to the
Hague Court, but sapped the strength of the Peace Movement
by inducing desertions. Lord Avebury and others retired from
Cremer's International Arbitration League at the height of the
war fever as early as June 1899. Joseph Chamberlain was
fêted even by Wesleyan pacifists. But Cremer and Darby both
denounced the war in their editorials, aided by Stead in his
paper *War on War*. Their three pens canvassed a petition
launched by the Press of six foreign countries for invoking the
mediation of President M'Kinley. The attitude of the Peace

---

[1] E. L. Whitney, *American Peace Society*, p. 263 ; F. Stratmann,
The Church and War, p. 211.

Party, voiced by Stead, was that the war must be stopped at once, even by the British Government confessing itself to have been in the wrong. "We have no responsibility for the mistakes and shortcomings of President Kruger. What we have to do is to ask whether our own policy has been free from reproach, whether we have acted throughout in a straightforward, honourable manner, being the superior and more civilised Power, and have used every available means of allaying the very distrustful Old Peasant with whom we had to deal." But on Stead's "Stop the War" Committee there was one body unrepresented: the Peace Society. Darby roundly condemned the agitation; not from the popular standpoint, that it was unpatriotic and would encourage the Boers to hold out, but because the Peace Society had never forgotten its own Crimean experience and Cobden's homily on the futility of striving to prevent a war once it had begun. "The temptation to 'do something' leads to mischief; misdirected zeal is not only weakness, it may even become harmful. . . . [Our] business is to work constantly, in season and out of season, for the promotion of our objects. . . . *Special* efforts in the direction of the restoration of Peace could only prove fruitless . . . and it [the Society] has therefore abstained from any." Other motives counted also. Stead was altogether too militant to work in harmony with the serene pacifism of Darby. So much so, that when an International Arbitration Union was formed by Stead at the close of the Inter-Parliamentary Conference of 1900, the Peace Society formally repudiated all connection with it, and scorned repeated invitations to join it.[1] In the same way Darby was later to obstruct the growing movement in favour of a federation of the British Peace organisations.

Nevertheless the Peace cry made itself universally heard, albeit the result was "a splendid failure." The other extreme pacifist flank, the Society of Friends, devoted itself to relieving distress on the battlefields of South Africa no less than to preaching Christian brotherhood at home. Most famous

[1] Howard Evans, *Cremer*, p. 216 ; *H. of P.* (1900), pp. 19, 30, 35, 44, 142 ; F. Whyte, *Life of W. T. Stead*, ii, 167, 169.

among the Quakers during the Boer War was Joshua Rowntree, the Scarborough manufacturer, whose meetings were frequently broken up by jingoist fanatics, and who undertook a mission to South Africa early in 1900 to succour the Boer women and children. His brotherhood received scant sympathy: the atmosphere was such that even Mr. Balfour regarded pacifist meetings as courting all the trouble they encountered.[1]

The Peace party, too, suffered heavy defeats in the General Election of 1900, though the most active pacifist leader, Cremer, regained the seat which he had lost five years earlier. Anxiety was increased, moreover, by the Fashoda Incident in Africa, which gave Cremer the opportunity to organise an exchange of addresses, followed by an exchange of visits, between the organised Labour of England and France. "Workers," ran the addresses, "the time has come when, in the interests of humanity, we should march shoulder to shoulder, proclaiming that the greatest interest of labour is peace." [2]

Within two years, as a result of diplomatic forces, the idea of an *entente* was being vigorously explored by the Governments of both countries. And again Cremer used his position to galvanise attention to the problem and to secure support in high places. In 1903, before the famous visit of King Edward VII to President Loubet, he went to France to familiarise the Chamber of Deputies with the idea of an Anglo-French Arbitration Treaty, simultaneously with the renewal of the agitation for a second Arbitration Treaty with the United States. The mission resulted in a meeting of British and French parliamentarians in London, attended by the Prime Minister (Mr. Balfour) and Campbell-Bannerman. And by the time of the return visit of British M.P.s in November, the cordial relations inspired by the King's visit had crystallised into the hoped-for treaty.

The Anglo-French Arbitration Treaty of 14th October 1903

---

[1] M. E. Hirst, *Quakers in Peace and War*, pp. 481–5 ; S. E. Robson, *Life of Joshua Rowntree*, chap. vi, pp. 107–32.

[2] Howard Evans, *Cremer*, pp. 208–10, 235–59 ; *H. of P.* (1900), p. 130.

is important chiefly for its repercussions. It became the model for the majority of the 162 arbitration treaties concluded during the next ten years. Its three articles, drafted according to the provisions laid down in the Hague Treaty of 1899, bound the two Governments for five years to submit to the Hague "differences of a judicial order, which it may not be possible to settle by means of diplomacy." But the fateful reservations of 1897 were still made, and a Foreign Office memorandum took pains to stress them; the treaty was to apply "only to such questions as do not involve the vital interests, the independence, or the honour of the two contracting parties, and do not affect the interests of a third Power." Nevertheless the treaty is a landmark. It became one of three models for future treaties. The other two were the draft used by Belgium in her treaties of arbitration (arbitrating only pecuniary claims and questions as to the interpretation of existing treaties) and the famous "all-in" arbitration treaty between the Argentine and Chile.[1]

For his part in securing the Anglo-French Treaty Cremer was awarded the Nobel Peace Prize for 1903. He used it to endow the International Arbitration League with £7000, on condition that at least two-thirds of its Council should henceforth be workmen; "for the industrial classes are, for weal or woe, going to be the future rulers of the world."

Between the French Treaty and the second Hague Conference four major issues occupied the British Peace Movement. The first was the attempt to engineer a new Arbitration Treaty with the United States. This will be noticed later. The second was the panic created by the Dogger Bank dispute with Russia in 1905, a crisis finally dispelled by recourse to the Hague machinery of Mixed Commissions. The third was a purely domestic disputation arising out of imperial and defence questions. All the Peace bodies were critical of the annual observance of Empire Day, which began in 1904. The Peace Society even stigmatised it as "mischievous, persistent propaganda," and allowed its own agent, John Gill, to paint a verbal

[1] *See* C. L. Lange, *Arbitrage Obligatoire en* 1913; G. Moch, *Hist. Sommaire de l'Arbitrage Permanent* (1910 edition), pp. 85 *seq.*

picture of British imperialism as "bands of banditti making a display of their robbery and holding it up to be admired." To the same end the Report of the Royal Commission on Compulsory Military Service, which appeared in July 1904, to be the inspiration of Lord Roberts' National Service League two years later, was hotly opposed by the whole of the Peace Movement and by the Trades Union Congress.[1]

But the most vital issue was the fourth and last—the problem of federation. When the practice began (see later) of holding National Peace Congresses in the different countries in preparation for the annual assembly of the Universal Peace Congress, a National Peace Council was established in London by C. P. Trevelyan and Ben Spoor (1904), and the question automatically arose of federating the whole Movement. This had already been done in France; and the National Congress at Manchester in June 1904 passed a resolution urging the same course in England. But the Peace Society obstructed. Darby, who would have nothing to do with sanctions, knew full well that he could never march level with the remainder of the Movement, which was less extreme in its pacifism. Sanctions to him were pernicious, impracticable, and unnecessary.[2] Accordingly the Peace Society eschewed federation, though anxious to continue to co-operate. "Co-operation and federation are quite distinct. . . . Co-operation implies freedom; federation involves control . . . mechanical. United action between the societies may mean much, but similar action by a small central body must necessarily mean much less in its moral effect upon public opinion. . . . Federation can rest only upon a common factor. It really means the greatest common measure of all the societies; and that can be obtained only by the elimination of what is most distinctive and imperative. . . . There cannot be two centres to one circle. For those whose Peace activity is identical with their Christian work the centre is already fixed. Combined action there may be; organic union there cannot be,

---

[1] *H. of P.* (1904), p. 225 ; (1905), p. 116 ; (1906), Annual Report.
[2] *Cf.* his arguments at Conference of International Law Association in October 1913 ; in *Proceedings of 28th Conference* (Madrid).

without the sacrifice of that which is dearest and best." The Society's annual meeting of 1905 resolved, therefore, that it would agree to federation only on condition that no decision taken by the central Council should be executed unless it secured a majority of three-quarters of the members present.[1]

Thus, paradoxically, the evangelical watchword of 1815 was being used as a brake on the Movement; and British pacifism was suffering (though in milder form) the distraction which had so nearly crippled the American Movement seventy years earlier.

(2) *America*, 1900–1907: *Pan-America and the New Anglo-American Arbitration*

In America, on the contrary, it was on its popular side that the Peace Movement was least active. Progress was greatest along the lines of legislative effort and Pan-America.

The concept of Pan-America became increasingly popular after 1900, when an *Associacion Americana La Paz*, founded in Buenos Ayres, spread itself throughout the southern republics of Bolivia, Uruguay, and Monte Video. And when the second Pan-American Conference assembled in Mexico in October 1901, at the invitation of President M'Kinley, sixteen out of the nineteen American States consented to sign a "protocol of adhesion to the Hague Conventions." As a result, a new Arbitration Treaty was negotiated among nine of the Governments represented, for the solution of all questions not involving honour or independence. This, the Treaty of Mexico, was the first "general" arbitration treaty concluded in America. Its adherents were fewer than in 1890, but its scope was vaster. And, moreover, its setting was more propitious; for the same month (January 1902) saw the establishment of a Central American Court of Justice, and in May 1902 there followed the "all-in" Argentine-Chile Treaty, which exhibited three unique features of tremendous significance. The reservations were negligible—questions affecting the Constitution of either party (extremely unlikely to arise); provision was made for a mutual

---

[1] *H. of P.* (1905), pp. 68, 83.

limitation of armaments; and there was specified a permanent arbitrator for all time (the British Government).[1] This represents the limit of arbitral achievement before 1914.

In the United States, Congress was frequently approached with a view to supplementing the work of the Hague Conference. From Massachusetts a memorial went to the House of Representatives in January 1903 embodying a plan for a "world legislature." But it thereupon took the old road—by way of the Senate, the Foreign Relations Committee, and a sub-committee—to oblivion. Likewise its renewal four years later; and likewise also a resolution for a Disarmament Conference among the naval Powers, aired in the Lower House in December 1903. Roosevelt's Presidential Address in the same month, however, warmly recommended the practice of arbitration. On the strength of it the question of an Arbitration Treaty with Great Britain was formally reopened at a National Conference on Arbitration convened specially in Washington (January 1904).[2]

The problem had already been reopened in England on the initiative of Dr. Thomas Barclay and the Chambers of Commerce in the summer of 1902; and strangely enough the agitation developed on a tide of reaction *against* the Hague Conference. It was widely felt that an independent arbitral authority like the Hague Tribunal was undesirable, for there were national motives that no court could adjudge — for example, the necessity for expansion due to pressure of population. Such questions would need diplomatic—that is, political —rather than judicial treatment. But, on the other hand, the international manifestation of the Peace Movement, concentrated in the Universal Peace Congresses, was utilising the Hague Court to the utmost in its recent resolutions;[3] though here again the British Peace Society dissented. Darby considered

---

[1] G. Moch, *Hist. Sommaire de l'Arbitrage Permanent* (1910 edition), pp. 71–5.

[2] E. L. Whitney, *American Peace Society*, pp. 249 *seq.*; *H. of P.* (1904), pp. 179, 192.

[3] *Cf.* U.P. Cong. (Rouen and Havre), 1903; and *H. of P.* (1902), p. 280.

the quest of a new treaty unnecessary. "Such a treaty has already been formed in the Hague Convention between the countries in question and also all the other countries in the civilised world, and it does not appear how any new treaty between these countries separately would be effective if that one be not."   And in no case would he subscribe to compulsory arbitration backed by force; for such a system would be "the old system revised, with a new label."   There could be no compromise between peace and war.[1]

The forces working towards a treaty ultimately produced effect.   The example of England and France, the mission of Dr. Barclay to America, the Washington Arbitration Conference, and the official efforts of Roosevelt bore fruit in the Hay Treaties of 1904–05 (all modelled on the Anglo-French Treaty of 1903), negotiated by the United States with thirteen foreign Governments.   The terms need no elaboration.   What matters most is that the Senate a second time intervened and ruined the enterprise.   Attacked in Congress and in the American Press as "pusillanimous" and unnecessary (in view of the Hague Convention), the treaties were rendered valueless when the Senate ratified them with an amendment designed to safeguard its own constitutional right to withhold consent from any arbitration.   In its new form the British Treaty was not transmitted to London; there was no need.   Three more efforts, indeed, were destined to be placed on record before the World War finally cut across the old international system and provided a fresh starting-point.   These efforts came at intervals of three years.

Meanwhile, by the time the second Hague Conference met Pan-America had inaugurated what Darby called "the first step towards the federation of the world."   This move, begun at a third Pan-American Conference held at Rio de Janiero in July 1906, was consummated at the close of the following year, when delegates of all the five Central American States, assembled in Washington, concluded seven vital treaties—one of which finally established the Central American Court of

[1] *H. of P.* (1904), p. 279.

Justice which had been projected in 1901. The body here constituted has frequently been cited as a local realisation of the dream of Ladd and Jay. Its importance in international jurisprudence cannot be over-stressed. It was to be made up of one full and two substitute judges from each of the member States, paid by equal contributions from their Governments. Five judges would form a legal quorum. Their jurisdiction covered both cases confined to the five States and also cases involving outside Governments. On these lines the Court functioned admirably until the end of its statutory ten years, when it expired in 1918. Its one disaster was a calamity quite outside its control, when its palace at Carthago was destroyed by an earthquake in 1910. Andrew Carnegie thereupon endowed it with a new building at San José.[1]

(3) *National Movements Elsewhere*, 1900–1907

Nowhere else was there either the popular activity of the British Peace Movement or the governmental success of American statesmanship. Nor does a study of the various national movements reveal everywhere the same progressive forces at work.

France alone offers a complete picture; for it was in France that there began, in 1902, the practice of holding annual or biennial "National Peace Congresses" as a preparation for the Universal gatherings, and it was in France that the Peace organisations were first federated. Langlade, one of the foremost historians of arbitration, urged at the first of these national congresses that the future could hold only two possible lines of advance—the fusion of the pacifist and internationalist bodies into a unity, or their federation. And though union offered the advantage of concentration, federation was to be preferred; for federation would not altogether remove the distinctive characteristics of the several societies. This view

---

[1] E. L. Whitney, *American Peace Society*, chap. xxix; G. Moch, *Hist. Sommaire de l'Arbitrage Permanent* (1910 edition), pp. 74, 111; G. L. Tryon, *Proposals for an International Court*, pp. 124–6. The title Pan-American Union was adopted in 1910.

forms an interesting contrast to Darby's attitude in England. It prevailed, as the French Peace Movement exhibited no sharp cleavage on religious principles. The great point of conservatism on which French pacifism stood firm was a product rather of the vicissitudes of French history. Voiced by Gaston Moch, it was to the effect that there must always remain, despite arbitration treaties and world courts, a right of legitimate defence against unprovoked aggression and against a Government that refused arbitration.[1] The records of the Movement, notably *La Paix par le Droit*, are for these years a record more of patient theorising in France than of concerted propaganda.

In Holland, on the contrary, fusion was the only salvation. The two Dutch pacifist bodies—the Peace League of 1870 and the Women's League of 1897—were only saved from dissolution by complete amalgamation in 1901. Their pooled strength functioned anew under the title (still living) of *Vrede door Recht*, with an initial membership of 1500. Propaganda was confined to the schools for some years, until the Movement had once more to be saved from disintegration in 1910. The new saviour, Professor van Vollenhoven of Leyden, rallied it to the cry that with Holland lay the moral responsibility for inducing a new Hague Conference. Apart from quadrupling the membership within the next three years, van Vollenhoven secured a revision of the history text-books in use in Dutch schools, eliminating all national bias. This was the first success of its kind achieved anywhere.[2]

Scandinavia, the birthplace of practical schemes for disarmament and neutralisation, underwent far greater trials, but Scandinavian pacifism on the whole throve on them. The Pan-Scandinavian Peace Congresses were held regularly (1901 and 1904). The Danish Government, inspired by agitations in the Chambers created by Frederic Bajer, and profiting from its national isolation and comparative security, contracted two "all-in" arbitration treaties, with the Netherlands (February

---

[1] National Peace Congress (Toulouse) *Report* (1902), pp. 64, 67, 100 *seq.*

[2] Van Beek en Donk, *Peace Movement in the Netherlands*, pp. 18, 33, and *passim.*

1904) and Italy (December 1906), for the peaceful settlement
of all disputes without reservation. Four other similar treaties
soon followed, including one with Great Britain.[1] Further
still, the three Scandinavian Governments had by 1904 reached
agreement on the question of the permanent neutralisation of
Norway-Sweden. The Norwegian Premier had carried the
project in his own Parliament two years previously, and had
at last won over the other two Storthings. But progress was
suddenly interrupted by the crisis of 1905 on Norwegian independence. It was here that the Scandinavian Peace Movement made its greatest exertion since its first five years. The
Swedish labour organisations, too, threatened a strike if the
revolution should lead to war. Bjornsen in Sweden, and
Hansen and Koht in Norway, undoubtedly contrived to allay
popular panics: until the Treaty of Karlstad, in September
1905, severed peacefully a political connection that had endured
for ninety years. From the general standpoint of international peace the treaty was a signal advance. Questions of
independence and "vital interests" were naturally excluded
from its arbitration provisions, but all other differences were
to be taken before the Hague Court in the event of deadlock,
and the frontier was demilitarised on the lines of the United
States-Canadian boundary. From the particular standpoint
of Scandinavian neutralisation, however, the settlement postponed action for two years. It was not until 1907 that Norway
was declared (by treaty) perpetually neutral, and the seal was
set on the work begun by Bajer in 1882.[2]

Elsewhere advance was spasmodic and unconcerted. New
Peace Societies born in countries hitherto without an organised
movement—notably Russia and Spain—laboured to escape
immediate collapse. The Tsaritsa had been sympathetic
towards pacifist doctrines since 1904, but lack of the means of

[1] *H. of P.* (1901), p. 114; (1904), p. 255; T. Marburg, *League
of Nations*, p. 124; L. S. Woolf, *International Government*, p. 48,
note.
[2] *H. of P.* (1902), p. 264; (1903), p. 52; (1904), p. 215; (1905),
pp. 136–7; (1906), p. 7; and facts supplied by Dr. M. E. Curti, drawn
from Scandinavian vernacular sources.

publicity hindered the formation of a Peace Society in Moscow until 1909, and in Poland until 1906. The same obstacle served to prevent both from ever flourishing. Their leaders, Nepluiev and Dolgoruki, remained but prophets.[1] Little is heard, similarly, of a body known as *Los Amigos de la Paz*, which Felix Moscheles founded in Granada during a Spanish tour in 1910. The only places where fresh creations flourished were outside Europe: in Australia, where the Movement (largely Quaker) was "non-sectarian and cosmopolitan," and in Japan, where there was already an active branch of the International Law Association.[2] In Central Europe the stagnation was partly due to intervention by the authorities. A placard issued by the Hamburg Peace Society in 1907, for instance, to emphasise the disasters that would ensue if the second Hague Conference should fail, was banned by the police. Student meetings throughout Austria-Hungary were likewise suspected and frequently treated as seditious. But despite repression a twofold Peace campaign was kept alive among the Czechs and Moravians—organised partly by the Students' Progressive Party and partly by the Women's societies, both of which groups had been articulate since 1890. Their combined programme was conditioned at first by anti-Semitic prejudice, which portrayed Jewish capitalism as the primary cause of wars. Later on their Peace propaganda became part of a political scheme to transform the Hapsburg monarchy into a federation—a "United States of Austria-Hungary," composed of seven independent units. From 1900 onwards this aspiration was popularised by two Czech leaders who afterwards gained world reputations—V. Psorn and Dr. Eduard Benes. Opposition drove it to assume after 1907 the more militant guise of a "congress of small and oppressed nations." From then till 1914 the most influential foundation in Central Europe was the Moravian Peace Union of 1910, an exclusively feminine body.[3]

[1] A. H. Fried, *Handbuch der Friedensbewegung* (1911 edition), pp. 299, 300; Suttner, *Memoirs*, ii, 120-2.

[2] *H. of P.* (1910), p. 38 ; (1906), p. 181.

[3] J. Grmela, *Peace Movement in Czechoslovakia* (English MS. trans.) ; and information supplied from Prague by M. Syrovy.

On the whole, then, it can be said of the national movements that where they could exert pressure on Governments in directions along which progress had already been made, they contrived to secure tangible results. This has been shown to be true for England and America. But in countries where popular internationalist thought ran in an opposite direction from official nationalist policy, the Peace Movement was either stifled or driven underground. In Scandinavia alone, for reasons of geography and race, were national interest and international sentiment at a maximum of identity.

(4) *The International Side,* 1900–1907

Encouraged by the potentialities rather than the achievements of the first Hague Conference, the annual musters begun in 1889 forged ahead with improvements in theory which might be offered to a second Hague Conference for translation into practice. This interim exploration was facilitated by the inauguration in certain countries of the preparatory National Congresses already noticed in England and France. The French example was taken up in 1904 in Great Britain, Italy, and Germany. The United States followed suit in 1907, Belgium in 1913. All were curtailed on the outbreak of war in 1914. Their importance is twofold. On the one hand they enabled the national groups to marshal their several contributions before setting out each year, and so made for briskness and resolution in the sessions of the Inter-Parliamentary and Universal Peace Conferences. In the second place, they have a historical value in revealing the diversity and the frequent cleavage in the world's organised Peace Movement, as well as the general unanimity which at the time was so powerful a stimulus.

We have already noticed in France the preference for federation as against fusion, and the insistence on a residuary right of self-defence. There emerged in 1904 a rough-and-ready compromise on sanctions; J. Dumas carried a resolution to the effect that arbitral awards should be enforced, if necessary, by "civil sanctions" that did not amount to war measures; for

17

example, the occupation of a disputed territory by a third Power pending the award.   Wherefore, with concrete bulwarks of this sort, the French Movement saw its way clear in the next year to recommend that the second Hague Conference should extend the practice of arbitral settlements to all disputes without exception, and make it universally obligatory. And from this there followed logically the conviction (recorded in 1906) that disarmament should be made the subject of a referendum in every country in which (for obvious reasons) women and children should take part.[1] The successive gatherings were dominated by the veterans of 1870–80 and by newcomers who later were to pilot the Movement through the War—Passy, Dumas, Prudhommeaux, and Ducommun.

In England fresh leaders emerged in the persons of the Hon. L. Courtney (later Lord Courtney of Penwith) and the Hon. Philip Stanhope (later Lord Weardale).   But, at least till 1907, the life of the congresses was concentrated in Darby, Cremer, and Felix Moscheles (the last named being Hodgson Pratt's successor).   Ninety-two organisations attended the first congress at Manchester in 1904.   Apart from routine resolutions on disarmament and against conscription, two distinctive features characterised these British gatherings, one of which was absent from the French deliberations, while the other was less hotly contested there. The first is the question of Parliamentary control of declarations of war.   Richard had first broached this in Parliament in 1886, to be echoed by Cremer two years later; and the Universal Peace Congress in London had recommended it in 1890.   It was now prosecuted by Sir James Macdonnell: though not until 1914 was the effort to achieve it crystallised into an organised agitation, and even to-day it is still unrealised.   The second problem was that of federation, advocated in the first instance by the Peace Committee of the Society of Friends.   Darby put up a stern fight against T. P. Newman, the Quaker sponsor, but he could do no more than register the Peace Society's qualified support.

---

[1] National Peace Congress *Reports*, Toulouse, 1902; Nimes, 1904; Lille, 1905; Grenoble, 1906, *passim*.

Federation was carried; and by the end of 1905 the National
Peace Council was fully organised as the quintessence of all the
Peace organisations in the country.   In this capacity it began
to seek a maximum of co-operation with the Trades Union
Congress.[1]

The parallel development in the United States was later and
slower.   The first American National Congress, indeed, was
not held until the year of the second Hague Conference.   But it
was more than merely a preparatory body devoted to canvassing
support for the Hague.   Its primary object was to educate
public opinion in America as to the significance of the Inter-
Parliamentary movement.   And its distinctive achievement was
the launching (also in 1907) of the American School Peace
League, which became perhaps the most influential of all the
juvenile propagandist bodies in the world.   Thereafter the
United States saw biennial National Conferences—with never
fewer than 1200 delegates—till 1915.[2]   Edwin D. Mead was
their most prominent and most indefatigable protagonist.

All these national groups and national programmes found
expression in the annual reunions organised by the Inter-Parliamentary Bureau and the International Peace Bureau set up in
1892.   To analyse fully the debates and resolutions preserved
in their reports is impossible.   All that can be done here is to
indicate salient lines of advance and trace the growth of threads
that ultimately survived the World War.

First and foremost, both series of conferences gained enor-
mously in respect.   Already ministers had been known to attend
their sittings.   After 1900 ministers invariably did so.   At Paris
in 1900 the Inter-Parliamentary proceedings were opened by the
President of the Senate, and the Universal Peace Congress was
attended by the Minister of Commerce; in 1902, at Monaco, the
Prince himself entertained the delegates; in 1905 in Brussels

---

[1] Its first adherents were the International Arbitration League
(Cremer), International Arbitration and Peace Association (Moscheles),
and Peace Society (Darby), with branches.   *See* Congress *Reports*,
Manchester, 1904; Bristol, 1905; Birmingham, 1906; Scarborough,
1907, *passim.*

[2] E. L. Whitney, *American Peace Society*, chap. xxxiv.

the Parliamentary groups were received by the King of the Belgians; and in 1906, when they met in London in the Royal Gallery of the House of Lords (Cremer's crowning triumph), the Prime Minister, Sir Henry Campbell-Bannerman, inspired them with an oration which denounced the race for armaments among the Powers and the quest of "a phantom security which continually vanishes as we approach."

Secondly, the gatherings no longer avoided, as of old, discussing current political problems. They realised by now that their task had reference to a present as well as to a future. Thus in 1900 both conferences passed strictures on Great Britain's refusal to arbitrate the Boer dispute as "an outrage on the conscience of mankind," though Darby urged that moderate condemnation would be equally valuable and far less dangerous to the prestige of the Movement. Three years later Hodgson Pratt carried through the Universal Peace Congress at Rouen a resolution condemning the British annexation of the Transvaal, annexations by force being "contrary to the fundamental principles of international justice." The Inter-Parliamentary Conference next year called on the signatories of the Hague Convention to intervene in the Russo-Japanese War. Even the age-long dispute between France and Germany over the Rhineland came up for discussion in 1906, and the Universal Peace Congress delegates of both countries agreed on the "inalienable right" of peoples "to dispose of themselves."

Thirdly, themes already familiar were gone over time and again with increasing definition and assurance. Projects were thrashed out for international Press unions; an international auxiliary language; a General Arbitration Treaty of universal scope and application (adopted by the Inter-Parliamentary Conference in 1906); an International University; Scandinavian neutralisation. The Belgian delegation, led by a newcomer, Henri La Fontaine, sought to restrict future arbitration treaties to matters not covered by the Hague Convention, and to make the Hague Tribunal the sole arbitral body. The French insistence, also, on the ultimate right of self-defence in certain circumstances, was vindicated: to the mortification of

Hodgson Pratt, who would have vetoed the discussion as outside the sphere of a Peace Congress. Darby subsequently quashed the resolution, however, when it came up for further discussion in the Berne Peace Bureau.

Fourthly, there were many innovations. Some were stillborn, by reason of inherent weaknesses. Stead proposed in 1901, for example, that in any country which refused all the four pacific means of settlement laid down by the Hague Conference, no religious services should be held that did not open with a confession of "blood-guiltiness" and end with an appeal to the Government to stop the war. Darby objected that such an "excommunication of humanity" would be a reversion to the Middle Ages, and held up the resolution until it was amended and rendered innocuous. Others were of wide significance for the future: in particular, a letter from Andrew Carnegie, read at the Universal Peace Congress at Boston in 1904, proposing a union of the Great Powers to declare that there should be no more war and to *enforce* the declaration. Eleven years later this paradoxical idea took shape in America as the League to Enforce Peace. It threw into relief the whole question of sanctions, on which there was no unanimity in either conference. La Fontaine and Darby fought out the question of sanctions at Milan in 1906, the former defending recourse to *pacific* constraint to effect an arbitral award—a strict economic boycott, the latter deploring *all* material constraint as unnecessary (since no award had ever been flouted) and pernicious (being a perpetuation of the War system). But the voting was so even that the day was not carried until a second count. Darby's opinion triumphed, by 78 votes to 71.

A second innovation, which the Inter-Parliamentary Conference actually nominated a committee to discuss (1905), was Ladd's project, long dormant, for a Permanent Congress of Nations. This got no further than the Committee's report, which recommended a World Congress of two houses, the Upper House the Hague Conference, and the Lower House the Inter-Parliamentary Union itself—executive and legislature respectively.

But the most arresting decision of the whole period was a lengthy document which did, in effect, what a fusion of the Kellogg Pact and the League of Nations Covenant will do at the present moment; that is, at once outlaw private war completely and buttress the outlawry with sanctions: abolishing private war, but consecrating the punishment of an outlaw State by the rest of the world.   The document was drawn up in 1902 by the Universal Peace Congress at Monaco.   It called itself a "Treaty of Pacigerant Alliance."   Its core lies in the third and ninth of its eleven articles.   Article 2 engaged the contracting parties "to submit to the Permanent Arbitration Court at the Hague . . . all disputes or differences which may arise between them, and which cannot be settled by diplomatic procedure, or by any other procedure chosen by common agreement, *whatever* may be the cause, the nature, and the object of these differences; and they, therefore, engage not to have recourse, directly or indirectly, to any act of war one towards the other."   Article 9 provided that in the last resort any State which infringed this solemn undertaking should be constrained to keep faith: all the contracting States would have the duty of aiding the Arbitrators "with the means of enforcing their award."   The vagueness of the concluding words was perhaps inevitable.   Sanctions were as yet an insoluble problem.   But, until the means of enforcement were specified, the Treaty could not be offered to Governments as a model draft.   Thus it had not yet become practical politics by the time the War came.   For the nature and effect of "pacific sanctions" did not begin to be definitively examined by the Universal Peace Congress until 1913, when the third Hague Conference was nearly due.   It exists to-day, therefore, as a prophecy and an anticipation.

(5) *The Second Hague Conference*, 1907

In so far, then, as the resolutions of both series of conferences were notified to Governments each year, there was ample material accruing to warrant a second Hague Conference.

The initiative for the summoning of the second Hague

Conference lies with a French statesman, the Baron d'Estournelles de Constant, as early as 1902: and for the very significant
reason that by 1902 the Hague Tribunal was beginning to be
regarded as a paper body only, imposing, quiescent, and harmless.
It had tried no cases, and it had been conveniently ignored by the
British Government in the Boer dispute (which was regarded in
England as a domestic question and therefore non-justiciable).
In September 1902, therefore, d'Estournelles de Constant prevailed on President Roosevelt to submit to the Court a minor
pecuniary dispute between the United States and Mexico.
The award was delivered within six weeks. As a result of the
precedent other cases were submitted: notably the financial
claims of ten Governments on Venezuela, which took over a
year to settle, and a protectorate dispute between Great Britain
and France in 1905 which was resolved in a fortnight. No
serious crisis was handled by the Hague Tribunal, however,
until 1909. The delicate Dogger Bank dispute between Great
Britain and Russia, during the Russo-Japanese War, was
composed by recourse to Commissions of Enquiry—the first
instance of its kind since the recommendation of such Commissions by the Hague Conference of 1899.[1]

It was in September 1904 that the first move was made
towards calling a second Conference, when an American,
T. E. Burton, carried through the Inter-Parliamentary Conference at St. Louis a resolution asking Roosevelt to take the
initiative. The President did so in a circular letter issued to the
Powers in the following October, but the proposal hung fire on
account of the Russo-Japanese War, and it was not until a year
later, after Roosevelt had facilitated negotiations to terminate
the war, that the Tsar issued a manifesto for the holding of a
second Conference (14th October 1905). It is noteworthy that
the American Peace Society had urged the President to offer
his services to end the war fully six months before he actually
did so.[2]

[1] See G. Moch, Hist. Sommaire de l'Arbitrage Permanent (1910
edition), pp. 80–2 ; L. S. Woolf, International Government, p. 49 ;
E. L. Whitney, American Peace Society, p. 212.

[2] Whitney, p. 252.

The Conference ultimately met at the Hague on 15th June 1907, and sat for four months, under the Presidency of the Russian politician Nelidov.　No fewer than forty-four sovereign States were represented, including nineteen American Republics which had not been invited in 1899.　As before, the work was done by Committees, behind closed doors, with plenary sessions at intervals to tabulate results.

As in 1899, the deliberations centred on arbitration and disarmament.　But of the ten additional Conventions that were added to those of 1899 there was not one that did not concern the Laws of War rather than the security of Peace: bombs, harbours, neutrals, balloons, right of capture at sea.　Of these conventions the most fruitful for future speculation was the Prize Court, which was established on a basis of compromise between two drafts, British and German.　For the rest, there was neither harmony nor clear perception on the two vital problems.　So that the findings of the Conference on arbitration and disarmament were embodied not in Conventions but in non-committal "recommendations."

The delegates confessed frankly that nothing could be done about the burden of armaments beyond urging Governments to "consider" it.　The question simply bristled with difficulties. No two nations were identically situated, politically, geographically, or spiritually.　In no country, either, did the military and naval budget give a reliable estimate of actual forces available. No general formula for limitation, therefore, could be found. And in the last resort the causes of war must first be removed.

How far they could be removed depended on how far the system of pacific settlement begun in 1899 could be developed. Here, again, the Conference did comparatively little.　Its "recommendations" included a Court of Arbitral Justice, planned in 35 articles without prejudice to the Court of Arbitration already in existence.　This was indeed an advance, for it amounted to a recognition of the fact that political disputes and legal disputes needed different treatment.　For the future, political disputes would go to the Court of Arbitration and legal disputes to the Court of Arbitral Justice.　But no line of demarcation was laid down—or even looked for—that would define when a dispute was, and when not, justiciable, or when primarily legal or primarily political. Perhaps such a line of division was impossible: but in any case the Conference was obsessed with National Honour. This obsession, again, hindered progress in the direction of *obligatory* arbitration. The Portuguese delegation submitted a general treaty of obligatory arbitration based on that drafted by the Inter-Parliamentary Conference in 1906. But its passage was obstructed by the German delegation, and in the end all that remained of it was a "general formula," adopted by only thirty-five of the forty-four States, declaring themselves "ready to have the common obligation of recourse to arbitration."

Chagrin, then, was the strongest sentiment inspired by the Conference when it rose in October. Its most hopeful provision, made at the instigation of Dr. Nicholas Murray Butler, who had stressed the point at the Lake Mohonk Conference earlier in the same year, was that a third Conference should meet at the Hague in 1915, and that the nations should together nominate a preparatory committee two years beforehand. The third Conference would thus be really international and not Russian in origin. But it was not destined to meet.[1] Within a year of the appointed time the unspoken fears and the half-realised dangers which had vitiated the work of both 1899 and 1907 produced a spectacle and an object-lesson which shook the faith of the Peace Movement throughout the world, temporarily disorganised and crippled it, and seemed for a time to have invalidated the consolidatory work it had done in the interval. That work was considerable.

(6) *Expansion, The Church Peace Union and Finance*

It is in a way ironical that the support most ardently desired by Peace workers since the earliest days of 1816 (and so urgently striven for in the face of apathy)—that is, organised backing

[1] *See* A. P. Higgins, *The Hague Conferences*, pp. 60–71 ; *Texts of Conventions*, etc., ed. J. B. Scott ; E. L. Whitney, *American Peace Society*, p. 227 ; L. S. Woolf, *International Government*, p. 51 ; N. M. Butler, *The International Mind*, p. 12.

from the Churches—was ultimately granted in the very year in which the World War began.   That it was secured then is due almost entirely to the persistence of one man, J. Allan Baker. Born in Canada in 1852 of Quaker stock, Allan Baker had lived in England since 1876, at first as salesman of his father's inventions, later as a temperance reformer and educationist, and after 1905 as Radical member for Finsbury.   His enduring work for Peace, spread over nine years, consisted in inspiring, organising, and in part financing the Movement which is known to-day as the World Alliance for Promoting International Friendships through the Churches.

The enterprise originated in 1906, in an idea of Baker's to use the Churches to solve one particular international problem— Anglo-German relations, which were growing tense on naval and colonial issues.   He planned and carried out reciprocal visits of representative British and German clergy throughout 1907; went to Germany himself in 1908 and interviewed the Kaiser; thundered in the House of Commons that the Churches must renounce their traditional attitude of "futile fatalism" towards war; secured financial support for his agitation from Andrew Carnegie; and welded together in 1909 an Anglo-German clerical committee to draw into the Movement the Churches of the whole world.

In December 1910 King George V received, after its inaugural meeting, the "Associated Councils of the Churches in the British and German Empires for fostering Friendly Relations between the Two Peoples."   At the same time, through the aid of the Peace Society, a more general organisation came into existence as the Church of England Peace League.   Both bodies suffered from Press criticism and public apathy during the Agadir crisis of 1911, but Baker had already crossed to America to begin the expansion of the Movement into a World Alliance.   The work of organisation was finally completed, simultaneously with the foundation of the American Church Peace Union and of branches in other national capitals, in 1914, when the Swiss Churches invited the Churches of the rest of the world to a Conference at Constance.

The Protestant section of the Constance Conference met on 1st August, despite the outbreak of war in Central Europe. It sent telegrams to all the rulers of Europe, and to the United States, imploring that war among the Powers might be averted. Then, after a hasty session which at last brought into being the World Alliance, the delegates hurried home on the last trains available before France and Germany entered the War. The Catholic section of the Conference, planned to meet at Liège on 10th August, was abandoned.[1]

Carnegie's munificence meanwhile had been expressed in a third channel, besides his gift to Baker's fund and his erection of a habitation for the Central American Court of Justice. He was the third financier to come to the aid of Peace, following Alfred Nobel in 1897 and Edwin Ginn in July 1910. The Carnegie Endowment for International Peace, administered by twenty-seven trustees, was started in December 1910, with a fund of ten million dollars. Three departments were set up—legal, historical, and educational. Among them were to be studied the causes of war, the record of pacifist efforts in the past, the development of international law, and the problem of influencing public opinion against war.[2] The Endowment functioned uninterruptedly during the World War, even after the entry of the United States. And it waxed continuously, until it is to-day the most influential, the most widely known, and the best respected of all the Peace organisations. Grants from it have kept alive many weaker pacifist bodies in Europe that would otherwise have perished with the War. And its two chief leaders, Dr. Nicholas Murray Butler and Dr. James Brown Scott, are among the world's greatest international thinkers of all time.

One other important attempt—this time governmental—to unite the international interests of the Powers was made before the outbreak of the War, in the International Parliamentary Commercial Conference, founded at the close of

[1] P. J. N. Baker, *Life of J. Allan Baker*, pp. 170 *seq.*, 206 *seq.*, 216 *seq.*; *H. of P.* (1909–10), *passim*; E. L. Whitney, *American Peace Society*, p. 265.

[2] See the Endowments' *Yearbooks*.

1913 on the initiative of the British House of Commons. The declared object was "to unite in common action commercial commissions, or legislation established in the principal Parliaments, in order to pursue a united front as regards the texts of laws on commercial affairs, and thus to assure to all nations participating . . . a more efficacious protection of their interests abroad."[1]   Nine Parliaments were represented at the first meeting in June 1914, but expansion was then curtailed (though not the meetings) until 1919.

(7) National Expansion Down to the War

It is impossible, again, to examine fully the history of the Peace Movement in its national centres during these last years before the War.   In all but the Anglo-Saxon countries no new threads emerged and no fresh successes were scored.   In England and America, on the contrary, the detail is so voluminous that only a broad comparative survey of vital developments is either useful or practicable.

The National Peace Congresses provide a key to what was happening.   Federation, the vaunted salvation of the Peace Movement, was soon being discussed in England as a possible salvation for Europe.   Victor Hugo's thesis of a United States of Europe, prominent for a time in and after 1867, was taken up by the Quaker section of the National Peace Council in 1910, and endorsed by the whole Congress in the following year,[2] to the glory of its spokesman, T. P. Newman.   Pacific sanctions and Parliamentary control of declarations of war at the same time brought into prominence two new champions, Ramsay MacDonald and G. H. Perris.   The Labour Party's threat, again, of a general strike in the event of war, was developed and endorsed in 1912.   Maurice Hewlett, the novelist, had vindicated the international strike as against "puerile" talk of disarmament in letters to the Daily News two years earlier. But in the United States, where the diplomatic horizon was less

[1] Report of the Conference of 1926 (London), p. 8.
[2] National Peace Congress Reports, Leicester, 1910 (p. 13), and Edinburgh, 1911.

clouded, speculation was more academic and less immediate. Moreover, the American Peace Movement had not yet settled the problem of its own organisation as in England and France. It was not till 1911 that the third National Peace Congress (at Baltimore) voted itself a permanent institution to be run by an executive committee representing every Peace organisation in the United States. Two years later the Congress was presided over by Woodrow Wilson.[1]

Thus both the national movements were now federated. Inside the federations, further, there were signs of new vigour infused by the younger recruits. The British Peace Society reorganised its propaganda in 1909 on a basis of four active sub-committees and a "consultative council." As part of the new efforts it launched next year a University Peace Movement from Aberdeen southwards. The American Peace Society moved its quarters by special legislative permission from Boston to Washington, where it became an agent of the Carnegie Endowment and hastened federation by taking under its own wing all the other pacifist bodies. Its revised Constitution was passed in 1912, with Arthur Deerin Call as Director.

It can be shown, too, that the argument against federation was not valid. The programmes and principles of the various component bodies were not levelled down to a dubious common factor. What federation did was rather to allow of specialised activity. The roads leading to international peace were the same for every society, but there were differences as to the kind of world that lay at the end of the journey. The ardent pacifist envisaged no constraint beyond the moral force of public opinion; the arbitrationist was more concerned to discover a system of combined sanctions—however extreme—that could be guaranteed to prevent war. Federation accommodated both philosophies by demanding of them not an identity of principle (which was impossible), but co-operation in action (which indeed they both desired).

And so it was. Cremer's fraternal addresses to the workers

[1] National Peace Congress Reports, London, 1912, Baltimore, 1911 ; E. L. Whitney, *American Peace Society*, chap. xxxiv.

of Germany during the last year of his life preached the means common to the whole Peace Movement but the standpoint peculiar to Labour. "Whatever may be the views of rulers, the producers of wealth have every reason for settling disputes without fighting each other. The quarrels of nations are not of their making, but they have to pay the cost of war and shed their blood." When he died in September 1908—"born in poverty but enriching humanity," knight, Nobel prize winner—his International Arbitration League passed under the direction of Frederick Maddison, who shepherded it through the War. J. Allan Baker, who (though the most active British pacifist in 1908–10) stood outside the societies, stressed rather the moral obligation of the Government to give the world a lead in disarmament. His Parliamentary speeches, apart from their emphasis on Anglo-German rivalry, repeatedly demanded a reduction in the Navy Estimates and a revision of foreign policy from a standpoint of "disarmament by international agreement." The Peace Society meanwhile fulminated against its own special bogeys—Lord Haldane's "Armed Nation," Lord Roberts's Territorial Army, the "Pan-Britannic Militia" of the National Service League, and even Baden-Powell's "insidious scheme" of Boy Scouts—from its own particular standpoint of Christian brotherhood. And E. D. Morel, the spokesman of "Democratic Control of Foreign Policy," unmasked the system of anarchic imperialism in his book *Morocco in Diplomacy* (1912), and founded a periodical on foreign affairs to educate the democracy that he would have take control.[1]

Anglo-American arbitration, however, provided the highest immediate goal for co-operation. But fortunately the statesmanship on both sides of the negotiations was so earnest and so truly internationalist that the feverish propaganda of old was not needed.

Had it not been for the jealous prerogatives of the United

---

[1] Howard Evans, *Cremer*, pp. 299–302 ; P. J. N. Baker, *Life of J. Allan Baker*, pp. 156, 163, 166–7 ; *H. of P.* (1909), p. 216 ; (1914), pp. 60 *seq.* ; S. Cocks, *Life of E. D. Morel*, pp. 178 *seq.*

States Senate, an arbitration treaty of triumphant proportions would already have been in operation for ten years, since 1897. Even now the Senate truncated two more drafts before 1914. The significance of the treaties of 1908 and 1911 lies, therefore, not in their eventual failure, but in their revelation of the enormous extent to which international understanding had grown as between the British and American Governments.

The treaties negotiated by Secretary Hay in 1904–5 had met the fate of their predecessor of 1897. The third attempt, in April 1908, resulted in twenty-seven treaties signed by Elihu Root with foreign Governments, to last for five years. Each of them contained two articles, providing that all disputes save the fateful reservations should be taken before the Hague Court in the event of deadlock. In each case the question in dispute was to be defined by prior agreement between the parties, together with the scope of the arbitration. Mr. Bryce, who signed the British treaty, included in his reservations "all questions affecting her autonomous colonies, which she will have the right to consult before concluding an agreement." The American Senate ratified all the twenty-seven after destroying their value by a formula asserting its right of "advice and consent."

Similarly in 1911. But the terms of the 1911 treaties far transcended those of 1908; and the reason for the advance is to be found in an epoch-marking speech delivered by President Taft on 22nd March 1910. Taft's words reveal how disastrously the Senatorial veto was stifling the cry for pacific settlement. "Personally," he declared, "I do not see any more reason why matters of national honour should not be referred to a court of arbitration than matters of property or of national proprietorship. I know that it is going further than most men are willing to go, but I do not see why questions of honour may not be submitted to a tribunal composed of men of honour, who understand questions of national honour, to abide by their decision, as well as any other questions of difference arising between nations." This was a mighty pronouncement. It amounted to a declaration of faith, by the head of one of the

Great Powers, in unconditional "all-in" arbitration. As such, it forms the link between the treaties of 1908 and 1911. Not only did Taft reiterate it at the Conference of the newly founded American Society for the Judicial Settlement of International Disputes in the following December, but it prompted declarations in the same spirit in Great Britain. Sir Edward Grey echoed it in the House of Commons on 13th March 1911, and Mr Asquith on 28th April.

Accordingly the Knox-Bryce Treaty of 3rd August 1911, and its counterpart between the United States and France, took a new line. The types of questions to be arbitrated were specified, and *all* others were to be left to Commissions of Enquiry as in the Hague Convention of 1899. The question of justiciability also (of whether a dispute fell into one of the arbitrable categories) was to be settled by a Commission of Enquiry should the need arise. This represents the climax of a century of Anglo-American arbitration.

But the Senate killed it. To allow a Commission of Enquiry to decide the justiciability of a dispute would be to allow a Commission of Enquiry to "bring a case to court"; and this was the Senate's own function and duty under the American Constitution. But, on the other hand, it was equally true that to allow the Senate to assume the function of grand jury in its own disputes was impossible. Nothing short of a constitutional amendment, destroying the Senatorial treaty-veto, could cut the knot. So that Taft bitterly declined to submit the amended document to the French and British Governments.

The form of treaty which finally passed the Senate, in August 1914, was a sorry travesty of the text of 1911, though it had the merit of remaining in force indefinitely until one of the parties should terminate it. Thirty treaties were negotiated altogether in the winter of 1913–14. The Senate ratified them all: and twenty-one of them were still in force in 1926. They provided that in all disputes which could not be settled by diplomatic means the parties should seek the "investigation and report" of a Committee of Enquiry, and not declare war or begin hostilities before the report appeared. The details were fixed of

how the Commission was to be chosen.   But *after* the issue of
the Commissioner's report the parties "reserve the right to act
independently on the subject-matter of the dispute."   They
were bound to nothing except to seek and wait for an impartial
report.   Nevertheless, this very interim period would be of
value in allowing national passions to cool down, and reason to
take the place of excitement.   And this is perhaps the strongest
argument behind the idea of arbitration.[1]

(8) *International Developments to* 1914

Meanwhile the expansion of the international work of the
Peace Movement was conditioned by four main sources of
strength: first, increased recognition—Edward VII received
the Universal Peace Congress in a deputation in 1908, and
Bülow, the German Chancellor, addressed the Inter-Parliamentary Conference; secondly, the presence of Trade Union
Congress delegates at the Universal Peace Congresses from 1908
onwards; thirdly, the steady formation of fresh groups of the
Inter-Parliamentary Union, until by 1914 there were twenty-five
national groups, totalling no less than thirty-seven per cent. of
the aggregate membership of the twenty-five Parliaments; and,
lastly, reorganisation of the Inter-Parliamentary Bureau under
a permanent chairman.

Beyond the annual review of fundamental problems like
obligatory arbitration, and of particular crises like that in
Morocco in 1912, new tendencies appeared from time to time,
to be either taken up or shelved.   The idea of a Pan-Europe, for
example, modelled on Pan-America, was very much in the air
during 1909–10.   The Berne Peace Bureau endorsed it on
behalf of the World's Peace Movement, and it was known to be
favoured also by Caprivi, the new German Chancellor.   On the
popular side, in the same year 1910, 18th May was chosen as

[1] Texts of all the treaties in W.P.F. pamphlet on *Arbitration*
(1926), pp. 521–41 ; see also G. Moch, *Hist. Sommaire d'Arbitrage
Permanent* (1910 edition), pp. 94–5 ; W. I. Hull, *The New Peace
Movement*, pp. 70–7 ; E. L. Whitney, *American Peace Society*, pp.
233, 296.

Peace Day (the anniversary of the first Hague Conference) to be observed in schools.

The one outstanding achievement between the second Hague Conference and 1914 occurred at the London meeting of the Universal Peace Congress in 1908, when four bases were laid down for a complete "Society of Nations." They were a Legislative Council to draft a Code of International Law, a Judicial Authority to apply it, an Executive to watch over common interests, and a reduction of armaments to a police minimum. But no committee was erected to investigate sanctions until 1913: and the Congress to which that committee was to report never met.

Most of the work of both conferences was carried out with a view to the third Hague Conference due to meet in 1915. The Hague Court of Arbitration had already scored its first real triumph in 1909 over the famous Casablanca dispute in Morocco, which was settled by it in three weeks after having at one time threatened to produce a European war. A conference of ten Powers in London, moreover, had endeavoured to furnish the Hague Prize Court (proposed in 1907) with a Code of Maritime Law for its dispensation. But to friends of Peace the very existence of a Prize Court pre-supposed a war system. And in point of fact, the Prize Court never came into existence; while the Declaration of London of 1909 was rendered obsolete as naval warfare developed during the War. In America the coming Hague Conference was heralded by three gigantic Peace Demonstrations during 1907-10, followed by a world-tour by Anna B. Eckstein to build up a universal petition. She had presented already a petition from 5,000,000 people to the Hague Conference of 1907. In England propaganda was intensified by the fact that the Peace Society's own centenary would arrive in 1916. Preparations were going on all over the world by the time the Palace of Peace was opened at the Hague in August 1913.[1] Then within a year all was chaos.

[1] G. Moch, *Hist. Sommaire d'Arbitrage Permanent* (1910 edition), pp. 80-2 ; E. L. Whitney, *American Peace Society*, chap. xxxv; *H. of P.* (1910), pp. 146-7, 164 ; (1913), pp. 36-7.

(9) *Summary and Estimate*, 1914

The causes of the War and the question of its inevitability are no direct concern of the present study; though it is noteworthy, in passing, that since the Treaty of Versailles statesmanship and diplomacy have been conditioned—at least officially—by the explicit assumption that war in the future can be prevented. What is of vital moment here is that the warnings uttered by statesmen just before 1914, when the "International Anarchy" was heading unmistakably to a crisis, had been current for just on a century; that the case against modern international warfare had been stated in turn, and with a steady increase in volume, by religious sectarians, economists, socialists, biologists, lawyers, strategists, and financiers; and that, although it cannot be claimed that the Peace Movement, popular or parliamentary, is to be credited with the sum-total of governmental action for World Peace prior to 1914, it is true that at many points the Peace Movement stimulated Government action, that at all points the Peace Movement popularised every step made towards international security, and that the greatest pre-war triumph of all, the Anglo-American Treaty of 1897, was the creation of organised pacifism.

The history of pacifism and internationalism during the century ended by the War resolves itself into three phases. First, the phase down to 1867, the period of the first and primarily religious movement, the period of exposition, culminating in the conferences of 1848–53. Secondly, the phase from 1867 to 1889, the years of the second and dominantly economic movement, in which governmental action was secured in the one direction of arbitration, and the Peace Movement was organised throughout the whole world; and thirdly, the quarter-century from 1889 to 1914, in which the theory of Peace was more and more explored by Governments, with the Peace Movement concentrated once more on exposition and popular propaganda.

And the record of achievement had been considerable. The problem was to find alternatives to war more reliable than ordinary diplomacy. By 1914 none of the alternatives discovered had ever broken down, whether the settlement was by "good offices," mediation, Commissions of Enquiry, Councils of Conciliation, formal arbitration in political cases, or judicial settlement in legal disputes.

But when the War came, to interrupt progress and devastate the Peace Movement, there was still much to do. Arbitration was "general" and "all-in," but it was not yet universally obligatory. Its record was but a list of individual cases and bi-lateral treaties; States were under no fixed obligation to have recourse to the Hague Tribunal. Nor was there in existence a precise Code of International Law available for impartial dispensation by the Hague or any other tribunal. Nor (most important of all) was there a definitely organised "Society of Nations" as envisaged over seventy years earlier by Ladd and Jay.

To put the matter in another way, progress had gone far along the two natural lines of law and politics, judicial tribunals and diplomatic conferences, but the potentialities of these two lines of advance had not been as yet completely realised except by the Peace Movement. Progress in both directions, if honestly pursued, led to the establishment of a League of Nations on a federal basis: not to a "Super-State," for national diversities and nationalist feeling were too pronounced for this, even if (and the point is doubtful) it were ideally desirable: but to a federal union of independent sovereign States, an organised Society of Nations, equipped with a Tribunal and a Code of Law. The work of both series of Peace Congresses was tending towards this goal. Precedents for its constitution and practicability existed in the British Empire and the Pan-American Union. The phrase "League of Nations" had been consecrated by both the Hague Conferences. And the principle of federation as against the "Super-State" had been the keynote of every Peace plan since the *Great Design* of Henry IV. The equality of sovereign States was fundamental to the peace of the world.[1]

It was left to the World War, by making certain the fear that an unorganised world would eventually mean the death of civilisation, to force a trial of this idea of a League of Nations as the only practical salvation. Meanwhile the shock of war staggered a Peace Movement comprising over 130 organisations in 26 countries, whose attitude to the crisis, when it came, had been resolutely indicated two years before. "Every pacifist ought to regard it as his sacred duty to oppose any war of conquest undertaken by the Government of his country, and he should endeavour, if need be at the peril of his life, by all the means at his command, to demonstrate, before public opinion and in the Press, the injustice of such a war and the possibility of recourse being had to one of the pacific methods of settling international disputes."[2] How the different sections of the Movement applied the phrase "war of conquest," and how their pacifism reacted to the outbreak of 1914, is left to the following chapter.

[1] For this subject see R. L. Jones, *International Arbitration* (1907), chap. ix, pp. 149–73 ; L. S. Woolf, *International Government* (1917), pp. 19, 64–5 ; W. I. Hull, *The New Peace Movement* (1912), p. 46 seq.

[2] Resolution of Nineteenth Universal Peace Congress, Geneva, 1912.

CHAPTER XI

"THE war psychology drives people against people until blood and slaughter appear the most human and natural things possible." August 1914 paralysed rational thinking, degraded the Press to the lowest levels of calumny and invective, and produced a state of hysteria in which nations rushed into action the first contingents of 38,000,000 men, the full mobilised strength of Europe.

So overwhelming was the convulsion, that from the very first moment the problem of the Peace Movement was one not of influence but of survival. Outside its ranks it met with suspicion and contempt, with the charge of "defeatism"; in all but a few countries, with ruthless suppression. Within its ranks it suffered disillusionments, heresies, and desertions. Two extremes rapidly swallowed up its moderates of a month before: despair, which issued in "an utter denial of the possibility of any true interstatal society"; and desperation, which saw no alternative to destruction except in "a League of Nations that should become a Super-State." Not that pacifist thought was dumbfounded altogether. It still functioned along its three strongest channels, religious, economic, and juristic. But its name was discredited, its ranks were thinned, and its articulate expression became a sheer physical impossibility. Blockades soon rendered it impossible for national groups to meet or correspond. Even bodies like the International Law Association, which were not fundamentally inspired by the "exploded conspiracy" of international peace, had to suspend their conferences.

The result was that, save for occasional furtive meetings in neutral countries, attended by every conceivable wartime risk, the Peace Movement, purged of its apostates, survived as disorganised isolated groups, faced with a task at once smaller and greater than before the cataclysm.   Smaller, in the sense that the immediate need was to act on public opinion to the utmost in order to make possible, at the close of this particular war, a peace treaty dictated by reason and not by rancour. Greater, in that the mass of theorising done since 1816 had to be re-examined and co-ordinated into a system on which could be erected the white hope of a Society of Nations.   It has to be shown how all this was done, and how far its performance influenced the League of Nations as ultimately constituted.

The general defence of pacifism during the War is to be found in an inspired passage in the London *Herald of Peace* in May 1915.   It is a defence based on the loftiest principles. "Is personal neutrality possible if your country is at war? Certainly.   Why not?   You are a separate entity by no means identical with your country, a moral being with responsibilities and an immortal destiny. . . . The pacifist has no chance when his country is at war. . . . Strict personal neutrality becomes imperative.   He cannot side *with* his country, for, being patriotic, he cannot assist her (or, rather, the political party which has temporarily the control of things) in destroying herself as well as her opponent; as a humanitarian he cannot join in the slaughter of human beings; and being a pacifist he dare not be an accomplice in the war.   He cannot side *against* her, for the same reasons accentuated a thousandfold.   It may be asked, Must he not, being patriotic, stand by her?   Yes, in higher matters and in the true sense, at the cost of any sacrifice, and with a glad readiness to sacrifice himself for her good.   But the insanity of war-making has no binding claim upon anyone to rational and moral obligation, and, outside and beyond that folly, there are a thousand links of affection that are untouched even by her crime.   A child is not filially bound to share in a parent's crime. . . . Finally, this is a personal question which each must determine, and in judging such ethical questions each is answerable at the bar of his own conscience, and there only."

(1) *Disorganisation of the International Movement*

As organised since 1889, the Peace Movement was thrown completely out of gear. Of at least sixteen non-governmental bodies which were in existence in 1914 to serve some purpose directly concerned with international peace, only those whose headquarters were in neutral countries remained active. Thus the Nobel Institute in Norway continued its work, though that work had always been confined to the purely academic side of the movement. Similarly the Carnegie Endowment in Washington—until 1917: when it threw in its lot with the Government on the entry of the United States into the War. But bodies like the two International Law Societies, the International Students' Union of 1898, "International Conciliation" of 1905, and sectional federations such as the International League of Catholic Pacifists (founded 1911) were in abeyance, as far as their administration went, until the end of the War.

The kernel of the whole Movement, the International Peace Bureau at Berne, was compelled to sublimate its energies in other ways than through the Universal Peace Congresses. The Congress planned to meet in Stockholm in the late summer of 1914 never met. Instead, the Bureau began to take advantage of its position in a neutral country surrounded by belligerents, to alleviate the plight of prisoners of war and interned aliens by means of a postal clearing-house. The Inter-Parliamentary Union, on the other side of the Movement, ceased to function altogether. The preparations for its Stockholm Conference were curtailed, the elaborate scheme evolved by its committees for a form of "permanent international jurisdiction based on obligatory arbitration" was interrupted, and the Bureau removed from Brussels to Christiania, where it maintained complete silence upon the War and confined its attention to exploring in isolation the bases of a durable peace. Of the twenty-six national groups, only those in Scandinavia, and in Great Britain and America, continued their national meetings. The Inter-Parliamentary Commercial Conference, however, remained nominally unaffected. It held its annual conferences through-

ANDREW CARNEGIE

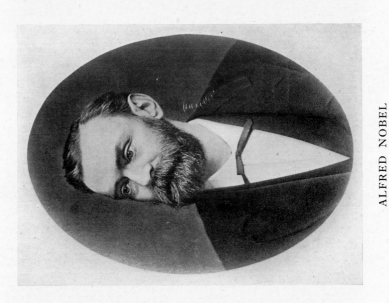

ALFRED NOBEL

out the War, even in belligerent capitals (in 1915–16 in Paris, in 1917 in Rome, and in 1918 in London); though the personnel was scanty, and the subjects discussed were commercial and not pacific.[1]

But despite the disruption of almost every link that bound the movement together, there emerged within twelve months of the outbreak an organisation which not only surmounted difficulties of travel and prohibitions by Governments, but recapitulated the whole history of the Peace Movement within three months. It began with no more than a score of people, all women, and in three short months it had reached the ear of President Wilson. Its influence on the Fourteen Points is undoubted.

The women, Belgian, Dutch, German, and British, met in the spring of 1915 to form a committee for the purpose of organising an International League of Women for Peace and Liberty. The congress in which the League was launched, on 18th April 1915, at the Hague, numbered over 1100 women from 12 countries. Many of the delegates—the British in particular—attended in spite of definite prohibition by their Governments. Their immediate task was to find a stable basis for peace at the close of hostilities. But when this had been done, the Movement broadened out and the organisation became permanent. At its head was Dr. Aletta Jacobs, the leader of the feminist movement in Holland. The League's programme is important as one of the earliest to be evolved during the War. Its terms were made known to all the Governments of Europe and America by the proven method of special deputations. And in this wise Jane Adams, who had presided at the opening congress, heard from Wilson's own lips three months later that "I have studied these resolutions, and I consider them the best proposals that have been formulated by any association."[2] There is at all events a marked coincidence of emphasis between the League's recommendations and the Fourteen Points: a concentration on the right of peoples to dispose of themselves, on democratic

[1] International Peace Bureau *Annuaire* (1924), *passim*.
[2] *Ibid.*, p. 66.

control of foreign policy, on the freedom of the seas, on open diplomacy, on State monopoly of munitions of war as the first step towards disarmament, and on a League of Nations "based on a constructive peace." All these principles were further defined by the bureau set up in Amsterdam, and in four other congresses held in neutral territory later in the War.

The output of similar speculations apart from this was phenomenal. But all of it, until co-ordination became possible through the medium of a committee established in Holland, was undertaken by pacifists in different countries independently of their allies abroad. Five projects stand out among many—one in each of the principal belligerent Powers, and one neutral— British, American, French, German, and Dutch. They will be noticed in surveying the national aspects of the Peace Movement during the four years.

(2) *National Endeavours*

(a) *Great Britain: Cleavage and Recovery*

The sections of the Peace Movement in Britain which remained true to their ideal were co-ordinated throughout, as since 1904, by the National Peace Council. Their attitude was determined largely by their judgment as to the origins of the War. They believed the War to have sprung from public ignorance on matters of foreign policy, from secret diplomacy, and from a "poisoned Press"—and they held that the responsibility of Germany and Austria-Hungary was immediate only. A war, moreover, precipitated by the anarchy of the preceding ten years would most likely fail to achieve the ends of Peace. The danger was that one military power would be put down only to give place to a stronger military alliance inimical to any League of Nations that might be created.[1]

Accordingly the first practical step taken towards preparing a national state of mind sane enough to conclude a durable peace when the time came, occurred in October 1914 in the foundation of the Union of Democratic Control. This was the first

---

[1] Cf. *H. of P.* (1920), p. 130.

organised effort to achieve that popular control of foreign policy which had been demanded in turn by Richard, Cremer, the Universal Peace Congress of 1890, the Manchester Peace Congress of 1904, and the Edinburgh Congress of 1911. The founder of the U.D.C. was E. D. Morel, already notorious for his book on Morocco, in which he had scourged both the British and German public for risking "finding itself involved in war without any real knowledge of the why and the wherefore." His three watchwords were Native Rights, Freedom of Trade, and open Diplomacy. In the last of these he had behind him the bulk of the Liberal Press. The *Manchester Guardian* in particular was of use to him at this juncture by its revelation of Lord Grey's official denial of an obligation to help France which really had existed. Morel founded the Union in company with Ramsay MacDonald, Norman Angell, C. P. Trevelyan, and Arthur Ponsonby. It was not a Peace society nor a stop-the-war movement, though the Press very soon vilified it as both. Its aim, beyond the principle inherent in its title, was to work out the bases of a lasting peace. And fundamental to such peace would be Parliamentary consent to all treaties, plebiscites in all provinces transferred at the end of the War, foreign policy working no longer for Balance of Power but for an international community, rationalisation of the production of armaments as a prelude to their reduction by international agreement, and (added in 1917) no continuance of an "economic war" after hostilities had ceased. But Morel would not be dissuaded from going further and airing the "causes of the war" to a public that had no interest but to win it. His mitigations of the invasion of Belgium only won him contumely, till in 1917 he found himself in prison for contravening the Defence of the Realm Act in sending a manuscript to Switzerland.[1]

The Peace Society from the outset remained passive. It never once wavered in its principles, but its existence during the War can be traced only in its annual meetings. The *Herald of Peace* virtually died. As early as 1891 the Society's attitude

---

[1] S. Cocks, *E. D. Morel*, pp. 191, 212, 225-6, and *passim*.

to an invasion of Belgium had been explicit. "If the people of England were foolish enough to consent to a war for the defence of that small country, such a conflict would be an incomparably greater evil and involve vastly more terrible sufferings and losses than the possible annexation of Belgium to France or Germany." To this the Society now held, though the President, the Right Hon. Joseph Pease, who was Minister of Education, proclaimed (and called upon the teachers to instil into their pupils) that England's cause in the War was just—self-defence "against the spirit of aggressive domination." He nevertheless remained for a time at the head of the Society. Darby, who had been its Secretary since 1890, resigned through sheer exhaustion at the close of 1915—a staunch pacifist to the end. One of his last articles was devoted to scorning the current talk of a "last war." "There is only one way to secure lasting peace, and that is to end the preparations and the conditions which make war possible." His place was taken by the Rev. Herbert Dunnico, M.P. The Society's active work dwindled to two travelling-agents. Beyond this its sole articulation was a scheme of peace passed at the annual meeting in May 1915, when Pease had been succeeded by J. P. Fry. This ran parallel to that of the Union of Democratic Control save in two respects: it made no reference to popular control of foreign policy, but it demanded a Court of Justice for the world and an International Council of Conciliation. Sanctions, of course, were ruled out; in its uncompromising pacifism the Society bitterly opposed the Compulsory Military Service Act of 1916.[1]

Furthermore, though some organisations went over to the War, the British Peace Movement as a whole was unanimous in the manifesto which it combined to issue in October 1914 on *The Duty of Pacifists in the Present Crisis*. The document was signed by Carl Heath (for the National Peace Council), Darby (for the Peace Society), Maddison (for Cremer's International Arbitration League), and J. F. Green (for Pratt's International Arbitration and Peace Association). It set out the duty of

---

[1] *H. of P.* (1891), p. 186 ; (1914), pp. 104, 107 ; (1915), pp. 113, 126, 157, 206, 235.

pacifists as twofold: a duty to humanity, to watch for the first reasonable chance to end the War by United States mediation; and a duty to their country, to provide for the wounded and the destitute ("we are not at war with individuals"), and to be tolerant towards enemy nationals "in our midst."

Some took this middle course. Allan Baker, for instance, went off to minister to the sick in distressed areas. But there were dissensions in the National Peace Council. G. H. Perris of the International Arbitration and Peace Association carried away from the Movement a large following, leaving as his last contribution to his society's journal a defence of his secession founded on the fact that he had never been a "Non-Resister." The Council as a whole, however, interpreted "war" in the widest sense and remained pledged to pacifism. To this extent its later name—National Council for the Prevention of War—is a misnomer; for there were no sanctions in the scheme for future peace which it subsequently evolved.

The Free Churches also went over. Above the signatures of J. Compton Rickett, F. B. Meyer, and J. Scott Lidgett they issued appeals for enlistment in June 1915. But the Baptist Union declined the responsibility of giving direction to its ministers in the matter of joining the colours. The Established Church, of course, had its duty to the State. "Can we admit for a moment," asked the Bishop of London at St. Paul's in July 1915, "that the soul of a nation which won Agincourt, which flung back the Armada, which withstood for many years the armies of Napoleon, is not so great as the soul of other nations?" And in reply to criticisms like that of the Peace Society, which railed at the "sorry figure" which Ecclesiasticism had cut in "this European horror," Father Bernard Vaughan objected that it was absurd to say that Christianity had failed, since Christianity was the one thing that had "never been tried." [1] And ministers rebuked the conscientious objector with an admonition that he might have shown a more robust Christianity by sharing the sacrifice of his fellow-countrymen.

It was not until the third year of the War that a movement was

[1] *Catholic Herald* (January 1916); *H. of P.* (1916), p. 2.

made, outside the Establishment, to consolidate Peace feeling in the Churches. But in the summer of 1916 "Peace Fellowships" were founded from four sources—the Baptists, the United Free Church, the Primitive Methodists, and the Wesleyan Methodists. All four fellowships passed resolutions against militarism in schools, and for the abandonment of a "knockout-blow policy" at the end of the War. Then, taking "peace by conciliation" for their keynote, they amalgamated in 1917 to form the United Peace Fellowship, inspired by the principle first voiced in 1816, that "war and preparation for war are contrary to the spirit and teaching of Jesus Christ." They appealed to the Government to make peace.

This was, of course, a purely national organisation. The World Alliance of 1914 had been out of action since its inaugural meeting. The other great religious pacifist society, the Society of Friends, stated its case unfalteringly at the opening of the War, and thereafter suffered for its faith. Its "War Message" in August 1914 reached as many as half a million people in the British Isles, and was circulated in four languages throughout the British Empire. Even under Government prosecution this pamphlet propaganda continued throughout the War, while individual Quakers answered a call to help in repatriating women and children, succouring destitute aliens, and recruiting the War Victims' Relief Committee.[1] In this work they were aided by the members of what later became the International Fellowship of Reconciliation, a secular Christian movement born in England towards the close of 1914, which by 1919 was to spread across two continents and become truly international.

Pacifism had meanwhile fought its supreme battle of Non-Resistance over the Conscription Act of 1914. As soon as compulsory military service in England became likely, late in 1914, attempts were made by the Socialist Fenner Brockway and his wife to collect the names of all British war-resisters. From this first step there grew up during the next year a No Conscription Fellowship; and though conscientious objection

[1] M. E. Hirst, *Quakers in Peace and War*, pp. 493–520.

was widespread in other countries, it was only in England that an organised passive resistance was developed. Led by Fenner Brockway, Clifford Allen, and W. J. Chamberlain, the No Conscription Fellowship contested the Conscription Bill until its passage into law rendered further propaganda illegal, and thereafter held to its faith by individual refusals to fight, which were dealt with by tribunals whose sympathy, never strong, rapidly gave place to ruthless repression. The standpoint of the Movement, outlined in its constitution, was that "because they consider human life to be sacred . . . they deny the right of Governments to say 'You shall bear arms.' . . . There is one interference with individual judgment that no State in the world has any sanction to tamper with—that is to tamper with the unfettered free right of every man to decide for himself the issue of life and death." That the Movement recruited many cowards and mere wasters is not material; for the cowards, when offered the alternative of some form of non-combatant service, accepted it. The heroes were the men who faced the tribunals unflinchingly, even to the extent of hearing their death sentences read out to them. Of these there were thirty. All their sentences were subsequently commuted, however, to imprisonment in England.

After the War the conscientious objection movement was erected into the present No More War Movement, founded in February 1921. The Labour Party, the Trades Union Congress, and the Co-operative Congress likewise became pledged to war resistance. Every member of the No More War Movement signed an individual declaration identical in substance with that of Burritt's League of Universal Brotherhood in 1846; and relations were opened up with war resisters in twenty-one other countries to form the War Resisters' International. The World War, therefore, brought into being a universal pacifist organisation of wider scope than any before founded.[1]

Theory, however, did not lag behind action. As early as the autumn of 1914 a body known as the "Bryce Group," led by

[1] See full account in W. J. Chamberlain, *Fighting for Peace* (1928).

Lord Bryce and G. Lowes Dickinson, was formed in London to study the future possible organisation of the world, which it ultimately pronounced upon in two sets of proposals "for the Prevention of Future Wars." At the same time, the realisation that at last some Society of Nations was necessary to collectivise the responsibility for preserving peace, set in motion forces which produced, in March 1915, the League of Nations Society. Here, in contrast to the plan of the Peace Society, the maintenance of peace was to be definitely enforced. A League of Nations was to be established at the end of the War, open to all civilised States, allied and enemy. Future disputes were to be taken before the Hague Tribunal if judicial and to International Commissions of Conciliation and Enquiry if political; and the sanctions to be used to compel aggressor States to have recourse to arbitration were to be the severest possible.[1] In short, the plan was essentially that of the later League to Enforce Peace formed in America.

Recourse to sanctions in violation of obligations was no doubt an inevitable provision. The example of Belgium was too convincing to be ignored. Lord Rosebery's famous utterance of November 1915 was typical of the thoughts current among disillusioned friends of peace. "In future it will be quite impossible to take note of treaty arrangements between Great Powers without obtaining some material guarantee for their observance. . . . Distrust must go beyond Prussia, because after what we have seen . . . no nation will feel itself safe if it bases its apprehension of Peace on anything but some material guarantee of its own—that is, in the long vista, force." In this way, when the pacific section of the Labour Party initiated a debate in the House of Commons in which they demanded to know on what terms the Allies would make peace, the occasion served only to amplify this very fear. Philip Snowden and C. P. Trevelyan, the Labour spokesmen, were powerless. The Allies' terms were subsequently reiterated by the Prime Minister in March: they comprised not only the evacuation of France, Belgium, and Serbia, with full compensa-

[1] C. L. Lange, *Société des Nations pendant La Guerre*, p. 26.

tion for the devastation, but the destruction of "the military domination of Prussia." In the eyes of the pacifists this last formula meant a war of attrition; for Germany had already taken it to imply the destruction of her independence. The Labour Party as a whole ultimately resolved to oppose the Government at the next election, when obstacles were placed in the way of delegates travelling from England to an International Socialist Peace Congress at Stockholm in August 1917. Arthur Henderson resigned from the Lloyd George War Cabinet.

But the most valuable contributions to Peace thought in England came from the pen of Leonard S. Woolf in 1916–17. His two books, *International Government* and *The Framework of a Lasting Peace*, form the culmination of his years of labour for the Fabian Society. The first went into the whole question of arbitration, whose scope it greatly widened by destroying the vital difference between legal and political disputes. The second applied his conclusions to the concrete task of organising a Society of Nations in an analysis of all the important plans hitherto advanced during the War. His *International Government* has been an invaluable source of guidance in the theoretical parts of this book.

Such in brief was the development of theory and practice in Great Britain in 1914–18. Its three outstanding manifestations were the principle of the Union of Democratic Control, the formation of the League of Nations Society, and Leonard Woolf's analysis. The final consummation of the League of Nations placed the Peace Movement in an altered position.

(b) *The United States : Disintegration*

Far more fundamental, though less disastrous at first, was the effect of the War upon the Peace Movement in America. At first there was little more than an interruption in the co-operation of American with European organisations. Neutrality allowed a detachment that the European bodies could not enjoy, and enabled American pacifism to express itself firmly without heavy responsibility. Thus, although the celebrations

19

which Allan Baker had been planning for the centenary of the Treaty of Ghent had to be curtailed, and Anglo-American friendship entered on its second century almost without comment, there was no searching of consciences in the United States Peace Movement until President Wilson entered the War in 1917.

The American Peace Society formally denounced the War in the autumn of 1914, and diagnosed its causes in the light of the preceding ten years' diplomacy. "The wonder is not that the war broke out this summer upon Europe, but that it did not begin years ago. . . . The real cause of the conflict is the piled-up armaments and war materials in Europe . . . for forty years, and the suspicions, jealousies, falsehoods, and ambitions which attended and vitalised them." And the moral was drawn—"No delusion was ever greater than that implements of war . . . are guarantees of peace and safety. This is the supreme lesson of the World War now devouring Europe and mocking civilisation."

But as the exigencies of the Government during the German submarine blockade became acute in 1916, and as American participation in the War grew more and more likely, the attitude of the Society changed, until it finally ranged itself behind the President and substituted war propaganda for peace propaganda. The reasons for the *volte face* form a remarkable parallel to the arguments on which the Society had risked schism in 1838. It never relinquished its condemnation of war as an institution, as representing "a barbaric, an unnatural, and a dying civilisation." But by April 1917 it had begun to recognise "that we are living in an ungoverned world." It admitted the possibility that the United States might enter the War, though it refused to accept any responsibility, one way or the other, for what the Government should decide. Two months later it was solidly behind the Government: whereafter its utterances became in turn explanatory, polemical, and bellicose. "Our first duty to Germany is to convince her, with all the power at our command, that we are launched upon this enterprise as a serious matter of business. We are at war. . . . We have a duty to perform, and we purpose to perform it. . . . This war is not a war of territory, of trade-routes, or of commercial concerns, but of eternal principles. . . . The American Peace Society stands for international peace and justice; [but] it finds nothing in that programme conflicting with the action of any American citizen in the present situation. . . . The American Peace Society supports the Government in this war, [and] will support and not obstruct the actions of that Government in the present situation so long as those actions represent the will of the majority. . . . The world has reached a situation where the judicial settlement of international disputes is for the time impracticable. This does not mean that our opposition to war is abated. Quite the contrary. We are opposed to any war. We are opposed to this war. [But] it is clearly within the realm of defensible duty that when our country is in danger we should rally to our country's support. The abolition of war is an international job. Were we to stop this war to-day, it would not mean that the disease of war would be cured, or even ameliorated. A universal disease requires a universal remedy. . . . We must now end this war by winning it. There can be no end of war until after the collapse of the existing German Imperial Government." [1]

Here, then, after just a century, came the parting of the ways for the British and American Peace Societies. The former found a lofty patriotism in its pacifism; the latter, faced with the same crisis, had at last to solve the Non-Resistance issue in the way it would undoubtedly have chosen, if necessary, in 1837.

As a result the American Peace Movement split. The bulk of its component bodies followed the lead of the American Peace Society. Pacifist activity in the United States dwindled almost to nothing. But from the standpoint of organisation the decision was disastrous. Nearly all the State Peace organisations disintegrated, and the Quakers seceded from the Movement practically everywhere. [2] The Carnegie Endowment for

---

[1] *A. of P.* (1914), p. 197; (1917), pp. 2, 99, 132–4, 230–1, 320–1; (1918), p. 40.
[2] E. L. Whitney, *American Peace Society*, p. 293.

International Peace, the only other body to remain unimpaired in vigour, supported the Government. As early as February 1915 the Endowment had declared that out of the War there must be fashioned a Peace in which "new sanctions are provided to compel respect for the judgments rendered." The trustees categorically added in April 1917 that "the most certain means of instituting a durable peace among the nations is to pursue the War against the Imperial German Government until the final victory of democracy, in conformity with the policy adopted by the President of the United States." But the Endowment went no further in actual belligerency than to put its offices at the disposal of the Government. Its work was concentrated rather in the direction of investigating the theoretical bases of a durable peace.

As in England, this theoretical discussion took effect in the foundation of a new society based on the theme of a League of Nations. The idea was first launched in September 1914 by the New York publicist, Hamilton Holt. It won the instant approval of prominent politicians and scholars—Taft, Roosevelt, Carnegie, and Prof. A. L. Lowell. But it is noteworthy that whereas the "League to Enforce Peace" finally emerged with a programme that bristled with sanctions, Hamilton Holt relegated armaments and force to purely police purposes.[1] An alternative body appeared, moreover, in May 1915, in the World Court League, founded to organise opinion in favour of the Tribunal recommended by the second Hague Conference in 1907.

The League to Enforce Peace is the most famous of all the organisations that heralded the League of Nations. It came into being at Washington on 17th June 1915, with Taft as President. Of the other societies, the World Peace Foundation accepted it, but the American Peace Society stood by Ladd's plan of a Congress of Nations fortified by moral sanctions alone, and refused the League's overtures as "tying around the neck of the whole enterprise at the outset the millstone of physical force." The fifth and last National Peace Congress in the

[1] *Ibid.*, p. 296.

autumn approved the League's programme: while the American Society for the Judicial Settlement of International Disputes had already played an integral part in drafting its terms. Hamilton Holt figured in the Executive Committee, along with A. L. Lowell and Theodore Marburg.

The declared objective was "a world organisation which will tend to prevent war by forcing its members to try peaceable means first . . . and to make immediate and certain war upon any nation which goes to war without a previous hearing of the dispute." The States within the organisation were to sign a compact pledging themselves to submit all justiciable disputes to an International Court for "hearing and judgment," and all non-justiciable disputes to a Council of Conciliation for "hearing and recommendation." No hostilities were to be begun before the promulgation of the judgment or hearing respectively: and violators of this pledge were to be attacked by all the other members in concert. The sole condition under which the right of private war would remain would thus be restricted to "the conviction," *after* arbitration, and in non-justiciable cases *only*, that "their interests demand it." In justiciable disputes there was the pledge in advance to accept the award. And the only other war would be international sanctions against an "outlaw" State.[1]

Together with this statement of its "platform" the League issued, when finally constituted a year later, a reply to objections. It met the argument that a nation must not surrender its freedom of action, with the retort that, on the contrary, no State should be allowed to enforce by arms a claim which it feared to submit to the judgment of a court. To strictures on its basis of organised force it pointed out that the force was in essence but a "police," and that what was enforced would be not conciliation (which could come from moral conviction alone) but merely a hearing. To the objection that the United States would stand aloof from any such League of Nations and eschew all entanglements, it recommended the "interdependence"

[1] Proceedings of the League (*Enforced Peace*), pp. 13-15, 131; E. L. Whitney, *American Peace Society*, chap. xxxiv.

argument: that the United States would be materially injured by any war in any part of the world. Suggestions were even offered for overcoming the veto power of the Senate without a Constitutional amendment. The League of Nations Council would not call on the United States to apply sanctions; it would merely declare that the time for sanctions had arrived, and leave Congress to issue the declaration of war. As to the Monroe Doctrine, inroads had already been made on that antiquated instrument by the obligations undertaken at the Hague Conferences. Finally there was swept away even the argument from human nature. A change in human nature, said Theodore Marburg, was not indispensable for the successful working of a League to Enforce Peace. "Altruism is a factor in its operations, but the plan still recognises self-interest as the governing motive of States, as of individuals." [1] And this, indeed, was the philosophical basis of the League.

The terms were fundamentally at one with those being evolved independently by the League of Nations Society in England and in other countries. But special prominence is given to the American League here because it was this, more than any other, that commanded the attention and influenced the post-war policy of statesmen. Theodore Marburg carried out in the remainder of 1916 a tour of six European countries. In the three principal belligerent capitals he produced the most epoch-marking pronouncements from leading statesmen. Sir Edward Grey, Aristide Briand, and Bethmann-Hollweg all endorsed his proposals. "I would like to say," said Grey to the foreign Press in October, "that if we seem to have little time to give to such ideas ourselves while we are engaged in this struggle, such a work in neutral countries is one to which we would all look with favour and with hope." Grey became, in Marburg's eyes, the best friend of the League to Enforce Peace: for his support induced also that of Asquith and Balfour. In France, Briand approved the plan of the League both in speeches and in letters. In Germany, Bethmann-Hollweg laid it down as an indispensable condition of future peace that "no more

[1] T. Marburg, *League of Nations* (1917), p. 66.

aggressive coalitions are formed. . . . Germany will at all times be ready to enter a league for the purpose of restraining the disturbers of peace." [1] In the three neutral countries, however, the support was not uniform: Switzerland and Spain were prepared to go at once to the length of a definite commitment, but the prevailing sentiment in Denmark was no stronger than sympathy.

The history of the American Peace Movement during the War produced, then, disruption throughout the bulk of the popular societies, involving a cessation of propaganda and the elaboration of a theory to explain the War as an "exception"; but, on the other hand, an organised movement among statesmen and publicists who had hitherto remained outside Peace bodies though favourable to their ideals. This last is a noteworthy fact, in view of the later influence of the League to Enforce Peace.

(c) *Germany: Restriction*

Outside the Anglo-Saxon countries pacifism was vigorously suppressed in all belligerent States. In Germany the pre-War Peace organisations were silenced by Government orders. There were three of these—the *Friedensgesellschaft* of 1892, the Inter-Parliamentary Group, and a "Group for International Understanding." Three others sprang up during the War, to correlate the plans of individual thinkers for a League of Nations: but their existence was furtive, and strict prohibitions forbade any public propaganda or addresses to the Chancellor.

Nevertheless German pacifism was not dead. [2] There had been a wide response to Anna B. Eckstein's appeal for support in her agitation for a third Hague Conference. In the critical summer of 1914, again, prominent thinkers like Leonard Nelson and Dr. Neucamp began to stress the need for some "international union of States." Pacifists came forward in books where pamphlet propaganda was impossible. Walter

---

[1] T. Marburg, *League of Nations* (1917), pp. 99 *seq.*
[2] See a study of German Peace Movement during the War, by E. Jäckh, in *L'Esprit International* (July 1929), pp. 393–415.

Schücking's *Bund der Völker* and *L'Union Pacifique Mondiale* served in Germany the purpose to which Woolf consecrated in England his *International Government*. Hans Wehberg's *Papacy and World Peace* provided a setting for the Pope's peace proposals of 1917. Encouragement was found, moreover, in Bethmann-Hollweg's response to the League to Enforce Peace: especially when it was echoed in the following year by jurists as pre-eminent as Mendelssohn Bartholdy.

The new societies themselves echoed and approved the League's programme. Led by Schücking, Wehberg, and Ludwig Quidde they evaded the military censorship whenever practicable. *Friedensgesellschaft* from the outset pledged itself to unite with pacifists in other lands to demand a peace free from recriminations. The Central Office of International Law boldly declared for the creation of some *super*national authority as the only means of laying the ghost of "national sovereignty" in future disputes, and of suppressing the "dangerous system of secret treaties and secret alliances." The foremost of the three newer organisations, *Bund Neues Vaterland*, evolved a "plan for a durable peace" as early as November 1914.

The Government's attitude to all this was not so obscurantist at first as the memory of the Hague Conferences would imply. Hollweg, indeed, told Schücking that he sympathised with pacifism but was powerless in the control of "constitutional militarism." His speeches in the Reichstag grew more truly internationalist after the second winter of the War. But when he was superseded as Chancellor in June 1917, the new Imperial Government was inoculated with Ludendorff's distrust of pacifists, and the work of the societies was sternly circumscribed. It was not till the last few months of the War that the new Chancellor, Prince Max of Baden, converted the Reichstag to the principle of a League of Nations in which national sovereignty should be hobbled. The prophets of the conversion were Ebert's Social Democrats, Erzberger's Catholic Centre Party, and the National Liberal Party.

By then three influential peace plans had been aired: that of the *Bund Neues Vaterland*, more or less identical with the

plan of the British League of Nations Society later; that of the
original German Peace Society; and the Reich's own Government plan, in which Schücking had a part. They were all
ultimately fused into the project of the German League of
Nations Society (*Liga für Völkerbund*) in 1918, led jointly by
Schücking and Erzberger.

(d) *France: Suppression*

Two forces combined in France to bring about an almost
complete cessation of pacifist activity: Government proscrip-
tion and internal debility. Pacifist organs—notably *L'Universel*
—were banned by the military censor, even when their keynote
was more religious than pacifist. The time to talk of love and
peace was temporarily suspended. Within the societies, in the
second place, there was lack of vigour. Militant patriotism,
supplemented by the Conscription laws, played havoc with
membership and funds. So that what propaganda the *Paix
par le Droit* bureau did undertake was clandestine; and the
most fruitful place in which to find records of its war-activity
to-day is the archives of the Paris Police.

This activity expressed itself in two directions; through the
ordinary channels of the society *La Paix par le Droit*, and
through a body not strictly pacifist, nor dominantly internationalist until now, the League of the Rights of Man, founded
in 1898. Between the two organisations was a permanent link
in the person of Théodore Ruyssen. Discussions between
them for a "durable peace" began in the summer of 1915, when
a "minimum" programme was drafted on the principles of
national self-determination, increased recourse to the system
of Hague Conferences, a League of Nations functioning by
means of pacific settlements and buttressed by "adequate
sanctions," and ultimate disarmament. The beginning of 1917
saw added to this a confession of faith to the effect that democracy was the form of government least inimical to world peace,
and (a significant contrast to contemporary British thought)
that judicial means could be made to settle *all* disputes of
whatever kind.

What is most distinctive of French speculation, however, is its emphasis on the necessity for sanctions in any future attempt at world organisation. The subject was dealt with most fully in a treatise published by Henri La Fontaine in 1917. Here the "means of constraint" were graded and classified into direct means (military and naval compulsion at the instigation of the International Authority, and indirect means (such as the rupture of diplomatic relations). On these lines the problem has been further explored since, when the Geneva Protocol of 1924 elevated sanctions almost into a gospel.[1]

As an organised propagandist movement, however, pacifism in France was degraded to the level of sedition and effectively silenced.

(e) *Neutrals: A "Clearing-House"*

With all international links put out of action, and with Continental Governments hostile to talk of Peace in war-time, the Peace Movement was compelled, in all countries, to seek some interim place for continued co-operation in neutral territory. To do so at first was comparatively easy. Facilities for travel were not immediately curtailed nor seriously endangered, and the Dutch Peace Society at the outset offered its services to the rest of the Movement throughout the world. "As soon as circumstances permit, we will be ready to resume the work of peace with more fibre and devotion than ever." It is thus of paramount importance that by 1916, when Governments began to refuse permits for delegates to travel to conferences abroad, there was already in existence in Holland an organisation representing the Movement from many countries— the Central Organisation for a Durable Peace.

On its domestic side the Netherlands Peace Movement felt the heavy responsibility that 1914 threw on it by reason of its neutral position. It established, in October, the *Anti-Oorlog Raad* (Anti-War Council) for the duration of the War, a special-

---

[1] H. La Fontaine, *Existing Elements of a Constitution of the United States of the World* (1917); also C. L. Lange, *Société des Nations pendant la Guerre*, pp. 30 *seq.*; *H. of P.* (1915), p. 141; (1917), pp. 58–9.

ised body devoted to finding Peace proposals "that should not
contain the germ of future wars." Every pacifist philosophy
was here represented—socialist, Christian, and economic—in a
purely temporary federation formed for that one particular
purpose. And the "Minimum Program" issued in November
1914, the most widely discussed of all the plans thrown up by
the War, commanded attention because it thus represented a
highest common mean, and because it harboured no futile
"stop the war" delusion. It is the earliest of the plans which
influenced Wilson in propounding the Fourteen Points.
Elaboration of its bases is not necessary here, since they coincided with those already noticed elsewhere, save for a few
peculiarities. Plebiscites were to be held in all regions transferred by the Peace treaties; there was to be liberty of commerce
in all colonies and protectorates; secret treaties were to give
place to parliamentary control of foreign policy; and the League
of Nations, when constituted, was to be provided with full
sanctions.

Out of this Dutch body there grew, in 1915, the Central
Organisation for a Durable Peace. For the rest, the *Anti-
Oorlog Raad* endeavoured at least to shorten the War by
keeping Governments informed of each other's official
utterances, in a monthly review issued in three languages.[1]
The review was impartial, but both sides naturally vilified it.
In 1917, further, an enterprising politico-pacifist committee was
set up to instruct parliamentary candidates in Peace matters.

The Central Organisation for a Durable Peace, founded at the
Hague in April 1915, was from the start an international body,
and the successor of the curtailed Inter-Parliamentary and
Universal Peace Conferences. Forty nations were represented
in it; and the delegates unanimously adopted the Minimum
Program as a basis of discussion, from which it recrystallised
out into nine points. Abroad the proposals found unqualified
support among the national groups except in America, where
Theodore Marburg, of the League to Enforce Peace, criticised
the plebiscite provision as involving logically the right of

[1] *Holland News.*

secession (which the American Civil War had been fought to dispel).[1]   In this way Alsace-Lorraine might declare for French rule now and for German rule at some future date, and Ireland might secede from the British Empire.   But, in the end, the principle found its way into the Peace treaties.

The supreme merit of the revised Minimum Program lies in its completeness.   There were no deadlocks, and no issues on which final recommendations were absent.   This is all the more remarkable in view of the fact that in the only other neutral countries in which Peace plans were evolved (in Scandinavia) the twofold crux of the discussions defied solution.   The three Scandinavian Inter-Parliamentary Groups, which met annually throughout the War, worked out by 1918 a Peace plan which to some extent ran parallel to the prevailing scheme for a League of Nations.   Its pacific settlements, for instance, were envisaged as falling into two categories: juridical (at the Hague) and political (effected by International Councils of Conciliation). But on the vital questions of obligatory arbitration and sanctions no decision was arrived at.   Opinions were too diverse.   The most useful deliberations, indeed, of the Scandinavian Peace Movement during the four years were devoted to an examination of the economic aspect of Peace.   It was to attack economic problems that the Netherlands-Scandinavian Socialist Congress of Stockholm was called in May 1917—the first public international Peace Congress of the whole War.   The result was a "general formula," recommended for the signature of all Powers at the Peace Conference, in which economic warfare was especially singled out for denunciation.   "In order to give Peace the character of durability, the contracting parties declare themselves ready to create a League of Nations on the basis of obligatory arbitration and general disarmament, with the suppression of all economic war, and with an extension of parliamentary control over foreign policy."[2]

[1] See his *League of Nations*, pp. 48–50.
[2] For the neutral countries see J. van Beek en Donk, *Peace Movement in the Netherlands*, pp. 35–48 ; C. L. Lange, *Société des Nations pendant la Guerre*, pp. 12, 39 *seq.* ; and information supplied from the Hague by M. van der Mandere.

Thus the northern European neutrals provided a clearing-house for pacific speculation, which found its common features in the Minimum Program. Elsewhere, save in one quarter, there was no activity worth recording—as a result partly of ruthless suppression, partly of inherent lack of strength. In Poland and Russia the Peace Movement had never been strong—nor in Spain. In Italy it was hedged about with restrictions as in France. In the nationalist provinces of the Hapsburg Empire (notably Czechoslovakia, where the Chelčicky Peace Society was articulate early in the War) it was stamped out. The one other voice that was raised was that of the Pope.

(f) *The Papacy*

Benedict XV earned the title "Pontiff of Peace" by his proposals to both the Central Powers and the Allies in August 1917. He was at heart a pacifist, in theory and practice together. He believed, on the one hand, and expressed the belief in his Encyclical Letter of May 1920, that there was only one and the same morality for States and individuals alike. On the other hand, he had faith in the practicability of pacifist doctrines. The first belief conditioned his refusal to bless the Austrian armies in 1914. The second prompted his Peace overtures three years later, when he postulated not only the re-establishment of Belgian independence and neutrality, but a future for international relations characterised by arbitration, the freedom of the seas, and a cancellation of all war debts. But in this, as in his later plan for a League of Nations, nationalists in all countries scented partiality. To-day, ironically enough, the only memorial to Benedict XV is one erected by the Turks.

Throughout the Church of Rome organised Catholic bodies grew up, extra-national in outlook despite their political duty to the State in which they resided. In France and Germany "White Cross Societies" were formed to work, as Catholics, for Peace, while the Pope himself did all he could in the way of exchanging and repatriating prisoners. The White Cross Societies achieved few conversions during the War, but in 1921 their many ramifications were united into the First

Catholic Peace Congress, at Paris, comprising delegates from twenty-one countries. Under the auspices of Benedict's successor, Pius XI, the Congress was repeated annually.

Peace at the behest of the Pope and Cardinal Gasparri was bound to fail. The Church "was impotent to enforce its behests." Political and religious cross-currents, too, complicated the tangle which the proposals of 1917 hoped to straighten out. There was the age-long feud between Italy and Austria-Hungary on the Adriatic seaboard; while the menace of Russian Orthodoxy in the Balkans had to be stemmed. The War years were for the Papacy a time of distraction, in which, somehow, it managed to preserve its reason in politics. Benedict at least let slip no opportunity to point the rational way to Peace.[1]

(3) *Contribution to the League of Nations*

President Wilson's formal endorsement of the idea of a League of Nations was circulated to the belligerent Governments on 18th December 1916, two days before the abortive German Peace proposals. The subsequent projects that were conceived by Governments are too voluminous for treatment here, important as are the differences between the official British draft, the Hurst-Miller draft, General Smuts' draft, Lord Cecil's plan, the draft of the Phillimore Committee, and the three drafts of Wilson himself. But it is instructive to take the several features of the League idea, and analyse the findings of the Peace Movement in relation to them, in the light of the Hague Conferences earlier and the League Covenant later.

Ten wartime Peace plans stand out among many. They all recognised the lesson of the previous century of international relations, that "national sovereignty," with its apotheosis of the State, must be reconciled with "interdependence" and the need for regulating common international interests by means of a common international authority. The War was accentuating this lesson. It welded together the national groups on each

---

[1] *See* L. J. S. Wood, "Benedict XV, the Pontiff of Peace," in *Dublin Review*, vols. 170 and 177 ; F. Stratmann, *The Church and War*, pp. 162-7 ; London *Times*, 28th January 1930.

side of the conflict to a degree never known before; and showed, in the process, the "limitations of State-sovereignty" and the "reality of interdependence."[1]

At the Hague Conferences a solution had been sought along lines well trodden already by pacifist theorists for just on a century. The "International Community" was regarded as needing a Legislature (to enact International Law), a Court, a system of arbitration and conciliation, sanctions to strengthen both, an Executive, a reduction of armaments, and provisions for altering the *status quo* when necessary.

The work of the Hague, already noticed, resolved itself as follows. Legislature—the Hague Conference itself, renewed every seven or eight years; Court (for justiciable disputes)—the projected Court of Arbitral Justice (1907) and a Prize Court —but the submission of disputes was purely voluntary; arbitration and conciliation (for non-justiciable disputes)—the Hague Court of 1899, and all the proved methods of mediation, good offices, and Commissions of Enquiry; sanctions—a national pledge of good faith alone; Executive—a Council consisting of the Diplomatic Corps accredited to the Hague; armaments—merely recommendations; altering the *status quo* —no special provisions.

On these fundamentals, in order, there was not by any means complete unanimity. Two of them—the International Court and the International Executive—were quite straightforward.[2] As to the Executive, six plans specified a permanent Executive secretariat to supervise ratifications, three made no recommendation, and one (the British League of Nations Society) vested executive power in the Council of the League. As to

[1] See discussion in C. Howard-Ellis, *Origin, Structure, and Working of the League of Nations* (1928), chap. i.

[2] The ten plans are : French League of Nations Society, British League of Nations Society, League to Enforce Peace, American Peace Society, World Court League, American Institute of International Law, Central Organisation for a Durable Peace (Minimum Program), International Peace Bureau (La Fontaine), British Labour Party, and the Fabian Society. See tabular analysis in American *A. of P.* (1919), pp. 216 *seq.* ; and L. S. Woolf, *Framework of a Lasting Peace* (1917).

the International Court for justiciable disputes, nine plans made a general recommendation (two going into details as to the number of judges, etc.), and one (the British League of Nations Society again) postulated a "Supreme Court, in which States sue and are sued, and whose decisions are enforced."

The Legislature was variously defined and qualified. Five plans recommended that the Hague Conferences reassemble at regular intervals; two excluded from the League all but self-governing nations; three made a majority vote necessary for the creation of international law; the Fabian Society gave the eight leading Powers a veto over the rest, and stipulated that every member State should have ratified a law before it could become operative.

The Hague machinery was chosen, again, by the same five plans in the matter of non-justiciable disputes. Only three of the others offered specific recommendations: and of these the Fabian Society and the British League of Nations Society outlined a "Council of the League," while the League to Enforce Peace suggested a Council of Conciliation and reserved that, if the Council's award were declined, the League as a whole should decide what was to be done.

Disarmament received attention in only six plans, of which three made provision for limitation by international control of the manufacture of armaments, and one (the Minimum Program of the Central Organisation) for limitation by agreement only.

Alterations of the territorial *status quo* were made conditional in eight plans, on the right of self-determination inherent in every national group. Two drafts, the Fabian Society and the American World Court League, advanced nothing. As Lord Bryce put it, there must be no perpetual clauses.

It was sanctions that produced real cleavage, as distinct from mere diversity. There was no middle way between two decisions: the sanctions behind the League's declarations and awards must be either moral, resting on good faith alone, as in the Hague Agreements, or material and unlimited, beginning with La Fontaine's "indirect" means of breaking off diplomatic relations, and ending (if necessary) with utter military and naval

WOODROW WILSON

subjugation at the League's direction.   Three of the American
plans declared for moral sanctions only; the other, that of the
League to Enforce Peace, agreed with the European drafts in
utilising full physical compulsion.

From this comparison a broad generalisation emerges which
an examination of the many other plans confirms.   It is
apparent that in the Continental plans the chief emphasis was
laid on a negative need, the need of preventing war; whereas in
the Anglo-Saxon plans the goal was rather positive—a desire,
as General Smuts defined it, for "permanent co-operation for
the service of the common interests of nations." [1]   Thus the
critical problem of sanctions was approached more optimisti-
cally by the older Peace bodies in the United States than by
their fellow-organisations in Continental Europe, where the
object-lessons of history postulated iron laws of compulsion to
preserve the Peace.

The League Covenant of 1919 was made to enshrine the
Continental philosophy of a system of sanctions so ruthless that
no State would dare, by aggression, to invoke it.   And this has
an important bearing on the attitude of the Peace Movement
in the post-War International Commonwealth to which we
now finally turn.

[1] *See* C. L. Lange, *Doctrine Pacifique*, p. 419.

PART FIVE

THE INTERNATIONAL COMMUNITY: 1918 onwards

Harmony of understanding in a world of unassailable diversity
ALFRED ZIMMERN

CHAPTER XII

(1) *The League System*

THE World War was fought at a cost of ten million lives and nearly forty thousand millions sterling; whereof the effect was to reinforce all the influences already tending towards some form of world organisation, by the addition of a world-wide fear for the future of civilisation itself. Desperation drove home the lessons already fashioned by reason and experience. Jean de Bloch's prediction as to the future of war had come true; the powers of destruction were gaining on the powers of creation. And the disastrous effects of modern war on the life of the world were soon laid bare in works like J. M. Keynes's *Economic Consequences of the Peace*, which appreciated problems ignored in the Treaty of Versailles. Both lessons, the moral of interdependence and the warning of science, are reflected in the League of Nations Covenant, signed on 28th June 1919, as an integral part of the Peace Treaty.

The problem that had to be solved was three centuries old. The conception of Sovereignty produced by the Renaissance, together with the conception of Natural Rights evolved during the French Revolutionary period, had made the nineteenth century an epoch of rampant Nationalism, in which international relations were determined by diplomacy, international law, and Balance of Power. Two solutions could be looked for as ideals infinitely far off—cosmopolitanism and world socialism. Short of them, the State's function of guarding the welfare of its citizens had to be harmonised, sublimated and purged from war, by some principle of association.[1]   But the difficulties were colossal.   Was the Community of Nations to be universal or restricted?   How was juridical equality to be secured for great and small nations alike?   Were *all* disputes to be arbitrated? If not, how was war to be effectually averted in disputes not open to judicial settlement?   And by what sanctions were pacific settlements to be enforced?   Above all, was the League to be a Super-State, transcending and destroying National unlimited Sovereignty?   And at all points, how could it overcome vested interests?   "So many vested interests were challenged by the League," it has been said, "and so many new forces had been liberated in Europe which were antagonistic to it, that unless it had been made part of the peace it might have been postponed for a generation." [2]

What was achieved was a democratic federation, analogous to the Pan-American Union and the British Commonwealth of Nations.   In aim the League was "but a more modern form of the unity of civilisation that haunted the minds of the great conquerors, inspired the 'universal' religions, and combined the two for a time in the concept of the Holy Roman Empire." [3] Its Covenant, anticipated in broad outline in the schemes noticed in the last chapter, contained to this end four innovations.   It attempted, for the first time in any international compact, to render arbitration *compulsory* in certain circumstances.   It declared, again for the first time, that the maintenance of peace necessitated a *reduction* of armaments. Thirdly, it was a *permanent* organisation; the International Labour Office and the Permanent Court were added to a permanent Secretariat.   And, fourthly, "secret diplomacy" was superseded at last by the security of *public* international relations.[4]   But the most distinctive feature of the League was

---

[1] *Cf.* C. Delisle Burns, *Short History of International Intercourse* (1924), *passim.*

[2] H. W. V. Temperley, in *History of the Peace Conference*, i, 276–7.

[3] C. Howard-Ellis, *League of Nations*, p. 61.

[4] Article 13, paragraph ii ; article 8 ; articles 6 and 14 ; articles 18–20.   Sanctions—articles 10 and 16.

its recourse to an inexorable system of sanctions. The Covenant was born of the war spirit; "good faith" had to be supplemented by provisions for "enforcing" peace if faith broke down. So that the philosophy of Henri La Fontaine and of the League to Enforce Peace triumphed.

In all this there were alleged, by benevolent critics, to be errors of both omission and commission. The League was certainly neither world-wide nor European, but midway between and irrationally incomplete. Its links were rather "mechanical" than natural. And its constitution seemed to cut across the historical process of human development into nations and groups of nations. More immediately, the danger was sensed that the League would degenerate into a "politico-military alliance"; that only the small States would accept it whole-heartedly (for the protection it assured them), while the Great Powers would acclaim it in so far as it tended to their several interests, but obstruct it when it ran counter to those interests. Thus during the Corfu crisis of 1923 the sardonic remark was current that Great Britain would not so complacently suffer the League to resolve a crisis in, for example, Egypt. And in 1924, critics of the League explained the acceptance of the Geneva Protocol by France in terms of the "military alliance" of Great Britain thereby entailed.[1]

Furthermore, the League did not rule out private war entirely. Apart from cynical reflections that "all the League's schemes are acceptable to the War Offices," the "gap in the Covenant" allowed three sets of circumstances in which nations were free to go to war if they chose. If a dispute was admitted by the Council of the League to be a domestic dispute of one of the parties, or if a dispute not subject to arbitration were submitted to the Council and failed to produce a unanimous Council decision, or if a dispute submitted to the whole Assembly did not secure decision by the necessary majority, then the contending parties reserved the right "to take such

---

[1] Criticisms of League in R. N. Coudenhove-Kalergi, *Pan-Europa* (1923), pp. 87 *seq.*; and C. C. Morrison, *Outlawry of War* (1927), pp. 130–1, 276.

action as they shall consider necessary for the maintenance of right and justice"—though a total of nine months' delay was provided for in each case. However unlikely to be realised, these three possibilities of private war remained. And the closing of the gap was from the start the League's most serious task—the legacy of "national sovereignty" and the war spirit.

Second in importance was the problem centred on the Permanent Court of International Justice, established at the Hague by protocol on 16th December 1920 to supplement but not supplant the Hague Court of 1899. There was no Code of International Law for it to apply, and it was precluded by its own statutes, moreover, from making International Law through precedents. Its jurisdiction comprised "all cases which the parties refer to it and all matters specially provided for in treaties and conventions in force"; beyond which it enjoyed a second, advisory, function in matters referred to it by the League Assembly or Council. But the jurisdiction was "voluntary"; dependent on States agreeing to submit their dispute to the Court, except in cases already provided for by treaty, or in any of the four classes of *legal* disputes for which Governments could, by signing the "Optional Clause," recognise the Court's jurisdiction as "compulsory *ipso facto* and without special agreement." These inevitable limitations were of significance for the future.

But the whole League machinery was at bottom only a beginning. The situation in 1920 has been admirably summed up by Dr. Hertz, Chief Rabbi of the British Empire. "All covenants, treaties, and pacts are in and by themselves mere machinery; and their practical beneficial results must remain infinitesimal when compared with the hopes they inspire, unless and until public opinion and public morality in the various signatory States have been educated up to the level of these treaties, covenants, and pacts." [1]

[1] At Preliminary Universal Church Peace Congress, Geneva, 1928 : *Report*, p. 12.

(2) *Modifications*

After 1918 it becomes a sheer impossibility to study, more fully than in the form of an epilogue, the developments within the League system and the attitude to them of the post-war Peace Movement. The events are too recent, their purport and direction are too little known, and the materials for investigating them have become overwhelming. The pre-war societies still exist, some of them still flourish; but their place in the front rank of organised Peace activity has been taken by the many League of Nations societies throughout the world, and their history has become, save on a few prominent occasions, purely a domestic matter.

It must suffice to attempt to indicate the salient developments in international relations within the League and the corresponding reactions among the various branches of the Peace Movement.

The problem before the League resolved itself into the famous formula "Arbitration, Security, and Disarmament," on whose solution the future working of the League was soon seen to depend. To many minds the three parts of the formula made a vicious circle which could not be broken anywhere. So inextricably were they interwoven that a satisfactory beginning in practice seemed impossible. The old system of Balance of Power, with its distrusts and its perpetuation of sanctions in the League, was so long in dying.

In point of fact all three parts were attacked concurrently. Disarmament began to be tinkered with at the Washington Five Power Conference in 1921, with concrete results, and Security by a Temporary Mixed Commission set up by the League. It was at the third Assembly of the League, in 1922, that a resolution was passed [1] linking up the two problems of Security and Disarmament. Thereafter discussions took a new turn, until, after the Draft Treaty of Mutual Assistance passed by the Assembly in the following year had been rejected by the

[1] Resolution 14.

British Labour Government, there came the Geneva Protocol (October 1924).

Here a bold step was taken to close the "gap in the Covenant." The standpoint was adopted that war must be rendered altogether unwarrantable except when waged by the entire League against an aggressor State. At every point at which deadlock seemed possible in the use of peaceful settlements, whether arbitral, mediatory, or judicial, some way out had to be found which would not leave a right of private war. Otherwise the fear that a State might some day have to fight *without* the help of the League would render its security under the Covenant illusory, and make all talk of disarmament mere lip-service. The Protocol accordingly outlawed "aggressive war," took cognizance of no hostilities except "in resistance to acts of aggression" or at the bidding of the League Council, and endeavoured to furnish a logical chain of peaceful machinery for settlement which would obviate deadlock. The solution chosen was compulsory arbitration—an innovation, but an extension of existing commitments to which the only insuperable objection was the unsavoury principle of absolute State Sovereignty. This complete system of arbitration provided, it was claimed, an "automatic test" of aggression. The member States relinquished their right of private war entirely, and recognised the obligation to be bound by all awards; and it was argued that the liability to compulsory arbitration would minimise the danger of aggressive and provocative national policies, and therefore increase the all-round security which was necessary for the compulsory principle to gain favour. The one danger remaining was the possibility of sudden and unprovoked attack. But *no* international agreement will ever guard against this further than by tightening up the system of sanctions (as the Protocol did). As for States outside the League, finally, they could either accept the newer machinery of the Protocol in settling their disputes with League members, or be dealt with under the older provisions of the Covenant.

Criticism of the innovation was immediate and strong. Compulsory arbitration was denounced as likely to inflame

passions and precipitate war rather than avert it. The definition of aggression as "resort to war" also was rejected as over-
simplifying the problem. In reply the twenty-one authors of the
Protocol maintained that their bridge across the gap was the only
structure that would at one and the same time promote security,
avoid deadlock, and act as a safety-valve. The Protocol, however, was finally rejected by the British Government and others.[1]

In substitution for it there were concluded the Locarno
Treaties of 1st December 1925, which marked an advance in
yet a fresh direction, that of increasing security by means of
"regional pacts." This principle was endorsed and recommended by the League Assembly which preceded the Treaties.
What Locarno did was to establish a régime of guarantees in
the two most disputed zones of Europe—the Rhineland and the
German-Polish frontier. Treaties of mutual guarantee against
aggression were concluded between the five Powers "interested
in the Rhine," and between France, Poland, and Czechoslovakia,
with ancillary Arbitration Conventions. And the moral effect
of this security in reassuring "the two strongest and most persist-
ently hostile States of Continental Europe"[2] was invoked as a
warrant for applying the expedient of regional pacts (within the
framework of the League Covenant) in other parts of the world.

This was an advance in one direction only—security.
Similarly the flamboyant Soviet proposals at the end of 1927
for complete, immediate, universal, simultaneous disarmament.
Similarly also the negotiations for a new Anglo-American
Arbitration Treaty to supersede the treaty of 1914. Peace
was not pursued again from an "absolute" standpoint until
December 1927, when a momentous resolution was passed by
the League Assembly denouncing aggressive war. Two months
later the Pan-American Conference at Havana went further
still, by renouncing aggressive war as between the American
nations: aggression being recognisable, as in the Geneva
Protocol, by hostilities after a refusal to arbitrate, or hostilities
in defiance of an award.

[1] See P. J. N. Baker, *The Geneva Protocol* (1925), *passim*.
[2] *Cf.* L. Sturzo, *The International Community*, p. 126.

Renunciation reached its climax in the Kellogg Pact of 27th August 1928, wherein fifteen States (subsequently joined by others) formally renounced war "as an instrument of national policy" and pledged themselves never to seek a settlement for their disputes save by pacific means. Both the strength and weakness of this commitment lay in its brevity and vagueness. Beyond the pledge to renounce war the Paris Pact stated only that violators of it should be denied "the benefits of this Treaty." All that could be said about it was by way of interpretation only. The most noticeable point was that it contained no sanctions. Faced with an aggressor, the signatories had only a moral obligation to ostracise that aggressor. Here, argued the more optimistic adherents of the Pact, was at last a bridge across the gap in the Covenant. For the moral duty of severing all relations against an aggressor, coupled with uncertainty as to how far or how little the member States would actually do so, would prove an effective deterrent to aggrandism and hostile acts. So that freedom of action, coloured by moral obligation, had been substituted for the elaborate system of the Protocol. The conduct of international relations was henceforth to be determined by a pledge "to rely on the peace machinery of the peace plans, and not on the war machinery."

Against this robust prediction, however, were ranged not only the British reservation—of areas (even outside the Empire) vital to imperial security—and the United States reservation safeguarding the Monroe Doctrine, but also the serious criticism that, even if most of the signatories had, as League members, the definite commitment to apply sanctions against an aggressor, it was still extremely doubtful whether the United States, bound only by the Pact, would co-operate in those sanctions or even allow them to prejudice her own commercial interests. There was "nothing save a somewhat problematical pressure of public feeling to prevent Americans from trading with the belligerents." [1]

[1] See J. T. Shotwell, *War as an Instrument of National Policy* (1929) ; D. H. Miller, *The Peace Pact of Paris* (1928) ; and *Survey of American Foreign Relations* (1930).

For the League the fundamental problem was to give the
Pact a definitely juridical value by harmonising its moral
atmosphere with the material sanctions of the Covenant
without prejudice to either.   The two documents seemed to
reflect two opposite and incompatible theories of Peace—the
two that had ranged the Peace Movement into two camps
during the War.   It is not necessary to follow the League
further in its quest.   Our concern is with the Peace Movement
in relation to the League.

(3) *The Peace Movement after* 1918

Two points may be noted at the outset.   One, that the Peace
Movement after the War was more truly international than it
had ever been before, though the International Peace Bureau
that constituted its common link declined in vigour.   Secondly,
that many of its aspirations had been at last realised.   There
were to be no more crusades for arbitration treaties; no more
frenzied petitions for the codification of International Law.
Within the framework of the League, Governments had now
taken up officially the work of preserving Peace by co-operation.
This does not mean that with the Treaty of Versailles the
raison d'être of the Peace Movement vanished.   There was
still ground to be broken in bringing pressure to bear on
public opinion and in combating too nationalistic tendencies
in education.   But the burden of the Movement was
henceforth lighter.   It was crusading, for the first time,
in a Peace *setting*, and with Peace the leading topic of the
day.

Symptomatic of this was the disappearance of the Netherlands
Anti-Oorlog Raad, which had saved international pacifism
during the War by setting up the Central Organisation for a
Durable Peace and facilitating the Minimum Program.   Only
the Dutch group of the *Raad* lived on after July 1919, to be
fused with the rest of the Netherlands Movement into one
Association for the League of Nations, which thereafter sought
the attention of a frankly sceptical public in "commemoration

assemblies" like that of 1924, when the quarter-century of the first Hague Conference was celebrated.[1]

In their national centres the Peace bodies without exception deplored the Treaty of Versailles. The more pacifist of them added strictures on the League Covenant as well. In England both the League of Nations Union and the pacifists were at one in desiring a revision of the Peace Treaties "in a European and a world sense." But while the League of Nations Union took its programme from Geneva, the older British Peace Movement, most articulate in the National Council for the Prevention of War and the No More War Movement, wished to see the League democratised and universalised into a real "World Parliament," run by peoples and not by Governments. Moreover, they eyed its sanctions askance, and joined with the Labour Party in condemning the economic calamities predicted in J. M. Keynes's *Economic Consequences of the Peace*. The Peace Society, now moribund, had its own standpoint of criticism for both Treaty and League. The Treaty was "a betrayal of the ideals in the spirit of which the War was presumably fought." The League Covenant "would have been greatly improved by the acceptance of its suggested amendments. . . . Still, the League does at least provide a foundation for a permanent edifice, and constitutes a landmark on the road to world peace. The machinery of the League is of secondary importance. . . . No scheme, however well contrived, will succeed in abolishing war unless it is written not only on parchment but in the hearts of men. Some supernatural sanction is required that will bind humanity into a new unity; and, apart from Christ, who can provide it?"[2] The Society of Friends, similarly, at the first All Friends International Peace Conference ever held (1920, in London), admonished the world that self-seeking must give place to sacrifice, co-operation supersede domination, and trust be substituted for fear and suspicion.[3] How far these ideals

[1] H. van der Mandere, *Nederlandsche Anti-Oorlog Raad* (1919); *Report* of Twelfth Congress of League of Nations Societies (Hague, 1928), pp. 68–72.
[2] *Annual Report* (1919); in *H. of P.* (1919), p. 105.
[3] M. E. Hirst, *Quakers in Peace and War*, pp. 521–5.

were being realised was revealed every year in the *Survey of International Affairs* issued by the Royal Institute of International Affairs, built up from the group of technical experts who had represented Great Britain at the Peace Conference— an academic body functioning under a Royal Charter.

Peace thought in France and Germany was no less chagrined at the Settlement of 1919. The French Movement diverged into two groups as in England. One, led by the League of Nations Associations, its direction determined by League policy, gathered into its orbit the old society *Paix par le Droit* and the group organisations of the Churches, of Catholics, and women. The League of the Rights of Man also aligned itself with this bloc. The other group comprised the pacifist bodies, not all of whose aspirations had been realised in the League Covenant. With them was ranged the venerable League of Peace and Liberty founded at Geneva in 1867, still canvassing among a small circle of members the blessings of a United States of Europe as an entity distinct from the League but not antagonistic to it.[1]

German pacifism, born of Suttner and Fried, regarded the Peace Treaties as a setback to international thought and to the very conception of a League of Nations. The realisation was acute that the barbarisation of modern war was inducing a bitterness among *peoples* that had been absent in earlier wars. The latter fear furnished the Movement with a general and universal exhortation. The former disillusionment resulted in a reproachful note pervading the manifestos of the *Deutsche Liga für Völkerbund* until the admission of Germany to the League in 1926, and thereafter until the final evacuation of the Rhineland in 1930. Then, for the first time in German eyes, the work of the League could become "the greatest political activity of the future."[2]

Elsewhere in Europe, Peace activity after the War came to be centred in national League of Nations Associations almost

[1] Information supplied by M. Prudhommeaux from Paris ; and *Headway* for April 1924, p. 76.

[2] *See* Valentin, *Völkerbundgedanken in Deutschland* (1920), pp. 154 *seq.*

exclusively. And in this way, by reason of the publicity which had been won for the League idea, societies were able to take root in countries where organised Peace Movements were hitherto unknown: notably the turbulent Balkans. But in these newer regions activity was limited and largely academic. Denmark alone produced an innovation. The Danish Government had urged, during the negotiation of the League Covenant, that the Scandinavian States might have the right to declare themselves neutral, participating in the economic but not in the military sanctions of the League if called upon.[1] The proposal was rejected, but the Scandinavian tradition of pacific internationalism continued to manifest itself in the Disarmament Bills that began to be introduced into the Danish Parliament in 1925.

In America, however, the opposite effect soon appeared. The United States had been the birthplace of the League, but the Government rejected the Covenant, and so did the American Peace Movement. The result was a wedge driven between the American societies. They became groups of "bitter partisan sectaries," often too deeply at war among themselves to work effectively for Peace. The Government's attitude towards the League was at first distrustful aloofness; President Harding's plea that the United States should adhere to the World Court (1920) was refused by the Senate, who were more concerned to strengthen the Pan-American Union than to risk being drawn into the stream of European politics and commitments. Nor, as time went on, did American interpretations of tendencies within the League allow this attitude to grow more cordial. The fact that *special* guarantees of the Rhineland frontier were exchanged in 1925 (at Locarno), instead of admitting Germany to the League with a security based entirely on the Covenant; and the scramble for Council seats in 1926, suggested that the "old balance of power system" was being continued "within the League itself," and seemed to belie the professions of goodwill contained in the Covenant.[2] And though

[1] *See* the German *Völkerbund*, April 1929, p. 32.
[2] *Cf.* discussion by C. C. Morrison, *Outlawry of War*, chap. xiv.

international thinkers like Professor J. T. Shotwell urged the President to co-operate with the League to the extent of letting it be clearly understood that the United States would not support a League outlaw, the Government's attitude remained one of guarded, if benevolent, neutrality; wherefore the ultimate adhesion of the United States to the World Court was hedged about with reservations.

The same fears pervaded the American Peace Movement. Disorganised as it was in 1919, all sections felt that the United States had been deceived in the War. And when the Senate rejected the League, the Peace question became gradually eclipsed in American politics and the League became neglected by the Peace societies. Of such societies there were one hundred and seventeen. They diverged into two extremist camps—one preaching peace-at-any-price, with the Women's Peace Society of New York City as its most strident contingent; the other, led by the American Defence Society, declaiming the old maxim *Si vis pacem, para bellum*—the motto of the Navy League in England.[1] The American Peace Society, adopting a middle position, on three occasions attempted to reconcile the principle of association inherent in the League with American reluctance to fight Europe's battles. In the Society's view this could be done by substituting for the League and its rigid commitments an International Legislature consisting in the Hague Conferences renewed. Later, when it was no longer feasible that the League could be supplanted, the alternative proposal was advanced that, by separating the Permanent Court from the League, American adhesion to the Court might be more readily secured. But the one signal contribution of American thought to Peace after the War was the idea of "outlawry," first articulated by S. O. Levinson in January 1922. The simple "outlawry" of war, placing the institution beyond the pale of international law (more explicitly than in the later Kellogg Pact), was a proposition very logically attractive. As will be seen later, it argued away the whole case for sanctions. Its official history began in the famous Borah resolution carried

[1] *See* American Peace Society *Annual Report* (1924), pp. 6–7

through the Senate on 20th December 1923, to the effect that war should be outlawed "by making it a public crime under the law of nations," and that nations should be encouraged to pledge themselves against it by treaty. This Borah resolution became one of the corner-stones on which the Kellogg Pact was erected.

In short, then, American Peace thought continued to disintegrate for lack of a common centre, with criticism of the League of Nations as one of its few points of contact. The European Movement, on the other hand, either rallied to the League or remained indulgently aloof, according as the Societies could discern in the Covenant a practical scheme of Peace or merely a few healthy signs of future progress.

Considered next from the standpoint of its international organisation, the Peace Movement after the War again appears in a double guise. On one side there grew up the International Federation of League of Nations Societies, directed from a central Bureau in Brussels and assembling annually for conferences in various capitals, since 1919. Many of the national groups were hardly more than small gatherings of intellectuals; but in some countries (Great Britain and France especially) their membership and their publicity became extremely wide. Each set itself the task of popularising the activities of the League in its own country, and of studying, at the annual conferences and in the various committees, current international problems. After some years the Federation laid itself open to the criticism of being too preoccupied with the problem of Minorities. Its propaganda began, too, to be endured with apathy; for the League idea had conquered at last, and "where there is no issue there is no interest." Therefore after 1928 the constituent bodies concentrated on unravelling those economic problems surrounding international relations which the League was not yet in a position to resolve.[1]

On the other side were the Universal Peace Congresses and Inter-Parliamentary Conferences, revived after the War in 1921.

[1] See quarterly bulletins of the International Federation of League of Nations Societies.

Their representation was limited at first to about half a dozen nations, but within four years there were assembled delegates from twenty-nine national Peace Movements, and Parliamentarians from forty-one countries. A comparative study of their reports reveals the same profound differences as before the War. The Universal Peace Congresses, by reason of their relatively "private" nature and lack of official responsibility, could discuss "actualities" with a freedom denied to the Inter-Parliamentary Conferences, and indulge both greater vigour in their denunciations and less patience in their demands. At their very first assembly the delegates set up a committee to flog the horse of War Guilt. They derided all talk of disarmament until the League of Nations should have become universal; though no harm would be done in the meantime by reducing all national forces to the level of Germany's, and abolishing conscription. They rejected the League's sanctions altogether. "No international agreements can lead to the goal of real world peace until every kind of military action, whether it be called offensive, defensive, or an operation of sanctions, is excluded." They demanded (year after year) the institution of compulsory arbitration in "*all* disputes without exception"; and, as a corollary, enthusiastically endorsed the advent of compulsory arbitration in the Geneva Protocol. "Only by the adoption of this Protocol can disarmament be achieved." They denounced the idea of semi-permanent seats on the League Council (and indeed the whole conception of permanent seats) as "contrary to the principle of equality among States." They urged the "abandonment of the traditional dogma of National Sovereignty, which is irreconcilable . . . with the organisation of permanent peace": and, as means, compulsory arbitration and a universal revision of history textbooks, to "unteach" the doctrine of State omnipotence. This educational reform they appealed for again and again.

In sharp contrast, the Inter-Parliamentary Conferences, with Dr. C. L. Lange as Secretary, were occupied more often in examining than in judging. Their most emphatic resolutions were concerned with expedients which would facilitate the spread of the League spirit—such as the cancellation of War Debts, the friendly settlement of the Reparations problem, the League's own system of "compulsory investigation and mediation" in non-justiciable disputes, and (a link between 1867 and the future) the practicability of a European Customs Union. Occasionally matters of principle provoked dissensions in the debates and abstentions in the voting. The United States delegation, for instance, dissented from a resolution on the "rights and duties of States" (1928) in which the declaration was made that "if a State were attacked all other States were bound to stand by it." Similarly the same delegation, as representing a Parliament which considered immigration a domestic matter, abstained from voting in a resolution of the Inter-Parliamentary Conference which treated it as an international matter. But the academic value of the work done in these conferences, and its significance as a medium of exchange and a road to common sympathy, is beyond all question. And concurrently with it, in a more academic and more specialised field, were resumed the annual gatherings of the International Law Association.

International Socialism, also, was interesting itself more and more in Peace questions. It had never been forgotten (as the International Congress of Trade Unions was at pains to point out to its nineteen national groups in 1922) that "the fight against militarism and war must be an integral part of the struggle to overthrow Capitalism." It was "the duty of the workers to *prevent* war by carrying out an International Strike on the outbreak of a war"—the desired weapon of Cremer since 1870. Sanctions were denounced, an international control of the manufacture of armaments was demanded, and the League of Nations was to be gradually transformed, by educational propaganda, into a *supreme* international authority run democratically. This democratic principle, and the right of self-determination for all national groups, became also the special mission of the Socialist League against Imperialism, a body whose militant demands on behalf of the subject races, however, were to be satisfied by no means in pacific directions alone.

Further, there were in existence group-organisations old and new which cut across the frontiers of States and the boundaries of class and made for international understanding in matters non-political. They range over every human interest. But they are all of the kind most completely curtailed in time of war, when politics determine entirely the loyalties and the passions of the mass of men.[1]

Finally, the awakening within the Churches which had produced (on the very eve of the War) the World Alliance for International Friendship through the Churches, began to manifest itself in three new forms—two national and one international. The international movement, originating in the Church Peace Union of America, was launched in 1928 at Geneva, when one hundred and ninety-one representatives of all the religions in the world met for a preliminary Peace Congress, "to consider how the forces of religion in all nations can be brought to act *concertedly* against war." There was no intention of setting up a formal league of religions. The objects were specifically limited to declaring the highest teaching of each religion on peace and war, to devise means by which men of all religions could clear a pathway to Peace, and to seek opportunities for concerted action against ominous national policies. Even here, however, shrewd circumspection was vital. All mention of the League of Nations was excluded from the statement of aims, lest the co-operation of United States religious bodies might be refused.[2]

The two national movements were British and American. Thirty-five religious organisations in the United States struck out in a new direction, best indicated in their own manifesto. "We hold that, since economic factors are primary causes of international suspicion and hostility and frequently lead to war, the Churches should engage in the most serious study of such vital problems as foreign investments, war debts, raw materials, tariffs, armed intervention for the protection of property, and

---

[1] *E.g.* student organisations, World Power Conference, Freemasonry.
[2] *See* Report, *The World's Religions against War* (1929), pp. 2, 5, 106, 110.

the whole question of the economic and political control of foreign peoples" ; that is, the work being done simultaneously by the Federation of League of Nations Societies.   In England, on the contrary, the Movement (begun in 1929) was the same in standpoint as that of the first Peace societies: namely, to end war as an abuse of force and unchristian.   Thus it crystallised into a "Council of Christ and Peace Campaign," sponsored by the Bishop of Chichester, and agitating, from its inaugural meeting onwards, that the Churches "should henceforward refuse to sanction recourse to war or allow themselves to be used as agencies in the support of war."   This, coming from within the Establishment itself, was a remarkable declaration. It was endorsed also by seven of the Free Churches—the Baptist, Congregational, Presbyterian, the three Methodist Churches, and the Society of Friends.   As later amplified, it appeared as a resolution appealing to the authorities of all Churches "to declare in unmistakable terms that they will not countenance any war, or encourage their countrymen to serve in any war, with regard to which the Government of their country has refused an offer to submit the dispute to pacific methods of settlement."   This was a less sweeping declaration. But nevertheless there was at last in existence a movement within the Churches such as pacifists had demanded since 1816.[1]

On a broad survey, then, the post-War Peace Movement appears as a series of gestures rather than a definitive movement; gestures put forth in directions sometimes too little explored even yet, for example compulsory arbitration, and sometimes running counter to mighty vested interests, for example in disarmament. No Peace advocate to-day believes that the possibility of war can be eradicated in practice; many feel that the point of "minimum risk" will never be reached until National Sovereignty gives way to a "pooling of Sovereignty" —Ladd's still unrealised dream of a Congress of Nations. Thus the organised Peace Movement functions in two ways: one international, retaining the theoretical basis of State Sovereignty, and therefore tending to support the League of

[1] Quoted in London *Times*, 1st January 1930.

Nations; the other rejecting State Sovereignty in favour of a
future ideal Cosmopolis, and therefore tending to discount the
League's political machinery though fostering its economic and
intellectual "federal controls." We have then, finally, to indicate the leading fundamental ideas on future peace that have
been confirmed or created by the War.

(4) *The Future in the Present*

The first of these, the idea of the League of Nations, has
already been outlined in its bases and development. It looks
to a future determined by positive co-operation among federated
sovereign States: in Dr. Alfred Zimmern's phrase, "harmony
of understanding in a world of unassailable diversity." The
other philosophies of Peace current to-day derive part of their
justification from doubts which the League idea fails to resolve
for them. Can the League achieve sufficient "moral, legal, and
political authority" to prevent war? Will it become a hegemony of Great Powers like the Concert of Europe after 1815?
Will the need of future guarantees for the development of civilisation allow of real disarmament "down to police strength"?
Will a bold lead by one Government in disarmament have the
happy result that attended a similar lead in abolishing slavery?
There are several alternative answers.

(a) *Organisation by Continents*

The first, in its philosophical form, consists in what has been
defined as Pan-Continentalism. On the practical side, its
adherents claim that it is being realised already in at least two
international federations—the Pan-American Union and the
British Empire. The theory holds that the hope of the world
lies in the welding of Pan-Continental Unions, which will in
time unite to form a world league. Continents, it is claimed,
have links of culture, race, political and economic interests, so
strong as to give them a homogeneity greater than can be enjoyed at present by any world organisation like the League of
Nations. The globe can be best conceived as comprising five

natural groups of peoples: Pan-Europe, Pan-America, the Russian Federal Empire, Eastern Asia, and the British Commonwealth. And the development of the five can be sought, in the opinion of Count R. N. Coudenhove-Kalergi, the leading exponent of the theory, even within the framework of the present League of Nations; the League being the "final world authority," and the administration of "local issues" being entrusted to the five continental organisations, three of which (the American, British, and Russian) are already fully developed.[1]

Pan-America is certainly a reality. We have watched its embryonic stages at 1826 and 1890, and its development since birth at 1908. After the War it was rapidly consolidated. To-day it enjoys a régime of all-in arbitration (since 1923), a code of the laws of peace (drafted in seven weeks in 1925), a categorical denunciation of aggressive war (1928), and obligatory arbitration of all disputes except civil wars, rebellions, and wars against non-American States (1928). In compulsory arbitration also Pan-America has advanced much further than the rest of the world. The value of all this as a conglomerate force tending to peace is admitted even by the severest critics of the Union, who fear, nevertheless, that the United States may strive to establish through the machinery of Pan-America a hegemony over the whole continent.[2]

The structure of the British Commonwealth of nations can be best illustrated in the Statutes of the Dominions approved at the Imperial Conference of 1926. "They are autonomous Communities within the British Empire, equal in status, in no way subordinate one to another in any respect of their domestic or external affairs, though united by a common allegiance to the Crown, and freely associated as members of the British Commonwealth of Nations." The hegemony of Great Britain is thus a moral hegemony only. And though the Empire has no geographical homogeneity, its solidity has contrived for it a

---

[1] See R. N. Coudenhove-Kalergi, *Pan-Europa* (1923), p. 99 and *passim*.

[2] See L. Sturzo, *The International Community*, pp. 70–71 ; C. E. Hughes, *Pan-American Peace Plans* (1930).

permanent place in Pan-Continental calculations. Its future relation to the rest of the world seems to be dependent on two great problems: the problem of its own markets, and its position in the League of Nations. The first of these can be solved by one of three extreme expedients—a Customs Union with the United States, involving a danger of ultimate subservience, or a Customs Union with Europe, involving a possibility of restricted prosperity on account of Europe's lower standards of productivity, or the quest of "Imperial economic unity." On the second question, the international status of the Dominions as members of the League, may hang the future of both the League and the Empire. The obligations of the Dominions under the Covenant may conceivably conflict with their constitutional obligations as British Dominions.[1]

Pan-Europe, however, has remained chimerical. Its history, as an ideal sought by organised effort, dates back to the Geneva League of Peace and Liberty in 1867, whose cry for a "United States of Europe" echoed the voice of Victor Hugo and Jeremy Bentham. Thereafter it was never long without articulation in high places. Signor Crispi would have erected it in 1891 on a basis of the Triple Alliance; the Universal Peace Congress at Berne endorsed it in 1892; Lord Salisbury dubbed it in 1897 "the only possible structure of Europe which can save civilisation from the devastating effects of a disastrous war"; the Baroness von Suttner and the Austrian Foreign Minister made much of it during the first Hague Conference; Stead canvassed it in England; the Berne Peace Bureau advocated it in 1909; and during the War its benefits were stressed by the Director of the Pan-American Union. After the War it began to appear in the form of definitive plans, not only by the Inter-Parliamentary Conference (1925) and the Universal Peace Congress (1924), but also by European statesmen: among them MM. Herriot, Stresemann, and Briand; while Count Coudenhove-Kalergi organised in Vienna the Pan-European League. Its advantages were claimed to be permanent peace, an all-round saving on

---

[1] *See* J. M. de Bornier, *L'Empire Britannique* (1930); and Lord Melchett, *Imperial Economic Unity* (1930).

armaments, a consequent rise in the standard of living, and
decreased racial prejudice.   Post-War thought, concentrating on
the need for economic recovery, and reassured politically by
the existence of the League of Nations, conceived as the first
step a European Customs Union, which might increase political
security as well as reducing tariffs.   But the obstacles to be
overcome were colossal.   The vested interests created by the
tradition of militarism, widespread mistrust of any new form of
international organisation as prejudicial to the League, and the
very race-hatred that the Union was to eradicate were material
and psychological factors that no paper agreement could write
away.   Logically the "United States of Europe" has the
supreme merit of no longer attempting "to drive two incom-
patabilities in double harness—political peace and economic
war."   But ideally, it has been condemned as "too big for
to-day, too small for to-morrow, and dangerous to both."   In
this last criticism, moreover, lies the ultimate criticism of Pan-
Continentalism itself.[1]

(b) American "Outlawry of War"

The second Peace idea to be considered entirely revolutionises
the League of Nations and simplifies it to an association of
nations based on *good faith alone*.   War, as a legal institution,
can only be abolished by being declared illegal and outlawed.
This is the theme on which Outlawry has developed in the
United States.   It was first expounded by S. O. Levinson in
1918, first endorsed by Congress in Senator Borah's resolution
of 1923, and crowned by the Kellogg Pact in 1928.   The
principle cuts away the League's system of sanctions altogether.
Its exponents hold that the outlawry of war can be sub-
stantiated only by substituting for war an institution of peace
"conceived not under political but under juridical categories,"

---

[1] *See* J. Novikov, *Fédération de l'Europe* (1901); Suttner, *Memoirs*,
ii, 295–6, 333 ; F. Whyte, *Life of W. T. Stead*, ii, 122, 326–7 ;
H. of P. (1891), pp. 321, 330 ; (1896), p. 162 ; (1897), pp. 325–6 ;
(1909), pp. 315–8 ; (1916), p. 34 ; the Swiss *Friedens-Warte* for
February 1916 ; R. N. Coudenhove-Kalergi, *Pan-Europa* (1923) ;
Review of Reviews (London) for August 1929.

since "any proposal in the name of peace which makes any terms whatever with war, which compromises with or tolerates it in any form or guise, is foredoomed to futility." This is advanced, it must be pointed out, not as a pacifist theory but as pragmatist realism. The project is claimed to be eminently practical, starting from the Paris Pact (reinforced by national plebiscites in favour of outlawing war), though the League Covenant, which does not preclude war altogether, would have to be revised and its sanctions article expunged. "National Sovereignty," moreover, would be accommodated and rendered innocuous; for "every nation . . . is safe in clothing with affirmative jurisdiction a court of peace founded on the outlawry of war, for the obvious reason that the scope of the jurisdiction of such a court is known in advance and agreed to by each signatory." The inalienable right of self-defence, again, is not so much *reserved* by the outlawry proposals as left *unaffected*. In short, outlawry aims at replacing war by law, and not by any scheme of world organisation based on the War System. War cannot be controlled; it is ruthless. Even the application of sanctions at the command of the League rests in the last resort on good faith. Outlawry therefore takes pride in extending the principle of trust—of moral sanctions alone—to the "whole enterprise of peace."

On its own showing the plan is inspiring. But it has to meet the trenchant criticism that, since not all disputes can be treated as purely legal and not political, and since the right of self-defence remains, outlawry of war would be no more conducive to ultimate disarmament and a "Peace Mind" than the League of Nations. The risk of unprovoked attack in a world quite unorganised (beyond its statute of outlawry) would perpetuate a need for armaments and alliances, and result in a legal peace system running counter to the old political war system. This objection reduces to the dictum that "faith is not enough," [1] and to that grim argument from human nature which is the fundamental barrier to all ideals.

[1] C. C. Morrison, *Outlawry of War* (1927) ; L. Sturzo, *The International Community*, pp. 242-3.

(c) *The Three Ideals*

Thus from practical schemes for the security of peace, whether from the lofty standpoint of trust or the shrewd standpoint of experience, we pass finally to the only three philosophies of Peace that are not bound down in time and space, that do not originate in a present geographical and political *status quo*, and that have real spiritual value. They are all frankly ideals.

The first is Cosmopolitanism, as expounded at its most popular by Mr. H. G. Wells. It postulates "a profound revolution in the nature of every existing government upon earth, and in the fundamental ideas upon which that government is based." State Sovereignty has no place in it, for State Sovereignty perpetuates war as in the past; but, on the other hand, a "pooling of sovereignty," as in the Constitution of the United States, is at least capable of maintaining peace. "Peace and national independence are incompatible," but in a federal World State (and there alone) common interests, replacing separate interests, can abolish the traditional causes of war. And to the objection that his wish for a "human solidarity overriding States" is unattainable, the cosmopolitan replies that the Nationalism of to-day is itself but an artificial product of education and politics, that it had a definite historical beginning, and that it may expect a definite end in the future. The assumption of Nationality is the supreme fallacy underlying the League of Nations, so disastrously as to obscure the aim which to the cosmopolitan is the one possible way to peace— "the creation of federal controls," abolishing frontiers and universalising every human link. The cosmopolitan rejects the appellation of idealist. He believes his cosmopolis to be inevitable, if very far off. But he descends to the plane of active preparation for it in one direction only—not political or juridical, but psychological. He exhorts the teacher to forswear old Nationalist education, the clergyman to be less acquiescent in the existing powers that be, and the Peace Movement to abandon its futile Internationalism based on

State Sovereignty. Thus only can there be created a "peace by coalescence" built on the moral conviction of a "cosmopolitan will." [1]

The second ideal can be called "Classic Pacifism." It finds its prophet in the German Alfred H. Fried, and its disciples in the No More War Movement and the Peace organisations of women, of youth, and of Labour. It expresses itself in individual declarations of faith and purpose—that war is unjust and a violation of the "unity of mankind," and that the pacifist will do nothing in any way to further any war, even defensive; but that, on the contrary, he will work by every means in his power to persuade his fellows to embrace Peace. This pacifism is practical in so far as it encourages and popularises all advances in arbitration and pacific methods of settlement, but idealist in its demands for trust and its transcendental scorn of sanctions.

The third and last ideal is the religious pacifism of the first Peace Societies; the inspiration of a long line of evangelists from Dodge and Allen to Darby, and of organised sects and churches from the seventeenth-century Quakers to the present-day Church Peace Unions. To all these a pacifism which does not preach brotherhood and love is narrow and shallow. Peace must have an ethical and religious basis, rooted in the soul.

Thus there have always been two types of Peace thought: one historical, the other philosophical; the former attempting to insure the immediate future by utilising past experience, the latter claiming to prophesy the ultimate future in terms of philosophical certitude. There is a wide gulf, for example, between abstract pacifism and the theory of the League of Nations. The League idea moves forward from the present. It starts from a geographical and political *status quo* which profoundly influences its life. It claims to make provision for altering that *status quo*, but only in terms of territory. The League idea cannot accommodate world-wide changes like the

[1] H. G. Wells, *Common Sense of World Peace* (1929) ; J. M. Holzman, *Pacifist Imperialism* (1930).

Fall of Rome or the Reformation.   These must be provided for as they come.   The goal of the Peace Movement, on the other hand, is the product of a fixed and unalterable state of mind, not bound by time or space.   Beyond their choice of parallel means to prepare for their future, therefore (arbitration, international co-operation, a new education), the two outlooks are different.   Internationalism (as in the League) can guarantee no more than that, starting from the present, Law will gradually supplant Force, and Power depend more on Law than on Force; that "force will not be abolished, but its predominance will." Pacifism (as in the Peace Societies) can guarantee nothing at all, unless mankind can be educated up to its ideal; but in that event it guarantees perpetual peace.

For the present the one quality that international man has in common is enlightened self-interest.   From this standpoint it is possible that a future can be assured in the terms laid down by the wider Peace Movement of 1867–1914: a world organised for peace on a basis of that very self-interest, long sublimated into interdependence, and working itself out as an automatic system of checks and balances within a World Federation from which the concept of unlimited National Sovereignty has been expelled.   And this is no more nor less than Ladd's "Congress of Nations."

BIBLIOGRAPHY

ARRANGEMENT

(1) BIBLIOGRAPHIES, STATISTICS, ETC.

CARNEGIE ENDOWMENT FOR INTERNATIONAL PEACE, *Select List of References [to Peace] prepared by the Librarian* (typescript), 1924.

FONTAINE, HENRI LA, *Bibliographie de la Paix et de l'Arbitrage International;* Tom. 1, *Mouvement Pacifique*, Monaco, 1904. *Histoire Sommaire et Chronologique des Arbitrages Internationaux*, 1794–1900, Bruxelles, 1902.

FRIED, ALFRED H., *Handbuch der Friedensbewegung* (pp. 425–62), Leipsic, 1911.

LANGE, CHR. L., *L'Arbitrage Obligatoire en* 1913, Paris, 1914.

NOBEL INSTITUTE, *Catalogue of Peace Literature in the Nobel Institute*, London, 1912.

U.S. CONGRESS LIBRARY, *List of References on International Arbitration*, Washington, 1908.

(2) WORKS ON THE PERIOD TO 1815

BALCH, T. W. (ed.), *The New Cyneas of Emeric Crucé*, Philadelphia, 1909.

BLANCHET, J. A., *Un Pacifiste sous Louis XV : La Société des Nations de l'Abbé de Saint Pierre*, Maçon, 1917.

DANTE ALIGHIERI, *De Monarchia*.

KANT, IMMANUEL, *Perpetual Peace*, ed. Mary C. Smith, London, 1909.

KNIGHT, W. S. M., *Life and Works of Hugo Grotius*, London, 1925.

LANGE, CHR. L., *Histoire de la Doctrine Pacifique, et de son influence sur le développement du droit international*, Paris, 1926; *Histoire de l'Internationalisme ;* Tom. 1 [to 1648], Christiania, 1919.

LANGLOIS, CH. V., *De Recuperatione Terre Sancte* (Pierre Dubois), Paris, 1891.

LOUIS-LUCAS, P., *Un Plan de Paix Générale et de la liberté de commerce au 17ᵉ siècle: Le Nouveau Cynée d'Emeric Crucé*, Paris, 1919.

MEAD, EDWIN D. (ed.), *The Great Design of Henry IV*, Boston, U.S.A., 1911.

NOVAKOVITCH, M., *Les Compromis et les arbitrages internationaux du 12ᵉ au 15ᵉ siècle*, Paris, 1905.

OGG, D. (ed.), *Sully's Great Design of Henry IV*, London, 1921.

PENN, WILLIAM, *Towards the Present and Future Peace of Europe*, 1694.

ROEDER, A., *L'Arbitrage International chez les Hellènes*, Paris, 1912.

ROUSSEAU, J. J., *Project of Perpetual Peace*, trans. E. M. Nuttall, London, 1927.

STAWALL, F. M., *The Growth of International Thought*, London, 1929.

TER MEULEN, J., *Der Gedanke der Internationalen Organization in seiner Entwicklung*, 1300–1800, The Hague, 1917.

YORK, ELIZABETH, *Leagues of Nations, Ancient, Medieval and Modern*, London, 1919.

(3) NEWSPAPERS AND PERIODICALS

Advocate of Peace [Organ of American Peace Society], Boston, 1836 to date.

Arbitrator [Organ of International Arbitration League], London, 1889 to date.

Bond of Brotherhood [ed. Elihu Burritt and Edmund Fry], London, 1846–56.

Calumet [ed. William Ladd], New York, 1828–35.

Christian Citizen [ed. Elihu Burritt], Worcester, Mass., 1844–51.

Concord [Organ of International Arbitration and Peace Association], London, 1887–89.

Evening Star, London, 1856–69.

Friend of Peace [ed. Noah Worcester], Boston, 1816–28.

Harbinger of Peace [ed. William Ladd], U.S.A., 1828–31.

Headway [Organ of League of Nations Union], London, 1920 to date.

Herald of Peace [Organ of British Peace Society], London, 1819 to date.

International Arbitration Monthly Journal, London, 1885–87.

Morning Star, London, 1856–69.

Peace Advocate and Correspondent, Newcastle, 1843.
The Times, London, *passim*.
War against War [ed. W. T. Stead], London, 1899.
And periodicals referred to in footnotes.

(4) WORKS BY PEACE ADVOCATES

(A select list of the more important only)

BALLOU, ADIN, *Christian Non-Resistance in all its Important Bearings, illustrated and defended*, Philadelphia, 1846.

BECKWITH, G. C. (ed.), *The Book of Peace : a collection of essays*, Philadelphia, 1845; *A Universal Peace Society*, Boston, 1844; *The Peace Movement : or War and its Remedies*, Boston, 1847.

BOGUE, DAVID, *On Universal Peace : a Lecture* . . . , October 1813.

BOLLES, J. A., *Essay on a Congress of Nations*, Boston, 1839.

BOUVET, F., *La Guerre et la Civilisation*, Paris, 1855.

BUCKINGHAM, J. S., *An Earnest Plea for the Reign of Temperance and Peace, submitted to Visitors to the Great Exhibition*, London, 1851.

BURRITT, ELIHU, *Lectures and Speeches*, London, 1869.

CHANNING, W. E., *Discourses on War*, ed. E. D. Mead, Boston, 1903.

CLARKSON, THOS., *Essay on the Doctrines and Practice of the Early Christians as they relate to War*, London, 2nd ed., 1817.

COBDEN, RICHARD, *Speeches and Writings*, ed. J. E. T. Rogers, London, 1878.

COUES, SAMUEL E., *War and Christianity*, Boston, 1842.

DARBY, W. EVANS, *What the Peace Society has Accomplished* (in *Pall Mall Magazine*), London, 1899; Nine Pamphlets on Arbitration, etc. (Pub. Peace Soc.), London, 1900.

DODGE, DAVID L., *The Mediator's Kingdom not of this World*, New York, 1809; *War Inconsistent with the Religion of Jesus Christ*, New York, 1815.

DUNCAN, PHILIP B., *The Motives of War*, London, 1844.

DYMOND, JONATHAN, *An Enquiry into the Accordance of War with the Principles of Christianity* . . . , London, 1823, Revised ed., 1824.

FIELD, D. D., *Draft Outlines of an International Code*, New York, 1872.

GIRARDIN, EMILE DE, *La Politique Universelle*, Paris, 1854.

GURNEY, J. J., *War : Is it lawful under the Christian Dispensation ?* London, 1860; *Address* . . . *on War and Peace* . . . , London and Norwich, 1840.

HANCOCK, THOS., *Principles of Peace, exemplified in the conduct of the Society of Friends during the Rebellion of 1798*, London, 1829.

HUGO, VICTOR, *The United States of Europe* (Presidential Address to Paris Peace Congress, 1849), Boston, 1914.

JAY, WILLIAM, *War and Peace: the Evils of the First, and a Plan for preserving the Last*, ed. J. B. Scott, New York, 1919.

JEFFERSON, JOHN, *The Unlawfulness of War: a discourse on Luke, ii*, 14, London, 1832.

LADD, WILLIAM, *Essay on a Congress of Nations*, ed. J. B. Scott, New York, 1916; (ed.) *Prize Essays on a Congress of Nations*, Boston, 1840.

LEVI, LEONE, *An International Code of Commerce*, London, 1851; *The Law of Nature and Nations as affected by Divine Law*, London, 1855; *War and its Consequences: with proposals for establishing a Court*, London, 1881.

MACNAMARA, H. T. J., *Peace, Permanent and Universal: its Practicability, Value, and Consistency with Divine Revelation*, London, 1841.

MARCHAND, P., *Nouveau Projet de Traité de Paix Perpetuelle*, Paris, 1842.

PASSY, FRÉDÉRIC, *Pour la Paix: notes et documents*, Paris, 1909.

PECQUEUR, CONSTANTIN, *Des Armées dans leurs rapports avec l'industrie, la morale et la liberté; ou, les devoirs civiques des militaires*, Paris, 1842.

RICHARD, HENRY, *Defensive War . . . a Lecture*, 5th February 1845, London, 1846; *Standing Armies and their Influence upon Nations*, London, 1868; *Relations of the Temporal and Spiritual Power in the Different Nations of Europe*, London, 1877; *On the Application of Christianity to Politics*, London, 1877; also pamphlets (Pub. Peace Society, Eastern Question Association, etc.).

ROBERTS, SAMUEL, *Thoughts on War . . .*, London, 1834.

SELLON, COMTE DE, *Nouveaux mélanges, politiques, moraux et littéraires*, Geneva, 1838.

STOKES, WILLIAM, *British War History during the Present Century*, London, 1869; *A Permanent European Congress in Lieu of War . . .*, 3rd ed., London, 1861.

SUMNER, CHAS., *The True Grandeur of Nations*, New York, 1845; *The War System of the Commonwealth of Nations*, New York, 1849.

SUTTNER, BERTHA VON, *Memoirs*, authorised English translation, 2 vols., Boston, 1910.

WALKER, AMASA, *Le Monde: or, In Time of Peace prepare for War*, ed. H. Richard, London, 1859.

WORCESTER, NOAH, *A Solemn Review of the Custom of War*, Greenfield (Mass.), 1817.

WRIGHT, HENRY C., *Defensive War proved to be a Denial of Christianity and the Government of God*, London, 1846.

(5) CONGRESS AND CONFERENCE REPORTS

American Peace Society, *Annual Reports*, 1828 onwards.
British Congresses of 1853 : Manchester *Report*; Edinburgh *Report*;
London, 1853.
Institute of International Law, *Transactions*, 1874 onwards.
International Law Association, *Transactions*, 1874 onwards.
International Peace Congresses: *Reports*, London (Convention),
1843; Brussels, 1848 and 1873; Paris, 1849 and 1878; Frank-
fort, 1850; London, 1851.
Inter-Parliamentary Union, *Work and Organization*, 2nd ed.,
Geneva, 1921; *Statutes, etc.*, Geneva, 1925; *Résolutions des
Conférences* (ed. Chr. L. Lange), 1911.
Inter-Parliamentary Conference *Reports*, see page 195, note, for list.
Lake Mohonk Conferences: *Reports*, 1895–1915.
National Peace Congresses: England, *Reports*, 1904–14; France,
Reports, 1902–14; U.S.A., *Reports*, 1907–14.
Peace Society (London), *Annual Reports*, 1819 onwards.
Universal Peace Congresses, *Reports*, see page 195, note, for list.

(6) YEAR BOOKS, ETC.

Annual Register, London, 1815 onwards.
Annuaire des Associations Internationales pour la Paix (International
Peace Bureau).
Bulletin of International Federation of League of Nations Societies
(quarterly), Brussels.
Carnegie Endowment for International Peace, *Year Books*, 1911
onwards.
Peace Year Book, London, 1911 onwards.
World Peace Foundation, *List of Peace Organizations in the U.S.A.*,
Boston.

(7) BIOGRAPHIES OF PEACE ADVOCATES

(Alphabetically by *Subject*)

J. ALLAN BAKER, by E. B. and P. J. N. BAKER, London, 1927.
SAMUEL BOWLEY, by F. SESSIONS, London, 1884.
JOHN BRIGHT, by G. M. TREVELYAN, London, 1913.
ELIHU BURRITT, by A. S. DYER, London, 1882; C. NORTHEND,
New York, 1879.
RICHARD COBDEN, Studies by W. H. DAWSON, London, 1926; J. A.
HOBSON, London, 1918; Biography by JOHN MORLEY, 3 vols.,
London, 1881.
W. RANDAL CREMER, by HOWARD EVANS, London, 1909.

JONATHAN DYMOND, by C. W. DYMOND, London (privately printed), 1911.

D. D. FIELD, by H. M. FIELD, New York, 1898.

W. L. GARRISON, by V. TCHERTKOFF and F. HOLAH, London, N.D.

J. J. GURNEY, by AUGUSTUS HARE (*The Gurneys of Earlham*, 2 vols.), London, 1895; by M. ALEXANDER, London, N.D.; by J. B. BRAITHWAITE, 2 vols., Norwich, 1854.

VICTOR HUGO, by A. F. DAVIDSON, London, 1912.

WILLIAM JAY, by B. TUCKERMAN (*Jay and Slavery*), New York, 1893.

WILLIAM LADD, by G. C. BECKWITH, Boston, 1841; by E. BURRITT, New York, 1873; by G. HEMMENWAY, Boston, 1865.

LEONE LEVI, by himself (years 1845–55 only), London, 1888.

SAMUEL MORLEY, by J. C. HARRISON, London, 1886; by E. HODDER, London, 1887 (5th edition, 1889).

ALFRED NOBEL, by H. SCHÜCK and R. SOHLMAN, London (trans.), 1929.

HENRY PEASE, by M. H. PEASE, London, 1898.

JOSEPH PEASE, Anonymous memoir, London, 1872.

HENRY RICHARD, by L. APPLETON, London, 1889; by RHYS T. DAVIES, Wrexham, 1925; by C. S. MIALL, London, 1889; by E. ROBERTS (in Welsh), Wrexham, 1907.

JOSHUA ROWNTREE, by S. E. ROBSON, London, 1916.

W. T. STEAD, by F. WHYTE, 2 vols., London, 1925.

JOSEPH STURGE, by W. CATCHPOOL, London, 1882; by A. DIAMOND, London, 1909; by S. HOBHOUSE, London, 1919; by A. PECK-OVER, London, 1890; by HENRY RICHARD, London, 1864.

CHARLES SUMNER, by E. L. PIERCE, 4 vols., Boston, 1876; by W. G. SHOTWELL, London, 1910.

GEORGE THOMSON, Anonymous memoir, London, 1878.

(8) WORKS ON ASPECTS OF THE PEACE MOVEMENT

BALDWIN, S. E., *The International Congresses and Conferences of the Last Century as Forces working towards the Solidarity of the World* (in *American Journal of International Law*, 1907).

BEEK EN DONK, B. DE JONG VAN, *History of the Peace Movement in the Netherlands* [1870–1915], Hague, 1915.

BIGGOTT, Sir F., *The Declaration of Paris of 1856*, London, 1919.

BOSANQUET, HELEN, *Free Trade and Peace in the Nineteenth Century*, Oslo, 1924.

BURNS, C. DELISLE, *Short History of International Intercourse*, London, 1915.

BUTLER, N. M., *The International Mind*, New York, 1912.

CASE, C. M., *Non-Violent Coercion*, London, 1923.

CHAMBERLAIN, W. J., *Fighting for Peace*, London, 1928.

CURTI, M. E., *The American Peace Crusade*, 1815–60, Durham, N.C., 1929; *Pacifist Propaganda and the Treaty of Guadeloupe-Hidalgo* (in *American Historical Review*, vol. xxxiii), 1928; *Non-Resistance in New England* (in *New England Quarterly*, vol. ii), 1929.

DICKINSON, E. DE W., *A Selection of Cases and other Readings on the Law of Nations*, M'Graw Hill, U.S.A., 1929.

DICKINSON, G. LOWES, *War: Its Nature, Cause, and Cure*, London, 1923.

DUCOMMUN, E., *Précis Historique du Mouvement en faveur de la Paix*, Berne, 1899; *The Programme of the Peace Movement*, London, 1898.

FERRERO, G., *Problems of Peace from the Holy Alliance to the League of Nations*, New York, 1919.

FREDERIC, KATHERINE A., *Early History of the Peace Movement in the United States* [1846–61], MS. thesis, 1928.

FRIED, A. H., *Die Grundlagen des Ursälichen Pazifismus*, 2 vols., Zurich, 1916; *Handbuch der Friedensbewegung*, Berlin, 2nd edition, 1911; *Pan-Amerika*, Berlin, 1910; Zurich, 1918.

HIRST, M. E., *The Quakers in Peace and War*, London, 1923.

HUGHES, C. E., *Pan-American Peace Plans*, New Haven, U.S.A., 1930.

HULL, W. I., *The New Peace Movement*, Boston, 1912.

KNOWLES, G. W. (ed.), *The Quakers and Peace*, London, 1920.

KOHT, HALVDAN, *Histoire du Mouvement de la Paix en Norvège*, Oslo, 1900.

LAGORGETTE, J., *Le Rôle de la Guerre*, Paris, 1906.

LENZ-FABIAN, *Die Friedensbewegung: ein Handbuch*, Berlin, 1922.

M'ELROY, R., *The Pathway of Peace*, Cambridge, 1927.

MARVIN, F. S., *The Evolution of World Peace*, London, 1921.

MORITZEN, J., *The Peace Movement of America*, New York, 1912.

NOVIKOV, J., *La Fédération de l'Europe*, Paris, 1901.

PASSY, F., *Sketch of the Peace Movement in Europe* (in *American Journal of Sociology*), 1896.

PERRIS, G. H., *Short History of War and Peace*, London, 1911.

PERRIS, H. S., *Pax Britannica: a Study in the History of British Pacification*, London, 1913.

PHELPS, CHRISTINA, *The Anglo-American Peace Movement in the Mid-Nineteenth Century*, New York, 1930.

PHILLIMORE, Sir W. G. F., *Three Centuries of Treaties of Peace and their Teaching*, London, 1917.

POLITIS, N., *La Justice Internationale*, Paris, 1924.

POTONIÉ-PIERRE, E., *Historique du Mouvement Pacifique*, Berne, 1899.

POTTER, P. B., *Introduction to the Study of International Organisation*, London, 1929.

STRATMANN, F., *The Church and War: a Catholic Study*, London, 1929.

TRUEBLOOD, B. F., *Historic Development of the Peace Idea*, Washington, 1924.

VALENTIN, *Völkerbundgedanken in Deutschland*, Berlin, 1920.

VEBLEN, T. B., *Enquiry into the Nature of Peace and the Terms of its Perpetuation*, New York, 1919.

WEHBERG, HANS, *Die Fuhrer der Deutschen Friedensbewegung*, Leipzig, 1923.

WHITNEY, E. L., *American Peace Society Centennial History*, Washington, 1928.

(9) WORKS ON INTERNATIONAL ARBITRATION

APPLETON, L., *Fifty Years' Historic Record of the Progress of International Arbitration*, London, 1882; *Historic Record of the Triumphs of International Arbitration* from 1789 *to* 1899, London, 1900.

ARNOLDSON, K. P., *Pax Mundi : Progress of the Movement for Peace by Means of Arbitration, Neutralisation, International Law, and Disarmament*, London, 1909.

BALCH, T., *International Courts of Arbitration*, Philadelphia, 1896.

BALCH, T. W., *Evolution de l'Arbitrage International*, Philadelphia, 1908.

DARBY, W. E., *International Tribunals : a Collection of the Schemes which have been Propounded*, London, 1899 ; 4th edition, 1904; *Progress of Arbitration in the Twentieth Century* (in International Law Association *Proceedings*), 1903.

DESCAMPS, E. F. E., *The Origin of International Arbitration*, London (translated), 1897.

DREYFUS, F. C., *L'Arbitrage International*, Paris, 1892.

DUMAS, J., *Les Sanctions de l'Arbitrage International*, Paris, 1905.

LA FONTAINE, H., *Pasicrisie Internationale : Histoire Documentaire des Arbitrages Internationaux*, 1794–1900, Berne, 1902.

GENNADIUS, J., *A Record of International Arbitration*, London, 1904.

JONES, R. L., *International Arbitration as a Substitute for War between Nations*, London, 1907.

LANGLADE, E., *De la Clause Compromissoire et des Traités d'Arbitrage Permanent*, Toulouse, 1899.

LAURENCE, T. J., *Principles of International Law*, 4th edition, London, 1910.

MACFARLANE, J., *War and International Arbitration*, London, 1896.

MANNING, W. R. (ed.), *Arbitration Treaties among the American Nations to the Close of* 1910, New York, 1924.

MOCH, G., *Histoire Sommaire de l'Arbitrage Permanent*, Monaco, 1905.

MOORE, J. B., *History and Digest of International Arbitration*, 6 vols., Washington, 1899.

Mougins de Roquefort, Ch. de, *De la Solution Juridique des Conflits Internationaux*, Paris, 1889.

Ralston, J. H., *International Arbitration from Athens to Locarno*, London, 1929.

Revon, M., *L'Arbitrage International*, Paris, 1892.

Rouard de Card, E., *Les Destinées de l'Arbitrage International*, Paris, 1892.

Russell of Killowen, Lord, *Arbitration: its Origin, History, and Prospects*, London, 1896.

Trueblood, B. F., *The Federation of the World: with a Bibliography of Works on International Arbitration*, New York, 1899.

Tryon, J. L., *Proposals for an International Court* (in *Proceedings* of the American Society for the Judicial Settlement of International Disputes), 1913.

(10) WORKS ON TWENTIETH-CENTURY PEACE QUESTIONS

Baker, P. J. N., *Disarmament*, London, 1926; *The Geneva Protocol*, London, 1925; *The League of Nations at Work*, London, 1928.

Barbeuse, Henri (ed.), *The Soviet Union and Peace*, London, 1929.

Church Peace Union (of U.S.A.), *The World's Religions against War*, London, 1929.

Coudenhove-Kalergi, R. N., *Pan-Europe*, London, 1923 and 1929.

Ellis, C. Howard, *The Origin, Structure, and Working of the League of Nations*, London, 1928.

Fachiri, A., *The Permanent Court of International Justice: its constitution, procedure, and work*, London, 1925.

Fleming, D. F., *The Treaty Veto of the American Senate*, New York, 1930.

German League of Nations Society, *Deutschland und der Völkerbund*, Berlin, 1926.

Hull, W. I., *The Two Hague Conferences*, London, 1908.

Ichihashi, Y., *The Washington Conference [1921] and after*, Stanford, U.S.A., 1928.

Jäckh, E., " L'Idée de Société des Nations en Allemagne pendant la Guerre " (in *L'Esprit International* for July 1929).

Keynes, J. M., *The Economic Consequences of the Peace*, London, 1919.

Lange, Chr. L., " Préparation de la Société des Nations pendant la Guerre " (in P. Munch, *L'Origine et l'Oeuvre de la Société des Nations*), Copenhagen, 1923–24.

Madariaga, S. de, *Disarmament*, London, 1929.

Mandere, Ch. van der, *Nederlandsche Anti-Oorlog Raad*, Hague, 1919.

Marburg, Th., *A League of Nations [to Enforce Peace]*, New York, 1917.

MILLER, D. H., *The Peace Pact of Paris*, New York, 1928.

MITRANY, D., *The Problem of International Sanctions*, Oxford, 1925.

MORRISON, C. C., *The Outlawry of War*, Chicago, 1927.

PERLA, LEO, *What is National Honour?* New York, 1918.

PHILLIMORE, Sir G. W. F., *Schemes for Maintaining General Peace* (Foreign Office Handbooks, No. 160), London, 1920.

SCOTT, J. B. (ed.), *The Hague Conferences and Declarations of 1899 and 1907*, Washington, 1908.

SHOTWELL, J. T., *War as an Instrument of National Policy and its Renunciation in the Pact of Paris*, London, 1929.

STURZO, LUIGI, *The International Community and the Right of War*, London, 1929.

WEHBERG, HANS, *Das Problem Eines Internationalen Staatengerichtshofes*, Berlin, 1912.

WHEELER-BENNETT, J. W., *Information on the Permanent Court of International Justice*, London, 1924; *Information on the Reduction of Armaments*, London, 1925; *Information on the Problem of Security*, London, 1925; *Information on the Renunciation of War*, London, 1929.

WOOLF, L. S., *International Government*, London, 1916; *The Framework of a Lasting Peace*, London, 1917.

(11) MISCELLANEOUS

ALEXANDER, F., *From Paris to Locarno:* 1919–25, London, 1928.

BARRY, W., and WOOD, L. J. S., "Benedict XV the Pontiff of Peace" (in *Dublin Review*, vol. clxx), 1923.

BURNS, C. DELISLE, *The Morality of Nations*, London, 1915.

DAWSON, W. H., *The Future of Empire: The World Price of Peace*, London, 1930.

DICKINSON, G. LOWES, *The International Anarchy*, 1904–14, London, 1926.

HOLZMAN, J. M., *Pacifist Imperialism*, London, 1930.

MILBURN, R. G., *The International Commonwealth*, London, 1927.

MURRAY, GILBERT, *The Ordeal of this Generation*, London, 1929.

NEWFANG, O., *The United States of the World: a Comparison between the League of Nations and the United States of America*, London, 1930.

PRESCOTT, D. A., *Education and International Relations*, London, 1930.

RAPPARD, W. F., *Uniting Europe: The Trend of International Co-operation since the War*, New Haven, U.S.A., 1930.

ROUSE, RUTH, *Rebuilding Europe: the Student Chapter in Post-War Reconstruction*, London, 1925.

SCOTT, J. F., *The Menace of Nationalism in Education*, London, 1926.

WELLS, H. G., *The Common Sense of World Peace*, London, 1929.

INDEX

345